Leslie Beck's
10 Steps to
Healthy Eating

HOW TO BOOST ENERGY,
MANAGE WEIGHT AND PREVENT DISEASE
WITH FOOD, DIET AND NUTRITION

Leslie Beck RD

Associate Researcher Anne von Rosenbach, B.A., M.L.S.

PENGUIN
CANADA

PENGUIN CANADA

Penguin Group (Canada), a division of Pearson Penguin Canada Inc.,
    10 Alcorn Avenue, Toronto, Ontario M4V 3B2

Penguin Group (U.K.), 80 Strand, London WC2R 0RL, England
Penguin Group (U.S.), 375 Hudson Street, New York, New York 10014, U.S.A.
Penguin Group (Australia) Inc., 250 Camberwell Road, Camberwell, Victoria 3124, Australia
Penguin Group (Ireland), 25 St. Stephen's Green, Dublin 2, Ireland
Penguin Books India (P) Ltd, 11, Community Centre, Panchsheel Park, New Delhi – 110 017, India
Penguin Group (New Zealand), cnr Rosedale and Airborne Roads, Albany, Auckland 1310, New Zealand
Penguin Books (South Africa) (Pty) Ltd, 24 Sturdee Avenue, Rosebank 2196, South Africa

Penguin Group, Registered Offices: 80 Strand, London WC2R 0RL, England

First published in a Viking Canada hardcover by Penguin Group (Canada),
    a division of Pearson Penguin Canada Inc., 2002
Published in this edition, 2003

1 2 3 4 5 6 7 8 9 10 (WEB)

Copyright © Leslie Beck, 2002
Copyright © 2002 Transcontinental Media Inc., recipes pages 185 to 221

Canadian Living and Tested Till Perfect are registered trademarks of Transcontinental Media.

Manufactured in Canada.

NATIONAL LIBRARY OF CANADA CATALOGUING IN PUBLICATION

Beck, Leslie (Leslie C.)
   Leslie Beck's 10 steps to healthy eating : how to boost energy, manage weight and prevent disease with food, diet and nutrition / Leslie Beck ; associate researcher: Anne von Rosenbach.

Includes bibliographical references and index.
ISBN 0-14-301602-4

1. Nutrition. 2. Health. I. Von Rosenbach, Anne II. Title. III. Title: 10 steps to healthy eating.
IV. Title: Leslie Beck's ten steps to healthy eating. V. Title: Ten steps to healthy eating.

RA784.B426   2003   613.2   C2003-903108-X

Visit the Penguin Group (Canada) website at **www.penguin.ca**

A journey of a thousand miles begins

with a single step.

—Chinese proverb

Contents

Acknowledgments x
Introduction xi

Step 1 Get Ready to Change Your Diet Permanently 1
Getting and Staying Motivated 2
Organizing Your Meals and Your Kitchen 10
10 Tips for Changing Your Diet 16

Step 2 Eat Enough Protein 19
Why Do You Need Protein? 20
How Much Protein Do You Need to Eat? 21
Protein in Foods 22
What Happens if You Don't Get Enough Protein? 24
What Happens if You Get Too Much Protein? 25
Animal versus Plant Protein: Should You Become a Vegetarian? 26
Concerns about the Safety of Animal Foods 29
Protein Foods You Should Be Eating More Often 35
10 Tips for Incorporating High-Quality Protein Foods in Your Diet 39

Step 3 Choose the Right Carbohydrates 41
What Is Carbohydrate? 42
A Grain of Truth about High-Carbohydrate Diets 43
The Whole Truth about High-Carbohydrate Diets 44
The Whole-Grain Story 45
The Carbohydrate–Insulin Connection and the Glycemic Index 48
Don't Forget about Fiber! 52
What about Added Sugars? 54
Are Artificial Sweeteners Safe? 57
10 Tips for Incorporating Healthy Carbohydrates in Your Diet 58

Step 4 Eat More Fruits and Vegetables 61

The Health Benefits of Fruits and Vegetables 62

What's in Fruits and Vegetables? 64

Strategies to Eat More Fruits and Vegetables 70

Should You Worry about Pesticide Residues? 73

What about Genetically Modified Foods? 76

30 Tips for Eating More Fruits and Vegetables 80

Step 5 Choose Healthier Fats and Oils 83

Fat Chemistry 101 84

Why You Need Some Fat in Your Diet 84

Eating Fat Can Make You Fat 85

Cutting Back on Dietary Fat 85

Fat and Your Blood Cholesterol 88

Get to Know the Different Types of Fat 89

Putting It All Together: How Much and What Type
   of Fat Should You Eat? 95

35 Tips for Choosing Healthier Fats and Oils 96

Step 6 Boost Your Vitamins and Minerals 101

Can Supplements Replace Food? 102

Focus on Calcium 103

Focus on Vitamin D 107

Focus on Iron 109

Focus on Folate (Folic Acid) 112

Do You Need a Multivitamin and Mineral Supplement? 115

25 Tips for Boosting Your Nutrient Intake 117

Step 7 Eat More Often 119

A Typical Day in a Hectic Life 120

Six Good Reasons to Eat More Often 121

How Often Should You Eat? 125

Should You Become a Grazer? 129

10 Tips for Eating More Often 129

Step 8 Don't Forget about Fluids 131

The Health Benefits of Drinking Water 132

How Much Fluid Do You Need Each Day? 135

What Counts as Fluid? 137

What about Caffeinated Beverages? 141
Recommendations for Alcohol 144
10 Tips for Boosting Your Fluid Intake 145

Step 9   Control Your Weight 147
Do You Need to Lose Weight? 148
The Pitfalls of Fad Diets 151
Successful Weight Loss 153
How Much Should You Eat to Lose Weight? 156
Choosing a Weight-Loss Program 158
Smart Strategies to Help You *Keep* the Weight Off 159
10 Tips for Managing Your Weight 161

Step 10   Be Active Every Day 163
Reasons to Exercise 164
Breaking Down Barriers to Exercise 167
Get Motivated and Stay Motivated 169
When to Check in with Your Doctor First 171
Putting Together Your Exercise Program 171
15 Tips for Getting More Active 177

Leslie's 14-Day Meal Plan for Healthy Eating 179
The Recipes 184

Endnotes 223
General Index 231
Recipe Index 239

Acknowledgments

I would like to thank the many people whose encouragement and valuable assistance made this book possible:

Anne von Rosenbach, whom I have now had the pleasure to work with on three of my books. Through her dedication and thoroughness, Anne sought after, gathered and organized the scientific research to support the information in this book. If it weren't for her amazing help, I'd still be writing this book!

The team at Viking Canada, especially my editor, Andrea Crozier, who has believed in my work from the very beginning. Your continued support and encouragement have made it possible for me to achieve my goals.

My clients, who, over the years, have inspired me to ask questions and continue my learning. The process never ends—for which I am grateful.

The fitness staff at the Adelaide Club in Toronto, especially my personal trainer, Tyrone Estabrook, who motivates me to work out even when it's the last thing I feel like doing. And a special thank you to Blair Larsen for providing relevant and scientifically sound information for the chapter on exercise.

And finally, my family and friends, who continue to put up with my periods of hibernation while I write books. They haven't written me off yet, and I hope they never do. I thank you for your love, understanding and friendships.

Introduction

They say it's never too late. After writing nutrition books for women and an A-to-Z nutrition encyclopedia, I've finally written a book for every Canadian who wants to eat healthier. And according to recent statistics, almost nine out of ten Canadians rank nutrition as important when it comes to deciding what to eat. This book sorts fact from fiction and tells you, in no-nonsense terms, what you need to eat to stay healthy.

You won't find any fads or gimmicks in this book, just smart eating strategies based on the latest science. It used to be that eating right was only a matter of common sense. But these days, many people want in-depth knowledge of nutrition, not only to help them shed pounds but also to keep up with mounting scientific evidence that certain foods may cause or help prevent disease.

Whether your eating habits need a tune-up or a complete overhaul, you'll get all the information you need in the chapters that follow. If you have high blood pressure or high cholesterol, you'll find plenty of tips on how to cut saturated fat from your diet and add vegetables, beans and soy foods. If you're genetically predisposed to illnesses such as cancer and osteoporosis, you'll learn how to lower your risk by eating the right foods and nutrients. Or if you're a frustrated yo-yo dieter, you'll find a specific meal plan and strategies that will help guarantee your success.

You may not have any health problems at all. Perhaps all you have is a nagging desire to revamp your diet to boost your energy level, optimize your nutrient intake and stay healthy. My *10 Steps to Healthy Eating* will help you do just that. You'll learn what foods you must eat more of, what you need to eat less of, and how often you should be nourishing your body. If you're concerned about getting enough calcium, iron and folate in your diet, you'll find out how much of each you need and how to get these key nutrients from foods and supplements.

How to Use This Book

Eat Healthy, Step by Step

This book will help you change your diet for the better, step by step. Each chapter represents a step, or goal, that you must achieve to reach your final destination of healthy eating. I begin each chapter by stating the goal, whether it's to eat the right carbohydrates, to choose healthy fats, to focus on key nutrients or to include regular exercise. My short *Nutrition IQ Quiz* gives you an opportunity to test your nutrition know-how before you read about the topic. You'll learn the answers as you read through the chapter, but I've also listed them at the end of the chapter for easy reference.

Improving your diet is a process, not a one-shot deal. It's important to take one step at a time. Once you master that step, you're ready to move on to the next. Although I have ordered the steps one through ten, you really can start wherever you like. For instance, getting more fruit and vegetables (Step 4) may be a bigger priority for you than including the right amount of protein in your diet (Step 2). Or you may decide to tackle exercise (Step 10) first. Do whatever is right for you.

However, regardless of what aspect of your diet you decide to improve first, I strongly recommend that you begin the process by reading Step 1. This step prepares you to make a change, whether that change involves your diet or your exercise habits. The strategies given in Step 1 will help you set realistic goals, overcome potential obstacles, gather the tools you need to accomplish your goals and, most importantly, stay motivated. Once you do the exercises in Step 1, you'll have a better sense of your priorities and what aspects of your diet you want to work on first.

165 Easy-to-Implement Tips

Within each chapter, I tell you what changes you need to make and why it's important to make them. Armed with this nutrition knowledge, you'll be ready to go into action and take one step forward. At the end of each chapter, I give you plenty of practical tips—smaller steps actually—that will help you achieve each goal.

A Two-Week Meal Plan to Get You Started

Let's face it, life is busy. Preparing healthy meals day after day and week after week can be a challenge, even with all the planning tools in place. That's why I've made it easy by giving you a starter kit. With help from the experts at The Canadian Living Test Kitchen, I've mapped out a 14-day plan for you—a meal plan that's based on the very principles you'll read about in this book. If you don't want to follow a structured meal plan, enjoy the recipes on their own. Incorporate them as you please into your family's meal times.

More Than 65 Recipes to Keep You Healthy

Each recipe in this book was developed and Tested Till Perfect by the experts in The Canadian Living Test Kitchen. They taste great, they're easy to prepare and, of course, they're good for you. Each recipe is accompanied by a per-serving nutrient analysis, a breakdown of its calories, fat, protein, fiber and so on. In addition to 14 days' worth of breakfast, lunch and dinner ideas, you will find great-tasting recipes for vegetables, whole grains, quick sandwiches and marinades.

I began my introduction by saying it's never too late to do something. In my case, that was writing this book, a book that I have wanted to write for a long time. In your case, it's never too late to eat healthy. Whether you're young or old, improving your diet and getting more active will help you feel better right now and years down the road.

Enjoy the path to healthy eating, each and every step of the way.

Leslie Beck, RD
Toronto, 2002

Step 1

Get Ready to Change Your Diet Permanently

LESLIE'S NUTRITION IQ QUIZ   CHANGING YOUR DIET

1. You've heard time and time again about the benefits of healthy eating. What statement below best describes how you feel about your current diet? (Choose one response.)
    - ❑ My diet is just fine the way it is. It may not be perfect; in fact, it may be far from perfect, but it's not doing me any harm.
    - ❑ I know my diet needs some work, but there are too many other stresses in my life right now for me to worry about it.
    - ❑ I know my diet needs some work and I do want to make some changes.
    - ❑ I am actively working on eating healthier.

2. Do you make time to grocery shop once a week? Yes ❑   No ❑

3. Do you usually shop from a grocery list? Yes ❑   No ☑ *sometimes*

4. Do you often come home from work without a plan for dinner?
    Yes ☑ No ❑

5. Do the tools (cookware, utensils) in your kitchen help you cook healthy?
    Yes ❑ No ❑

ow many times have you vowed to start eating better, only to find that your motivation has quickly disappeared? Or perhaps your desire to eat healthy is alive and well, but too often you come home from work, tired and hungry, to an empty fridge. You probably didn't plan on dining on a bowl of cereal, or worse, a pepperoni pizza. (Not that a bowl of cereal is a terrible choice, but if this is your usual evening meal, I'm willing to bet that your diet is suffering from a severe lack of protein and vegetables.)

Eating healthy *as a way of life* is much more than knowing what foods to eat and when to eat them. The very first step to changing your diet for the better is *getting organized*: knowing what you want and need to change in your diet, how to make those changes and, most importantly, how to stick with them through thick and thin.

Over the past 14 years, I have helped many people achieve their diet- and nutrition-related health goals. I've provided the necessary tools and encouragement to help clients lose weight, gain weight (yes, there are a few people out there who need a little extra padding!), lower blood cholesterol, reduce blood pressure, manage an irritable bowel or simply just eat better. But I have come to realize that successful clients tend to share a few characteristics: they believe in their ability to change, they don't beat themselves up when they get off-track and they are persistent. Throughout this chapter you'll learn strategies that will help foster these important characteristics that define success.

Getting and Staying Motivated

Changing your eating habits is a process—it's not a one-step event that leads to a dramatic transformation. It takes the right attitude, internal motivation, an action plan and long-term commitment. Behavioral scientists believe that people who make long-lasting dietary changes pass through a series of stages. Each stage determines where they are in terms of being ready to make a behavior change, and what they need to do to move forward. Even people who quit something "cold turkey" evolve through these stages without realizing it.

To form a new healthy habit (or break an old bad habit), read about each of the stages of change listed below. Then determine where you fit and work on skills that you need to make change last.

Pre-Contemplation Stage

Almost half of all people who need to make a change are at this stage. If you are here, you may not know that your diet or your weight are hazardous to your health. Even if you do recognize this, you may not be able to admit that you need to make a change. Or perhaps you are too discouraged to make a change because your previous attempts have ended in failure.

The challenge is that pre-contemplators usually don't want to talk about their problem. It's tough to help someone if he or she is not ready or willing to listen. I hear this complaint often from my clients who are concerned about the health of a loved one. For the past five years, I've helped Mary, a 46-year-old businesswoman, lose 50 pounds and keep them off. She's made many healthy changes to her diet and she exercises four times each week. But what she really wants now is for her husband, who has a family history of heart attack, to follow suit. "If I bring up the subject of losing weight, he'll shut me down … I can't even get him to go to the doctor … he says he feels fine," she despairs.

Many people in this stage start to pay attention once they acknowledge the real risks of their behaviors. Unfortunately for Mary's husband, this meant suffering a mild heart attack while on vacation in Mexico. For others, a wake-up call to action can be as simple as a low-key, nonjudgmental message from a friend or family member ("Take a look at this story on the dangers of stress and high blood pressure"). Inspiration can also come from a significant birthday. I can't count the number of times I've heard that a 40th birthday prompted an analysis of health habits.

Contemplation Stage

In this stage, you know you should change your diet, or lose weight or exercise more. But you find too many reasons not to do so: "I'm too busy to work out … I'm too rushed in the morning to eat breakfast … I don't like vegetables … I'm too tired to cook a healthy dinner"… and so on. We've all made these kinds of excuses before, myself included.

The key to getting out of the contemplation stage and moving forward is to convince yourself that the benefits of making the change are worth the sacrifices. You need to weigh the pros and cons. Make a list of the changes you'd like to make, along with the short-term and long-term benefits. Think about the physical, mental and emotional benefits.

When I asked Mary to do this during our first meeting, she was surprised at how long her list was. She'd actually never thought about these things before—she just knew she wanted to lose weight. For Mary, losing weight meant she'd be able to lower her blood cholesterol, fit into a size 10, have more energy, come home from work in a good mood for her family, feel more self-confident and feel comfortable around her slim friends at their annual beach holiday.

If you've been stuck contemplating change for years, listing the negatives of continuing on your current path just may move you to action. If you don't make a change, how will you feel in 10 and 20 years? What will you be doing? Or more importantly, what won't you be doing? Occasionally I have clients who come to see me looking for motivation. They are in the contemplation stage, hoping that I will wave a magic wand over their heads to make them ready for action. But only you can make change happen. Knowing why you want to change will empower you to get to the next stage.

Preparation Stage

By now you not only realize that you need to make a change; you've also listed all the pros and cons. But you may still need a nudge to get started. This gentle push may be the setting of a starting date, or the voicing of your healthy intentions to your family. You might even decide on a compromise. If revamping your entire diet seems overwhelming, you might be more likely to embrace a halfway measure such as eating breakfast each morning, or skipping the cookies after dinner.

These strategies are meant to prepare you for action. Preparing yourself will make you feel in control. And feeling in control will bolster your confidence to proceed.

Action Stage

You're ready to go for it. The will, the motivation and the confidence are all in place. Now all you need is a road map. How do you plan to make healthy changes to your lifestyle? Some people change their diet and lose weight on their own. They might follow a nutrition book or they might implement dietary changes they have decided on by themselves. Others find it helpful to enlist the support of an established program or consult a qualified nutritionist like myself.

Regardless of how you do it, the following five strategies are essential for your long-term success.

1. Set Realistic Goals

Have you ever heard the saying, "If you don't know where you are going, any road will take you there"? In other words, all roads are the wrong roads. Your goals should be guidelines that give you direction and focus.

One of the common characteristics of highly successful people is that they are goal oriented. Successful people know what they want to achieve in life and they have a clear plan to get there. Their road map to success is the list of goals they have written down.

Your goals to pursue a healthier lifestyle must be for *you*, and only you. You can't set goals to please other people. You can only truly succeed at eating well or losing weight because you want to, not because your spouse, or your doctor for that matter, says you should. It might be worthwhile to take a moment to identify the motivating forces driving your desire to make healthy changes. Answers such as "to manage a health concern," "to lose weight," "to control my stress level" and "to boost my energy level" can all be powerful motivators for change. If this exercise reveals that the *only* thing motivating you to get healthy is the influence of someone else, chances are you'll be less successful.

It's one thing to have goals, but it's another to write those goals down on paper. There are plenty of reasons why documenting your nutrition and health goals is the first step to lifelong healthy eating.

Written goals will increase your odds of success. Researchers who study employee motivation have learned that *specific* goals consistently lead to better on-the-job performance than general goals or no goals at all. Can you imagine an Olympic athlete training for years without any goals? Can you imagine yourself succeeding at losing weight or lowering your blood cholesterol without a road map? Probably not.

Written goals will enhance your motivation. By knowing your final outcome, be it a specific weight goal, a healthy blood pressure reading or eating a low-fat diet, you will be able to measure your progress. And as you take notice of your progress, you'll be motivated to continue working toward your goals. If you are highly committed to your goal, you will perform better.

Written goals will bolster your self-confidence. As you observe the progress you are making toward achieving your goals, you will be more confident in your ability to do so. People who believe they can achieve their goals are much more committed to those goals.

Written goals provide clarity and direction. Just as a business plan is a road map for an organization, showing the destination it seeks and the path it will follow to get there, your nutrition goals are your driving force for dietary change. Goals help you know what you need to do to achieve the results you want.

Now it's time for you to write down your goals. Use the framework below to help you craft realistic, achievable goals.

SMART Goal Setting

Specific Avoid making vague or general goals. It's not enough to say you want to "eat better" or "lose weight." That's not specific enough! But saying you want to "eat lower-fat meals" or "eat more fruit and vegetables each day" or "lose 15 pounds" is specific. Once you crystallize what it is you want to achieve, it becomes much simpler to figure out how you're going to get there.

Measurable If you can't measure it, you can't monitor your progress. If you want to start exercising, you need to write this goal so it is measurable. You might say "I will exercise for 30 minutes after work, four times a week." Now you have a way to track your progress.

Attainable Set a goal that you know is possible for you to achieve. There's no sense setting your sights on adopting a complete vegetarian diet if your family won't eat soy foods or beans! Can you really see yourself preparing two separate menus at meal time?

Realistic Make sure your goals are realistic for you to accomplish with your given resources, lifestyle and time frame. You might have weighed 30 pounds less when you played varsity football 20 years ago, but is that weight really achievable today? You need to assess your current lifestyle and have a clear sense of what you are willing and what you are not willing to change.

Time frame Goals must have a target date for completion. My client Mary wanted to lose 50 pounds. We determined that this was a realistic goal based on her current lifestyle and her weight history (it was over the past ten years that she had gained her excess weight). She was also realistic about her time frame. She was content to lose five pounds each month. She started her nutrition plan in February, so her target date was set for ten months later, some time in November. (Mary actually achieved her goal three months ahead of schedule—another benefit of being realistic about goal setting. There was no disappointment, only a great sense of accomplishment.)

Target dates can be short term, say weeks or months down the road, or long term. Depending on who you are and what your goal is, a short time frame may be all it takes to get accustomed to your new healthy habit. For others, a longer time frame may be more realistic.

Keep in mind that change takes time. It may take longer than you expect. But the longer you work at changing your habits, the more likely you'll break those bad habits for good. And some people like to have goals ever-present—by succeeding at achieving your goal, you'll stay motivated and continue making those healthy choices for a lifetime.

Get out your pen and paper. Write down three nutrition/diet/health goals that you would like to achieve. It's important to write your goals in *positive terms*. Your goals should tell you what you are going to do, instead of what you're not going to do. Rather than telling yourself, "I'm not going to eat any sweets after dinner this week," tell yourself, "I am going to have fruit and yogurt for dessert every night this week." And remember, your goals must be specific, realistic and measurable. Here's an example of a SMART goal:

> I would like to be able to prepare tasty vegetarian meals for my family three times each week. Over the next month, I will replace one animal-protein-based meal (meat, chicken, eggs) with a vegetarian-protein meal (soy, beans) each week. In two months' time, my family will be eating three vegetarian meals each week.

Remember, these things don't happen overnight. You need time to find recipes and incorporate them into your family's menu plan.

Now, make your list. Write three goals, like this: "Specifically, I would like to (fill in the blank) by the following date: (fill in the blank)."

After you've made your list, choose one goal to work on first. Once you feel you've mastered that area in your diet, move on to your next goal (but don't stop working on what you have just accomplished!). Too much of a change too soon can be overwhelming, so make it gradually. And remember, eating healthy and exercising is not an "all or nothing" endeavor. What I mean is, you don't have to do everything perfectly to be on track.

Too often I see clients who can't meet their exercise goals because of a demanding work schedule and, as a result, they feel that they've failed. And then you know what happens?

That good old dieting mentality takes over: "Well, I've blown it now so it really doesn't matter what I eat today … I'll start fresh next week." Lose that attitude! You'll make progress even if you accomplish 50 percent of the things you set out to change.

When I see clients for their follow-up visits, I always ask how they have been doing. Sometimes I hear, "Oh terrible … I've only managed to work out once this week and I've been out for dinner three times … I know my weight is up." But guess what? They still manage to lose a pound or two. That's because small changes add up. You are not expected to be perfect (even I'm not perfect … well, most of the time I come pretty close!).

2. Identify Your Barriers to Success

It's important to recognize obstacles that may prevent you from achieving your goals. Make change easier by avoiding cues that spell trouble. This may involve simple things like banning cookies from the house, planning a weekly dinner menu or grocery shopping on a full stomach. Sometimes, though, it may require more significant adjustments, like changing jobs or making new friends.

You can get a few clues as to how you might overcome potential barriers by thinking about the things you're doing well at right now. What makes it easy for you to eat healthy? Take a few moments to answer these questions:

1. Think about several healthy eating choices you are making now and of which you are proud. *What things make it easy for you to maintain these healthy eating choices as a part of your lifestyle?* I'll give you a few of my own personal gold stars:

    -   I always exercise at least four times each week. This is easy because fitting exercise into my life is convenient. My fitness club is right across the street from my office, I have a StairMaster at home and I live in a neighborhood with many wonderful running trails.

    -   I eat plenty of vegetables—at least five servings each day. This is easy for me because I love vegetables, I have plenty of tasty quick-cooking methods for veggies and I shop for fresh vegetables twice a week.

2. Now think about the goals you have just set. *What things might prevent you from making and maintaining these healthy eating choices in your lifestyle?* Here are a few of the obstacles I most commonly hear about from clients, along with a suggestion of how to overcome each (I address all of them in more detail in the chapters to come):

    -   "I don't have time to exercise." (If you really want something, you have to make time for it. If you truly can't schedule a 30-minute workout into your day, what about finding time for two 15-minute power walks—one at lunch and the other after dinner?)

    -   "There's no healthy food in the house … work is too busy for me to have time to grocery shop." (Get your groceries delivered to your home once a week.)

- "I can't resist ... the cookies are in the house for the kids' lunches." (The kids don't need cookies every day—either don't buy them, buy a brand you don't like or hide them!)

- "For me, watching television and snacking go hand in hand." (One of my clients canceled her cable so she won't watch so much television.)

- "I'm starving at 4 o'clock ... the vending machine is so handy." (Plan for a midday snack. Throw a piece of fruit or an energy bar into your bag each morning.)

3. It's time to brainstorm. *What are some ways you can see yourself overcoming each obstacle?* If you give this some thought, you'll be more prepared to deal with each barrier when (and if) the time comes. Bottom line: you'll be much more likely to succeed if you have a plan in place to deal with obstacles as they arise. I call it risk management!

3. Establish Rewards

Your goals for improving your diet and your health should be enjoyable and fun. It's important to decide how you will reward yourself for accomplishing your goals, as well as the smaller steps along the way. Rewards make you feel good about your accomplishment and give you incentive for carrying on with your plan for change. Write down when you plan to reward yourself and how you plan to do it. A new CD? A tube of lipstick? New clothes? A weekend getaway? Dinner at your favorite restaurant? You get the idea.

4. Enlist Support

A big key to making change stick is receiving encouragement and support from those around you. Support comes in many forms. If your goal is to lose weight, you might benefit from the support of a group like Weight Watchers. In fact, I have a number of weight-loss clients who come to see me to get one-on-one counseling but also attend weekly Weight Watcher meetings. It's motivating to talk to other people who are dealing with similar issues.

Support can also come from coworkers. They can share healthy recipes with you or act as workout partners at lunch. Exercise classes are another place to find support. Many people find it more motivating (and more fun) to work out with a group of people rather than walking alone on a treadmill.

It's important to determine who your support person(s) will be. Think about someone who is ready to listen to your request for help and is able to make an effort to offer positive support. Sometimes the people we think should be our best support are not the most appropriate people to seek help from. A close friend whom you enjoy socializing with may have a hectic schedule that leaves little time for providing the assistance you need.

Undoubtedly, support means getting encouragement from a partner and friends. You have to let your support person know how you want them to help you. Perhaps you need to tell your spouse not to pull out the bag of potato chips after dinner. Or you might need to ask your best friend to offer motivating comments from time to time. Getting positive reinforcement from those around you, in whatever form it may take, is a crucial element in achieving your goals.

5. Track Your Progress

How can you know how you're doing if you don't keep tabs on your progress? If you don't monitor your weight or your body measurements, how do you know your plan is working? If you don't keep track of your food intake, how can you be sure you're eating five to ten servings of fruits and vegetables each day? You can't. You must keep track along the way.

One of the biggest assets in making dietary change is a *food diary.* I strongly recommend that you keep a journal—whether it's a pad of paper or a bound journal—to track your food intake for at least the first month you embark on your plan for change. Document the foods you eat each day. Write down what times you ate, what you ate and how much, your hunger level prior to eating and any overriding emotions that were present at the time. Record your food intake after each meal. Don't wait until the end of the day to do this or you'll likely forget a few foods.

Your food diary helps keep you focused on and committed to your goals. It highlights in black and white the foods you *are* eating and the foods you *are not* eating. It will make you think twice about eating that extra helping at dinner or that handful of potato chips. At the very least, it will make you aware that you are doing these things. Often, much of our eating is "mindless eating." We don't pay attention to what we are putting in our mouths because we are always in such a hurry—we grab a bite as we run out the door, or while we read the newspaper or while we watch television.

A food diary can provide a huge amount of self-awareness. Assess your food record each day. What did you notice? No fruit? No vegetables? No breakfast? Too many sweets? Portion sizes larger than you thought? Your diary may also reveal emotions or behaviors that trigger overeating, areas that you may need to work on. You may even decide to keep a food diary for a few weeks before you decide what nutrition goals you want to work on. I am willing to bet that the process of recording your food intake will illuminate a few problem areas (and a few areas in which you are already doing great that you may not have realized!).

For those of you intent on shedding some extra body fat, keep track once a month of your body measurements (bust, waist, hips) and clothing size. Monitor your weight once a week (no more!), preferably at the same time each day (first thing in the morning is best). If your goals include lowering blood cholesterol or blood pressure, leave room for charting these important health measurements once every three months. I also recommend that you track your exercise sessions in your food diary.

Maintenance Stage

Perhaps you've managed to lose those nagging ten pounds, but now you feel them creeping back on. Or after last year's efforts at cutting back on fat and lowering your cholesterol to a healthy level, your recent visit to the doctor revealed your blood cholesterol sliding upward. Most of us know that achieving our nutrition goals is often not the hard part—maintaining them over the long term is.

As I have said before, making a permanent lifestyle change is a process, not a single event. And the path you follow will not always be a smooth one. Slip-ups are bound to happen—we're only human, after all. The key is to not let temporary setbacks get you down. How you deal with lapses can determine whether your mistake turns out to be inconsequential or leads you to return to your old habits (a relapse).

The most important rule is: *do not pile blame on yourself or treat a momentary lapse as if it's a catastrophe, signaling the end of all your efforts.* If you get down on yourself, you will lose confidence in your ability to carry on. An occasional lapse or slip won't hurt your progress. But if you let lapses accumulate, you may find yourself back at square one.

Following these tips will help you prevent a relapse:

- If you feel yourself slipping, *keep a food diary* to maintain perspective. A food diary will show you the big picture. It will help you to see all the things you are doing right—the things you're likely to forget about if you focus on the negative.

- *Have an action plan* to deal with lapses. Keeping a food diary is one way to refocus your efforts. But you might also resort to other measures: stepping up the exercise, cutting out desserts for a few weeks, adding one new healthy recipe to your menu plan each week … do whatever works for you. An action plan is intended to refocus and remotivate you to get back on track.

- Identify exactly what set you off course. A bad day at the office? Junk food lingering after a party? Feeling grumpy and fatigued at the end of a tough week? Thinking that you deserved that donut because you've been "good" all week? Once you've determined the cause of your lapse, *think of ways you can cope with these lapses*, with actions that don't involve food. This will prepare you for the next time you encounter a trigger. (And we all know there will be a next time—the trick is to learn from your mistakes.)

- Tell yourself that one mistake does not make you unable to change. Just pick up where you left off.

Organizing Your Meals and Your Kitchen

You can have all the good intentions in the world, but if you are not organized to follow through with those intentions, they're pretty much useless. Not being organized in the kitchen is a surefire way to sabotage your healthy plan. To be successful at eating healthy you need to plan ahead and have the right foods and cookware on hand.

Trust me, I know how busy your lives can be. My head often spins after hearing about my clients' hectic weekday schedules. With both spouses working, and having to rush home to pick up kids or deliver them to extracurricular activities, it can be downright challenging to put a nutritious meal on the table. And if you leave it to chance, let's face it: it isn't going to happen. Too often, the fast food drive-through saves the day.

Strategy #1: Plan Weekly Menus Ahead

Most people don't plan menus—that is, they don't write them down in advance. Menu planning means thinking about what foods you will eat together for a meal, for a day or for a week. I encourage you to sit down on the weekend (before you grocery shop) and map out your family's meals for the week. You'll need to think about your family's scheduled activities, that is, who will be home for meals and who won't. This will help you decide whether you need to cook ahead on the weekend or whether you need to plan for leftovers. And once this is done, it's easy to prepare your grocery list.

You don't have to be feeding an entire family to benefit from planning your meals ahead of time. I have plenty of clients who cook for one and find menu planning extremely useful. They don't need to think when they get home from work; no last-minute decisions are necessary because they have the foods ready to go. Devising a menu plan helps my single clients eat restaurant or take-out foods less often, and save money.

Planning ahead may sound like a lot of extra work, but believe me when I tell you that it will save you heaps of time during your busy week. Healthy foods will be on hand, which means fewer stops at the grocery store during the week. Planning for leftovers also cuts down on preparation time. And best of all, you'll be eating wholesome, healthy meals. Writing down your weekly menus in advance means you can plan for a variety of nutritious foods.

You may decide to use my 14-Day Meal Plan I've included in this book. If you are looking for ways to incorporate more fish, soy foods and beans into your family's diet, this meal plan ought to get you started (don't worry, there are meat and chicken recipes too!). These delicious recipes come from The Canadian Living Test Kitchen. The recipes are fast and healthy; most can be prepared in 30 minutes or less.

Strategy #2: Schedule Time for Once-a-Week Grocery Shopping

If you've completed your weekly menu plan, you essentially have your grocery list. Your meal plan tells you what foods you need to buy each week. You may need to restock your supply of fresh vegetables and fruit midweek, but you should have all the essentials on hand to last through the week.

To save trips to the grocery store, take advantage of your freezer. I encourage my clients to eat more fish, but buying fish is often seen as an obstacle. You don't need to buy fish fresh the day you plan to eat it. I visit my local fish store every Friday and buy what I need for the next seven days (I usually eat fish four times a week). I just freeze what I won't be eating over the next two days and defrost it as I need it. If you go through bread quickly, buy a few loaves and store those in the freezer too.

A weekly trip to the grocery store is important even if you don't have a menu plan. You still need to have healthy foods in the house. When you shop, stick to the perimeter of the store—the outer aisles are where you'll find the healthy, fresh foods. I don't even bother going down the snack food or frozen entrée aisles. Never shop on an empty stomach; you'll come home with more food items than you planned, some of them not so healthy. If you find you really don't have time to visit a grocery store (or perhaps you just don't like to grocery shop), take advantage of a home delivery service. Today, many supermarkets and specialty food shops deliver for a small fee. Some stores offer on-line ordering and will even deliver in the evening.

Here's a list of staple foods to have on hand for preparing quick healthy meals (your tastes may vary; these are only some of the foods I keep on hand):

Grain foods Brown rice, whole-wheat pasta, couscous (a really quick side dish), kasha, quick-cooking oats (if you buy instant, choose plain, unsweetened), brown rice crackers (a great low-fat snack for kids), whole-grain breads (look for whole-wheat flour as the first ingredient), whole-rye or -pumpernickel bread, cold cereals with at least 4 grams of fiber per serving (check the nutrition panel), whole-wheat frozen waffles.

Vegetables Fresh veggies: broccoli, bell peppers, carrots, zucchini, cucumber and mushrooms will all store well in the crisper for up to a week, sometimes longer; baby greens and bagged salads are fast and convenient; winter squash and turnip last for weeks on your countertop; sweet potatoes, onions and garlic keep well in your vegetable bin; frozen veggies (skip the brands with added sauce): green beans, spinach, peas, corn; canned veggies (I prefer frozen, but if you buy canned, choose sodium-reduced): canned tomatoes are a must!

Fruit Fresh fruit: apples, oranges, grapefruit, lemons and limes keep well in the fridge for days, even weeks; bananas (a staple for me with my morning bran); dried fruit: apricots, apples, currants, raisins, cranberries (great additions to hot cereal and salads); canned unsweetened fruit and applesauce; unsweetened fruit juices (that means no sugar added!).

Fish, poultry, meat and eggs Salmon fillets, halibut fillets, chicken and turkey breast, ground turkey, extra-lean ground beef, canned tuna and salmon, sardines, omega-3 eggs. If you buy more fresh meat or poultry than you need for the week, be sure to label and date it before you add it to your freezer. It's easy to forget what's in there. I've often had to throw away chicken breasts suffering from a bad case of freezer burn. I prefer to buy only for the week ahead.

Beans   Canned beans: chickpeas (for salads and pastas), black beans (great for tacos), white and red kidney beans (for soups, salads and chili), lentils. Dried beans and lentils are great but require a little extra prep time (see page 38, Chapter 2). I like to keep dried green lentils on hand for soup, salad and casserole recipes.

Soy foods   My protein staples are fish, beans and soy. Firm tofu is great steamed, stir-fried and grilled (I often chop it, then add it to hot and sour soup). Soy ground round can be added to pasta sauces, chili and tacos; you can buy it plain, or Italian or Mexican seasoned (you'll find it in the produce section). Veggie burgers can be grilled three minutes per side for a fast meal. Soy beverages are an alternative if you don't drink cow's milk (make sure you buy a brand that's enriched with calcium). Always check the expiry date on soy foods.

Dairy products   1 percent or skim milk, yogurt with 1 percent milk fat or less (I avoid the brands with artificial sweetener), cheese, cottage cheese, butter (I always keep some in my freezer in case a recipe calls for it; I don't use margarine).

Oils and dressings   Extra-virgin olive oil for salad dressings and sauces; canola oil for cooking and baking; sesame oil for flavoring stir-fries (add it at the end of cooking); walnut oil for salad dressings. Oils can go rancid quickly, so avoid the urge to buy an economy-sized bottle. Buy small bottles of oil and store them in a cool, dark cupboard (walnut, sesame and flax oils should be stored in the fridge). I usually make my own salad dressings, but if you do buy a commercial brand, avoid fat free (we need some fat for good health). Fat-reduced versions are fine, but check the type of oil used.

Spices and condiments   The list is long, but a few essentials for me are black pepper, red pepper flakes, thyme, oregano and basil. Capers, oyster sauce, hoisin sauce, fish sauce, tandoori paste, curry paste, Dijon and grainy Russian-style mustards are great flavor boosters for vegetable, fish and meat dishes. Red wine vinegar, balsamic vinegar and rice vinegar are the types I use the most.

Beverages   All that's in my house is bottled water, green and black tea (I buy a few varieties from my local tea shop) and unsweetened citrus juice (I have a small glass each morning with my bran cereal—the vitamin C enhances iron absorption). I don't buy soda pop of any kind. I admit that you will find a bottle of wine in my house on weekends.

Sweets   The sweetest foods I have on hand are fruit bottom and vanilla yogurts (oh, and of course fresh fruit!). Desserts come into my house only when I entertain guests for dinner, and even then, it's usually fairly healthy (fruit and sorbet, fresh fruit crumbles). As for spreads, sugar-reduced jams are good to have on hand for toast, pancakes and waffles. Maple syrup and honey are handy to have in case a recipe calls for them.

Strategy #3: Buy It Pre-Prepped

Nothing is more time consuming than chopping, slicing and dicing food. This step often presents a major obstacle when it comes to deciding what to eat. If you don't mind spending a little extra money, take advantage of time-savers at the grocery store: prewashed, precut fresh veggies such as baby carrots, broccoli florets, cauliflower, shredded cabbage, grated carrot, cubed butternut squash, chopped lettuce, even fresh fruit salads. Cherry and grape tomatoes need only a quick wash before they're ready to toss into a salad or enjoy as a snack. You can also buy your cheese grated, turkey sliced and garlic minced.

If you want to save money, do it yourself on the weekend. I often spin my lettuce as soon as I get it home from the grocery store and then store it in vegetable bags. You might spend 15 minutes on the weekend chopping carrots, celery and bell peppers to have handy for snacks and salads. With everything sliced and ready to go, you can throw together a meal in no time.

Strategy #4: Plan for Leftovers

Leftovers may have a bad reputation in your house, but cooking more than you need for the next day's meals saves an enormous amount of time. And it's a great strategy when you know the next night's schedule is going to be hectic. I'll often double a casserole recipe so I will have extra for lunch and/or dinner the next night. Or I'll bake an extra fillet of salmon and enjoy it cold on a bed of greens the next day. If I'm making a salad, I will intentionally make more for the next few days (I just skip the tomatoes and add them fresh each day).

Many of my clients grill a few extra chicken breasts on the weekend to serve up in sandwiches or salads the following day. Batch cooking on the weekend is a big time-saver—soups, casseroles and grilled vegetables all work well. If you love brown rice but don't have time to cook it on a weeknight (brown rice takes longer to cook than white rice), prepare a batch on the weekend.

Divide your leftovers into freezer containers to make nutritious "TV dinners." Store your meals in containers that can be reheated: disposable aluminum containers for the oven or baggies and airtight plastic containers for the microwave. I think you get the idea: *plan for leftovers* to save time during the week.

Strategy #5: Surround Yourself with Healthy Tools

Now that your cupboards and fridge are stocked with nutritious foods, it's time to look at kitchen equipment that has good nutrition (and convenience) in mind. I am sure you can think of a piece of cookware or a gadget that you can't be without. The list below is what I have on hand in my kitchen:

- *Nonstick pots, pans and baking sheets.* Make sure you buy good-quality cookware and bakeware. They're expensive, but they'll last for years and years. And always use plastic utensils so you don't scratch the surface.

- *Wok, electric or stovetop.* The round bottom of a wok allows food to be stir-fried with a minimum of oil. Choose a wide (14 inches/35 cm is good), deep wok so you can keep foods moving while stir-frying.

- *Steamer baskets.* I couldn't be without my steamer; in fact, I have three: two made of stainless steel and one made from bamboo. I steam everything from vegetables, to fish, to tofu. And steamers are great for reheating that brown rice you cooked in advance the day before!

- *Blender.* This is an invaluable tool for whipping up a quick breakfast smoothie and healthy fruit shakes for the kids after school, or for puréeing soups.

- *Food processor.* This is great if you need to shred, chop or grate a large amount of food. It saves time. I have one myself, but I find I rarely haul it out of the cupboard (it's heavy!).

- *Stock pot.* This type of pot is great for making large batches of soup or cooking pasta.

- *Hot-air popper.* Use the popper to make a low-calorie, low-fat, high-fiber snack. Forget about that microwave popcorn that's loaded with hydrogenated fat!

- *Sharp knives.* If you don't own any, do yourself a favor and invest in a few good knives. You will be amazed at how efficient you become in the kitchen. And who knows? You may even enjoy chopping those veggies!

- *Grater.* Buy a multiplane grater for versatility. Use it for carrots and zucchini, lemon and orange zest and Parmesan cheese.

- *Meat thermometer.* A thermometer allows you to cook your meat to just the way you like it, and safely too. The best ones are those that give a digital temperature reading.

What about larger appliances for cooking? I rely on my stovetop and oven and take full advantage of the barbecue in the warmer weather, but many people say they can't live without a *microwave oven.* A microwave will allow you to reheat or defrost in minutes. And it's handy to have for cooking vegetables and fish. If you're single and cooking for one, you might invest in a *toaster oven.* I have many clients who toast, bake and grill with this space-saving appliance. Portable *indoor electric grills* are popular, too. They come in many shapes and sizes; some wipe up easily, and cleaning other models can be cumbersome. Do your homework before you invest.

Congratulations! You're now ready to embark on your healthy eating journey. By now you've set your goals, you're ready to track your progress in a food diary and you're starting to plan your meals and stock your pantry accordingly. The following chapters will teach you what you should be eating and when you should schedule those meals and snacks. From carbohydrates, fats and protein foods to vegetables, fluids and supplements, the learning begins. Enjoy!

10 TIPS
FOR CHANGING YOUR DIET

1. Make a list of the changes you'd like to make to your diet and/or your health. Beside each, write down what the short-term and long-term benefits would be of making these changes.

2. Ask yourself what is motivating you to make these changes. Does your motivation come from inside yourself or from someone else?

3. Write down three of your desired changes as SMART goals (specific, measurable, attainable, realistic and time-dated). Turn to page 5 if you need a quick review on goal setting. Remember, keep your goals positive: list what you are going to do instead of what you are not going to do.

4. Think about the things that will make it easy for you to make these lifestyle changes. Think about the things that might prevent you from making or maintaining these changes. Write down ways you can see yourself overcoming each obstacle.

5. Determine who your support person(s) will be. Let them know exactly how you want them to help you achieve your goals.

6. Keep a food and exercise diary for the next four weeks (or longer). Assess it each day. If your goals include weight loss, record your weekly weight and body measurements once a month.

7. Plan and write down your weekly menus in advance.

8. Schedule time for grocery shopping once a week. Shop on a full stomach and use a list.

9. Do whatever you can to save time in the kitchen: batch cook on the weekend, buy pre-prepped produce and plan for leftovers during the week.

10. Take an inventory of your cooking equipment. Make sure you have what you need to prepare quick nutritious meals.

ANSWERS TO LESLIE'S IQ QUIZ   CHANGING YOUR DIET

There are no right or wrong answers! Your answers will reflect your attitudes and behaviors about your diet. For instance, if you answered the first question by saying that "I know my diet needs some work and I do want to make some changes," you're motivated to begin. Chances are you'll be more successful at making dietary change. On the other hand, if your response was, "There are too many other stresses in my life right now to worry about my diet," it's worth remembering that starting a nutrition program does not have to be an all-or-nothing endeavor. Start slowly by making one small change at a time. Once you see success, you'll feel ready to tackle another area of your diet. Depending on how you answered questions 2 through 5, you may need to brush up on your organization skills. If you plan ahead, healthy eating requires very little effort!

Step 2

Eat Enough Protein

LESLIE'S NUTRITION IQ QUIZ   PROTEIN

1. True or false? A high-protein, low-carbohydrate diet will build muscle.

2. True or false? A low-protein diet may increase your risk of osteoporosis.

3. Which food contains the most protein (in grams)?
   a. 1 ounce (30 grams) beef   b. 1 whole egg
   c. 1 PowerBar®   d. 1/2 cup (125 ml) cooked lentils

4. Which food is considered a complete protein?
   a. tofu   b. yogurt
   c. veggie burger   d. nuts

5. True or false? Organic meat and poultry is produced without the use of hormones and antibiotics.

With high-protein diets all the rage, it might seem odd that I have to remind you about the importance of protein-rich foods. Yet, there's more to healthy eating than just making sure you eat enough protein. And as you'll read below, there are health hazards associated with eating too much protein and with eating too little. What's more, some protein foods may be better for your health than others. Before you opt for your usual dinner of meat and potatoes, take a moment to learn the ins and outs of dietary protein.

Why Do You Need Protein?

Foods like meat, poultry, eggs, milk, beans and tofu all supply your body with a rich source of protein, a nutrient essential for life. During the process of digestion your body breaks down food proteins into their individual building blocks, amino acids. These amino acids are then absorbed by your intestine and eventually make their way to your body's cells. Here, amino acids are repackaged into between 10,000 and 50,000 different kinds of body proteins, each one playing a unique and important role in your health.

Proteins form structural components in the body—muscle tissue, connective tissue and the support tissue inside bones and teeth are all derived from the protein we eat. Scars, tendons and ligaments are made of collagen, one of the body's key structural proteins. The cells of your skin, hair and fingernails consist mainly of protein. Many of these body proteins are in a continual state of breakdown, repair and maintenance. If your diet is chronically low in protein, protein rebuilding and repair slows down.

Amino acids in food are also used to make hormones, important proteins that regulate hundreds of body processes. Thyroid hormones control your metabolic rate, the speed at which your body burns calories. Hormones called insulin and glucagon closely regulate the level of sugar in your bloodstream. When your blood sugar rises after eating, insulin ensures that this sugar enters your cells, where it's needed for energy. On the flip side, if you haven't eaten for hours and your blood sugar becomes too low, glucagon helps release sugar that's stored in your liver into your bloodstream.

Enzymes are another group of proteins that control billions of chemical reactions taking place in your body every day. Enzymes not only break down large molecules into smaller ones, but they also build compounds and transform one substance into another. The digestive enzyme lactase breaks down lactose, the natural sugar in milk, into smaller sugar units so they can be absorbed by your small intestine. If you're a marathon runner, chances are you've heard about glycogen synthetase, the enzyme that rebuilds your muscle glycogen (carbohydrate) stores. During a run, your muscles break down glycogen to get fuel. If it weren't for glycogen synthetase (and recovery foods!), your muscles wouldn't be prepared to go out and run the next day.

Protein also helps your immune system defend your body against viruses and bacteria. Amino acids derived from foods are used to make antibodies, giant protein molecules that attack foreign invaders and prevent infection. If you're a healthy person, your antibodies work so quickly that most diseases never have a chance to develop. Without enough protein, your body cannot maintain its resistance to illness. Other types of body proteins help maintain your fluid balance, transport nutrients in your bloodstream, aid in blood clotting and enable you to transform light into visual images.

Your body uses protein for energy, too. In Step 3, Choose the Right Carbohydrates, you'll learn the important role carbohydrate plays in providing energy (glucose) to all your body tissues. But if your diet doesn't supply enough carbohydrate, your liver is forced to take the protein you eat and convert it to glucose. Turning protein into glucose for energy is a normal process that happens inside your body every day. It happens whenever you skip a meal and go for a long period without eating.

If your diet is chronically low in calories and carbohydrate, your body will break down muscle and other important proteins to make needed glucose. The end result can be muscle wasting, a sluggish metabolism, delayed healing from an injury and a weakened immune system. And if you're a body builder who doesn't eat enough carbohydrate-rich foods, you won't get the results you're looking for in the gym. That's because some of the protein you eat has to be used to make energy for your body, rather than for building muscle.

How Much Protein Do You Need to Eat?

With the exception of growing children, we need to consume enough protein each day to make up for the amount our body loses. The amount of protein in your diet has to be matched with the amount you lose in urine, skin, hair and nails and in your muscles during exercise. If you eat more than your daily requirements, excess protein gets stored as body fat (not muscle!). As you'll see below, your daily recommended protein requirements are based on your body weight and your activity level.

DAILY PROTEIN REQUIREMENTS FOR HEALTHY ADULTS

No regular exercise	0.8 grams per kilogram (0.36 grams per pound) body weight
Recreational exercise	1.1–1.5 grams per kilogram (0.5–0.7 grams per pound) body weight
Endurance athlete	1.2–1.4 grams per kilogram (0.5–0.6 grams per pound) body weight
Strength trainer	1.6–1.7 grams per kilogram (0.7–0.8 grams per pound) body weight
Elderly	0.8–1.0 grams per kilogram (0.36–0.45 grams per pound) body weight
Maximum for healthy adults	2.0 grams per kilogram (0.9 grams per pound) body weight

Position of the American Dietetic Association, Dietitions of Canada, and the American College of Sports Medicine: Nutrition and Athletic performance. *J Am Diet Assoc.* 2000.

Manual of Clinical Dietetics, 6th ed. American Dietetic Association, 2000.

To find out how much protein you have to eat each day, first calculate your daily protein needs by multiplying your weight by your recommended protein intake. For example:

- A 135-pound woman who does not exercise: $135 \times 0.36 = 49$ grams protein
- A 135-pound woman who takes aerobic classes: $135 \times 0.5 = 68$ grams protein
- A 135-pound woman training for a marathon: $135 \times 0.6 = 81$ grams protein
- A 180-pound man who lifts weights: $180 \times 0.7 = 126$ grams protein

Protein in Foods

The next step is translating these numbers into daily servings of protein-rich foods.

PROTEIN CONTENT OF FOODS

Food	Protein (grams)
Meat, Poultry, Fish and Eggs	
Egg, 1 whole, large	6 g
Egg, 1 white, large	3 g
Meat, 3 oz (90 g)*	21–25 g
Chicken, 3 oz (90 g)	21 g
Salmon, 3 oz (90 g)	25 g
Sole, 3 oz (90 g)	17 g
Tuna, canned and drained, 1/2 cup (125 ml)	30 g
Dairy Products	
Cheese, cheddar, 1 oz (30 g)	10 g
Milk, 1 cup (250 ml)	8 g
Yogurt, 3/4 cup (175 ml)	8 g
Legumes and Soy Foods	
Beans, baked, cooked, 1 cup (250 ml)	13 g
Black beans, cooked, 1 cup (250 ml)	16 g
Kidney beans, cooked, 1 cup (250 ml)	16 g
Lentils, cooked, 1 cup (250 ml)	19 g
Soybeans, cooked, 1 cup (250 ml)	30 g
Soy ground round, cooked, 1/3 cup (75 ml)	11 g

Food	Protein (grams)
Legumes and Soy Foods (continued)	
Tofu, firm, 6-cm x 4-cm x 4-cm piece, about 3 oz (90 g)	13 g
Veggie dog, 1 small, about 1.5 oz (46 g)	11 g
Veggie burger, 1, about 3 oz (85 g)	17 g
Nuts and Seeds	
Almonds, 1/2 cup (125 ml)	12 g
Mixed nuts, 1/2 cup (125 ml)	13 g
Peanut butter, 2 tbsp (25 ml)	9 g
Peanuts, 1/2 cup (125 ml)	18 g
Sunflower seeds, 1/3 cup (75 ml)	8 g
Tahini (sesame seed paste), 2 tbsp (25 ml)	2 g
Other Foods	
Bread, mixed-grain, 1 slice	3 g
Pita bread, whole-wheat, 1 pocket	6 g
Bran flakes, 3/4 cup (175 ml)	4 g
Fruit, 1 piece	1 g
Oatmeal, cooked, 3/4 cup (175 ml)	4 g
Pasta, cooked, 1/2 cup (125 ml)	3 g
Potato, 1 medium, baked with skin	3 g

*3 oz (90 g) of meat is approximately the size of a deck of cards.

PROTEIN CONTENT OF FOODS (continued)

Food	Protein (grams)
Other Foods (continued)	
Rice, long-grain, cooked, 1/2 cup (125 ml)	3 g
Vegetable juice, 1 cup (250 ml)	2 g
Vegetables, 1/2 cup (125 ml)	2 g
Nutrition Supplements	
Energy Bars, high-carbohydrate (e.g., PowerBar, Clif)	7 g
Energy Bars, 40/30/30 (e.g., Balance Bar, Zone Bar)	14–18 g

Food	Protein (grams)
Nutrition Supplements (continued)	
Energy Bars, high-protein (e.g., Pure Protein, ProMax)	21–35 g
Soy Protein Powder, plain, 1-oz (28-g) scoop	25 g
Soy Protein Powder, flavored, 1-oz (28-g) scoop	14–16 g
Whey Protein Powder, 1-oz (32-g) scoop	22–25 g

Special stages in the life cycle will increase your protein needs. During pregnancy, women must eat an additional 5 grams of protein each day during the first trimester, an extra 20 grams per day during the second trimester and an extra 24 grams per day during the third trimester. Breastfeeding moms need to make sure their diet includes 65 grams of protein each day during the first six months (and more if they exercise regularly).

For most of us, eating too little protein is not an issue. You can see how these numbers add up, especially since most people eat more than a 3-ounce (90-gram) serving of meat or poultry. It's estimated that the average North American male consumes 105 grams of protein each day and that females get roughly 65 grams. Here's what a typical food day looks like in my life; you can see how easy it is for me to meet my protein requirements (based on my exercise routine, I need 95 grams of protein each day):

A TYPICAL DAY IN LESLIE'S FOOD LIFE

Breakfast	Protein (grams)
Whole-grain cereal, 1 1/2 cups (375 ml)	8 g
Skim milk, 1 cup (250 ml)	8 g
1 piece fruit	1 g
Lunch	
Whole-grain bread, 2 slices	6 g
Chicken breast, 3 oz (90 g)	21 g
Vegetable juice, 1 cup (250 ml)	2 g
Vegetables, 1/2 cup (125 ml)	3 g
Water	

Snack	Protein (grams)
Low-fat yogurt, 3/4 cup (175 ml)	8 g
1 piece fruit	1 g OR
Soy milk, 1 cup (250 ml)	9 g
Dinner	
Fish, 5 oz (150 g)	45 g
Assorted vegetables, 2 cups (500 ml)	8 g
Water	
Daily protein intake	**111 g**

What Happens if You Don't Get Enough Protein?

There are some people who find it challenging to meet their daily protein requirements. You may be at risk for not getting enough protein if:

- You live alone and rarely cook meat, chicken or fish.

- You frequently grab quick carbohydrate meals during the day—bagels, pasta, low-fat frozen dinners.

- You're a vegetarian who doesn't eat animal foods *and* you don't incorporate high-quality vegetable protein sources into your daily diet.

- You engage in heavy exercise *and* fall into any of the above categories.

Eating too little protein day after day, week after week, will hamper your body's ability to repair itself, slow down your metabolism and weaken your immune system. I have counseled many clients whose main concern was a lack of energy and catching one cold or flu bug after another. There was a common thread in all their diets: they lacked a sufficient amount of protein. After a few months of following a higher-protein diet, these clients not only felt better, but they also reported being sick less often.

Researchers are learning that there may be other consequences of not getting enough protein. Compared with healthy older adults who eat the most protein, those who consume the least don't score as well on memory tests.[1] Although the reasons are unclear, protein seems to play a unique role in brain power. A study from the University of Toronto determined that older adults were able to recall a paragraph more accurately after they had consumed a protein drink.[2]

A low-protein diet may also increase your odds of getting osteoporosis. The Framingham Osteoporosis Study reported that among 600 elderly men and women, those with the lowest protein intakes showed the greatest loss of bone in the hip and spine—about 1 percent was lost each year.[3] On the other hand, people eating the most protein had bone losses about one-quarter of that.

A lack of protein not only may cause thinner bones but also may lead to bone fracture. A study of 35,000 Iowa women aged 55 to 69 years revealed that, compared with women who ate the least amount of protein from meat and dairy products, those who got the most were 69 percent less likely to suffer a hip fracture.[4] And it also seems that a little extra protein helps bones heal faster once they do break. When Swiss researchers studied hip-fracture patients, they found that those patients who received a protein supplement recovered faster and were discharged from the hospital sooner.[5]

If your diet is low in protein, don't wait until you're older to fix it! Scientists from the Mayo Clinic think that the amount of protein you eat when you are young may be an important predictor of your bone density. (Much of our bone density is achieved by the time we are 16 years old.) Their study found that higher intakes of dietary protein were linked to greater bone density in premenopausal women, but this relationship was not seen in older women.[6] The bottom line is clear: *don't skimp on protein*. Getting enough is an important strategy for keeping your bones strong and healthy.

What Happens if You Get Too Much Protein?

If eating too little protein is not a good thing, are high-protein diets the way to go? The answer is no. Studies reveal that consuming more protein than you need can bring about a host of health problems. Here's a glimpse of findings that have been reported in the medical journals:

- High-protein diets may put you at risk for high blood pressure. American researchers found a significant relationship between protein intake and blood pressure: high-protein diets were linked with higher blood pressure readings.[7]

- While skimping on protein may not be good for your bones, overconsumption may be just as harmful. The Nurses' Health Study from Harvard University followed almost 90,000 women and learned that those who ate more than 95 grams of protein each day had a 22 percent higher risk of forearm fracture compared with women who ate less than 68 grams.[8] (The average 130-pound/59-kg woman needs about 50 grams each day.) What's more, compared with women who enjoyed red meat less than once per week, those who ate five or more servings each week had a significantly greater risk of bone fracture.

  It's thought that too much animal protein causes a build-up of acid in the body. Your kidneys respond to this acid load by excreting calcium in the urine. Research findings from the University of San Francisco support this notion. In a study of 1035 post-menopausal women, those whose diets were the highest in animal protein and the lowest in plant protein lost more bone than did women whose diets had lower amounts of animal protein and more plant protein.[9] Furthermore, women with a high intake of animal protein were almost three times as likely to fracture a hip than were those who ate less.

- Mothers-to-be who follow a low-carbohydrate, high-animal-protein diet late in pregnancy may influence the future health of their children. The results of two Scottish studies suggest men and women born to mothers who eat a high-protein, high-fat diet late in pregnancy have a higher risk of diabetes and high blood pressure.[10,11]

- Eating too much meat might increase your risk for certain cancers. According to Harvard scientists, women who eat meat at least once a day have a twofold risk of developing non-Hodgkin's lymphoma compared with women who eat meat less than once a week.[12] Italian researchers compared the diets of healthy people with those of 7990 cancer patients. They found that frequent red meat eaters (at least seven times per week) had a higher risk of colon, breast, stomach, pancreatic, bladder, ovarian and endometrial cancers than did those who ate red meat no more often than three times per week.[13]

The harmful effect of meat may be due to its saturated fat content or the way it's prepared. Cooking meat to a high temperature forms compounds called heterocyclic amines, which have been shown to cause cancer in animals. Until we know more about the effects of cooked meat, cancer experts recommend that if you do eat meat, you should limit your intake to no more than 3 ounces (90 grams) per day and avoid eating charred meat.

- Getting more animal protein than you need could put you at risk for heart disease. That's because some animal foods, such as cheese and fatty meats, can pack a hefty amount of saturated fat, the artery-clogging fat that raises blood cholesterol levels.

Animal versus Plant Protein: Should You Become a Vegetarian?

After reading that too much animal protein can leach calcium from your body and that a steady diet of red meat may increase your risk of cancer, you might be wondering if it is healthier to become a vegetarian. It certainly seems to be the case. A number of studies report that vegetarians are leaner and healthier. Being a vegetarian appears to protect from constipation, type 2 diabetes (adult onset), heart attack, high blood pressure, gallstones and certain cancers.

Researchers from Loma Linda University in California have been busy studying almost 35,000 Seventh-Day Adventists. Most Seventh-Day Adventists don't smoke or drink alcohol, and many are vegetarians. Compared with meat-eating men, vegetarian men had a significantly lower risk of heart disease, colon cancer and prostate cancer.[14]

That vegetarians enjoy unusually good health is also evident in the Oxford Vegetarian Study, an investigation of 6000 vegetarians and 5000 nonvegetarians living in the United Kingdom. After 12 years of study, the researchers found that compared with nonvegetarians, vegetarians experienced a 28 percent reduced risk of heart disease and 39 percent lower risk of certain cancers.[15]

These findings raise three important questions:

1. Are vegetarians healthier because they have a healthier lifestyle (e.g., they don't smoke cigarettes and they exercise more)?

2. Do vegetarians suffer from chronic diseases less often because they avoid unhealthy foods and food components (e.g., meat, saturated fat)?

3. Do vegetarians experience better health because they include more healthy foods and food components in their diet (e.g., fruits, vegetables, nuts, antioxidants)?

Current evidence indicates that the answer to each question is YES! While giving up red meat may have something to do with lower rates of heart disease and cancer, it's not the whole story. A steady diet of whole grains, nuts, vegetables, fruit, beans and soy foods is low in fat and offers plenty of protective plant chemicals, antioxidants and fiber.

The road to good health and longevity is not necessarily paved by a vegetarian diet. What seems to be most important is that you adopt a *plant-based* diet. Eating a plant-based diet means that your meals emphasize grains, vegetables, fruit and legumes and de-emphasize animal foods, like meat and poultry. Eating a plant-based diet means eating smaller portions of animal foods. It means substituting vegetable proteins for animal proteins more often.

For some people, making the transition to a plant-based diet means eating a 4-ounce steak instead of their usual 10-ounce cut. For others it means adding lentils to pasta sauce instead of ground meat. And for some, it might mean pouring calcium-enriched soy beverage over their breakfast cereal instead of milk.

There's one more important point to make: A healthy vegetarian diet does not mean only giving up animal foods. Too often I see clients who make the mistake of avoiding animal products and not including good sources of vegetarian protein. A daily fare of toast and jam, a vegetable sandwich, and pasta with tomato sauce isn't nutritionally superior, even if it is free of animal foods. Where's the protein? The beans? The soy foods? The nuts?

Types of Vegetarian Diets

Surprisingly, only 4 percent of Canadians consider themselves to be vegetarian.[16] And many of these people still include some animal foods in their diet. Vegetarian eating covers a wide range of eating styles; some vegetarian diets avoid all animal foods, others include only a few. Take a look:

- *Semi-vegetarians* avoid meat, but they do eat poultry, fish, eggs and dairy products.

- *Pesco-vegetarians* avoid meat and poultry, but they do eat fish and seafood.

- *Lacto-ovo vegetarians* avoid meat, poultry, fish and seafood, but they do eat eggs and dairy products.

- *Lacto vegetarians* avoid meat, poultry, fish, seafood, and eggs, but they do eat dairy products.

- *Vegans* avoid all animal products, including meat, poultry, fish, seafood, eggs and dairy products. These vegetarians need to plan their diets carefully to get enough protein, iron, calcium, vitamin D, vitamin B12 and zinc.

Depending on what vegetarian lifestyle you choose to follow, make sure you add enough protein to your diet. If you give up meat, poultry and fish, you'll need to include beans, soy products, nuts and seeds in your daily diet.

Protein Quality and the Vegetarian Diet

Protein-rich foods supply your body with 20 amino acids, all of which are needed for good health. Eleven of these can be manufactured by your body and are called nonessential amino acids. The remaining 9, however, must be supplied by your diet because your body cannot synthesize them on its own. They are called, as you may have guessed, essential amino acids.

If your diet does not supply enough of these essential amino acids, your body's rate of protein building will slow down. Eventually your body will break down its own proteins (remember those muscle tissues, hormones and enzymes!) to get these amino acids.

Essential Amino Acids	Nonessential Amino Acids
Histidine	Alanine
Isoleucine	Arginine
Leucine	Asparagine
Lysine	Aspartic acid
Methionine	Cysteine
Phenylalanine	Glutamic acid
Threonine	Glutamine
Tryptophan	Glycine
Valine	Proline
	Serine
	Tyrosine

Animal and plant proteins have very different amino-acid profiles. Animal protein foods contain all the essential amino acids in sufficient quantities to support growth, repair and maintenance of body tissues. For this reason, animal proteins are considered complete proteins, or high-quality proteins. Plant proteins, on the other hand, are always low in one or more of the nine essential amino acids. In some cases, a plant food may even be lacking an essential amino acid completely. The proteins from plant foods are considered incomplete proteins, or low-quality proteins.

Most of us eat enough protein to get ample amounts of essential amino acids. But strict vegetarians (vegans) must take care to combine their plant-protein foods so that the essential amino acid missing from one is supplied by the other. By doing so, vegetarians are able to consume all nine amino acids essential to their bodies. When two or more vegetarian protein foods are combined in this way, they are called complementary proteins.

COMPLEMENTARY VEGETARIAN PROTEINS

Food	Limiting Amino Acids	Food to Combine	Complete Protein Meal Ideas
Legumes, Soybeans	Methionine	Grains, nuts, seeds	Tofu and brown rice stir-fry
Grains	Lysine, threonine	Legumes	Pasta with white kidney beans
Nuts and seeds	Lysine	Legumes	Hummus with tahini (sesame seed paste)
Vegetables	Methionine	Grains, nuts, seeds	Bok choy with cashews
Corn	Lysine, tryptophan	Legumes	Black bean and corn salad

Nutritionists used to think it was important to combine proteins in the same meal. We now know that this is not necessary. As long as you are eating a variety of vegetarian proteins throughout the course of the day, you'll meet your body's needs for essential amino acids.

Combining proteins in the same meal is important, however, for growing children. To support growth and development, infants and preschoolers need 35 percent of their protein from essential amino acids. For this reason, it's very important to carefully plan the meals of young vegetarians to ensure they get all the essential amino acids they need.

Concerns about the Safety of Animal Foods

Most of us are not strict vegetarians. In fact, most Canadians include meat, poultry and fish in their diet. At the same time, there's a growing concern that these foods might harbor chemicals that are harmful to our health. I often get asked questions about hormones and antibiotic residues in foods. Are these foods completely safe to eat? Should you buy organic? These are tough questions to answer. As you'll read below, factors other than health enter the picture. Political and economic factors can also play a role in shaping the safety of our food supply.

Despite the fact that both the government and food industry tell us we have one of the safest food supplies in the world, an increasing number of Canadians remain concerned. An Ipsos-Reid survey conducted in 2001 revealed that 74 percent of Canadians are concerned about food safety.[17] According to another recent survey, 42 percent of Canadians said they were very concerned about animal treatment on farms and 55 percent were very concerned about antibiotic residues in animal foods.[18] Some scientists and public health watchdogs have voiced the following concerns.

Growth Hormone Residues in Beef

It is true that hormones are routinely used to speed up the growth of beef cattle, ensuring they gain more muscle and less fat. Once calves reach a weight of 900 pounds (409 kg), they're moved from the farm to a feedlot operation, where they're given free access to grains and water, bulking them up to market weight. It's here that beef cattle will receive growth hormones, often in a preparation called Revalor-H. A pellet is implanted behind the animal's ear, which then slowly releases the hormones into its bloodstream. Growth hormones may also be added to the animals' feed.

Health Canada allows six different growth hormones to be used in beef cattle: three natural and three synthetic. Revalor-H was approved in 1997, despite concerns that residues in meat could potentially disrupt the hormonal balance and immune systems of vulnerable people such as pregnant women and prepubertal children. Some scientists feel that eating hormone-treated beef may cause girls to reach puberty earlier, increasing their risk for breast cancer.

Concerns about the use of growth hormones in North American cattle can also be heard abroad. The European Union has banned the import of Canadian (and American) beef because their scientists believe that one commonly used growth hormone, estradiol, can cause cancer. (The use of growth hormones in cattle is banned in Europe.) Health Canada has stated firmly that there is no good evidence that these hormones cause cancer; in fact, the World Health Organization considers all six hormones safe. The government argues that Europe's ban on our beef has more to do with trade issues than health issues.

Some consumers don't find this too reassuring. If there is uncertainty and disagreement among the experts about the potential health hazards of hormone residues, should we not proceed with caution? Some watchdog groups feel we should stop using these hormones until we have plenty of proof that they are indeed safe to use.

Hormone residues in meat and meat products are certainly monitored. For starters, they are kept to a minimum by ensuring that cattle producers follow a specified drug withdrawal period, or treatment-free period. This means that the drug must be stopped a certain period of time before the animal is slaughtered. The Canadian Food Inspection Agency (CFIA) then randomly tests meat and meat products for hormone residues at federally registered slaughterhouses and processing plants. This testing ensures that the producers have obeyed the drug withdrawal period. Maximum residue levels have been set that include many safety margins. According to data from the CFIA, meat samples tested between 1994 and 1999 were virtually free of synthetic hormone residues. Hormones are not used in poultry.

Antibiotic Residues

Cattle, poultry, hogs and farm-raised fish are routinely given antibiotics in their feed and drinking water to promote growth and prevent infection by disease-causing bacteria. The use of antibiotics has increased substantially since intensive farming practices have become common, with large numbers of animals confined together. A report in the *Canadian Medical Association Journal* stated that 90 percent of antibiotics used in agriculture are given to promote growth and prevent disease, rather than to treat an infection.[19] The researchers also found that levels of antibiotics in animal feeds have increased 10- to 20-fold since the 1950s.

Many of the antibiotics given to animals are also used to treat illness in people. The question debated is whether or not resistant bacteria from animal foods can make human illness more difficult to treat. Resistant bacteria can make their way to people through residues in food as well as through rivers, streams and wells that run off animal farms. There is also concern that antibiotic residues in animal foods could cause allergic reactions.

To minimize antibiotic residues in food, producers must comply with an antibiotic withdrawal period before the animal goes to slaughter. Positive antibiotic residue tests can occur if the farmer does not adhere to this treatment-free period or if drug-label instructions are not correctly followed.

Studies from Europe and the United States have found evidence of antibiotic-resistant bugs in supermarket foods. American researchers recently published a report in the *New England Journal of Medicine* that tested 400 samples of ground beef, ground pork, ground turkey and ground chicken for the presence of salmonella.[20] Testing revealed that 20 percent of the samples were contaminated with salmonella. Of the strains isolated, 84 percent were resistant to at least one antibiotic and 53 percent were resistant to three or more.

Many scientists believe that resistant strains of bacteria that cause illness in humans—*Salmonella, E. coli* and *Camplyobacter*—are linked to the use of antibiotics in animals. In 1998, Health Canada urged farmers to reduce the use of antibiotics, saying that if they don't, the government will pass regulations to require them to do so. This means that farmers with large operations will have to improve their management practices on the farm. Improved ventilation and better cleaning and animal handling practices could improve livestock health with less use of drugs.

There's also concern about carbadox, an antibiotic used in hogs that's been shown to cause cancer in rats. Banned in Britain in 1986, then in the rest of Europe in 1999, Health Canada finally issued a stop sale on carbadox in 2001. But it is possible that some hog farmers are still using the drug. Although they can no longer buy it in Canada, they may have stockpiled it or they may purchase it across the border in the United States, where its use is legal. Carbodox residues may be more of a concern in the meat of younger animals (e.g., baby back ribs) that are taken to market before an adequate drug withdrawal period can be observed. Unfortunately, there are no tests that can detect carbadox residues in pork.

Toxins in Fish

Fish is an excellent source of high-quality protein, and I encourage you to incorporate it into your diet (read more on this below). Yet there are a few things you need to know about fish in order to make wise choices. There are some concerns with farmed fish, fish raised in confined areas and given prepared feed. I've already discussed the issue of antibiotic use to treat infection, though the amount of antibiotics used in aquaculture is reported to be much less than the amount used to raise livestock. It is true, however, that when one fish gets sick, all the fish are given medicated feed. So there remains the potential for antibiotic resistance to be passed to people.

There's also the issue of synthetic dyes in farm-raised salmon. Dyes are used to produce that reddish pink color we associate with wild salmon. If it weren't for artificial dye, your Atlantic salmon would be white. While there's no evidence that these dyes are harmful, the possibility of mild allergic reactions exists.

The biggest concern, however, is over mercury contamination in certain species of large fish. In 2001, Health Canada and the U.S. Federal Drug Administration issued advisories recommending people to limit their intake of swordfish, shark, king mackerel and fresh and frozen tuna. These species of fish can accumulate high levels of mercury that can be harmful to the developing fetus, young children and breast-fed babies. Mercury is a naturally occurring metal found in very low levels in the air, soil, lakes, streams and oceans. But it can also make its way into the environment from industry: pulp and paper processing, mining operations and burning garbage and fossil fuels all release mercury.

Pregnant women, women in their childbearing years and children under the age of 15 are advised to eat these fish *no more than once per month*. Other people should limit their consumption to no more than once per week. According to Health Canada, mercury is not an issue with canned tuna since the tuna used for canning is young and hasn't had time to accumulate mercury. However, in July 2002 an advisory panel to the U.S. FDA recommended that pregnant women and women of childbearing age limit their intake of canned tuna while more studies are done.

How Is the Safety of Our Food Supply Monitored?

It's possible that drug residues in animal foods can cause allergic reactions, hypersensitivity, hormone imbalances, immune function problems and toxicity. But the truth is that we don't know the full effects of chemical residues in food, whether they're from hormones, antibiotics or toxins.

Health Canada holds the main responsibility for food safety. The minister of Agriculture and Agri-food assesses the effectiveness of the CFIA's inspections. The CFIA is responsible for testing food for potential contaminants and ensuring they don't exceed safety standards. The CFIA has the authority to inspect food-producing facilities, sample and test food products and enforce federal standards. They also inspect animal feeds for drugs such as growth hormones and antibiotics, and they randomly test food produced at federally registered slaughterhouses and processing plants. When findings from these tests or other scientific studies reveal potential health hazards, it's up to the government to take measures that ensure our safety.

There are other players in our national food safety program as well. Livestock and fish farmers share responsibility in ensuring their animals end up as food products that are safe to eat. Producers are responsible for deciding to use medicated feed products and for correctly reading and interpreting label instructions. And they're accountable for the cleanliness of their animals, equipment and facilities. Farmers must also ensure that animals intended for food meet the required amount of withdrawal days from veterinary drugs before being sent to slaughter.

When it comes to animal foods, veterinarians play an important role too. They are responsible for ensuring that food animals receive veterinary medications only when required, and in the proper amounts and ways.

Health Canada places a fair bit of responsibility on the food industry itself. According to the government, it's up to the industry to ensure that it not only sells safe, high-quality products but that it also provides product information to allow consumers to make informed decisions when buying a food product. In addition, our food safety is ensured by the work of food scientists and researchers who develop residue tests and conduct analyses of toxic contamination of food.

While this is all good, scientists at Environmental Defence Canada (EDC), a nonprofit organization established to inform Canadians about food safety, argue that the government should make the results of their food inspections public knowledge. After all, how can consumers be sure the meat or poultry they're buying at the grocery store is free of residues? For now, it's a matter of trust: we put our faith in the Canadian Food Inspection Agency and assume it is doing its job to keep our food supply safe.

EDC believes that Canadians have the right to information about toxic contaminants and food safety in order to make informed food choices. In an effort to help consumers, they have made government food test results available to the public through their web site, www.foodwatch.ca.

What You Can Do at Home

The Plant-Based Diet Option

If the information above leaves you with niggling doubts about the safety of animal products, there are a few things you can do to give yourself some peace of mind. For starters, eat meat less often. To minimize your exposure to hormone and antibiotic residues, take my earlier advice and adopt a plant-based diet. Don't eat animal protein every day, and when you do enjoy it, keep your serving size small. Incorporate more vegetarian-protein foods into your weekly menu plan (my 14-Day Meal Plan includes plenty of the all-star protein foods listed in the section below). Eating a variety of protein foods will help you minimize your exposure to any one potential contaminant.

The Organic Option

If you're willing to spend a little more money, your next option is to buy organic animal foods. Organic meat and poultry are raised on certified organic farms. That means when the animals are young, they graze on organic pastures. When cattle need to bulk up to market weight, they are given certified organic feed rations that have been produced without the use of synthetic chemicals or genetically modified crops. Organically raised beef cattle are not given hormones, but antibiotics may be used to treat sick animals. Otherwise, the use of vaccines and veterinary drugs is not allowed. As well, the organically raised animals are slaughtered according to certified organic regulations.

When buying organic meat or poultry, look for a label that bears the name of an independent certification body (see page 76, Chapter 4). This ensures that the meat has been produced according to organic standards.

Safe Food Handling

Whether you choose to go the organic route or not, it's imperative that you handle your foods safely to prevent food poisoning from the likes of *Salmonella, E. coli* and *Camplyobacter*. Here are a few tips to practice once you get your food home from the supermarket:

- Always wash and thoroughly dry your hands before and after handling foods.

- Avoid cross contamination:

    - Store juicy foods in metal or glass containers on the lowest rack in the fridge to prevent juices from leaking onto other foods.

    - Clean your cutting board thoroughly between uses.

    - Never put cooked food on a dish that previously held raw food.

    - Wash cooking utensils that handled raw food before using them on other foods.

- Use a digital read meat thermometer and cook foods thoroughly to kill harmful bacteria:

    - Cook red meat to an internal temperature of 160°F (71°C) (medium rare).

    - Grill your burgers (beef, chicken and turkey) until they are no longer pink inside and the juices are clear, not pink (to 160°F/71°C).

    - Cook whole chicken to an internal temperature of 180°F (83°C) and chicken pieces to 170°F (77°C).

- Cook pork to an internal temperature of 160°F (71°C).

- Salmonella can grow inside fresh unbroken eggs. Cook eggs until the yolks and whites are firm, not runny. Don't use recipes in which eggs remain raw or only partially cooked.

- When you cook ahead of time, divide large portions of food into small, shallow containers for refrigeration to ensure safe, rapid cooling. Reheat your leftovers until steaming hot.

- Read best-before dates. Don't forget that once you open a package, the best-before date no longer applies.

Protein Foods You Should Be Eating More Often

Whether you choose to eat animal foods or not, there are a few top-notch protein foods that deserve a place on your dinner plate. Set goals to include the following foods in your diet each week.

Fish

Fish is a great source of protein without the high saturated fat found in fatty meats. We've known for years that populations that eat fish a few times each week have lower rates of heart disease. Special fats in fish, called omega-3 fats, can lower high levels of blood fats called triglycerides and reduce the stickiness of platelets, the cells that form blood clots in arteries. *Aim to eat fish three times each week.*

If you already have heart disease, consider eating fish more often than this. The American Heart Association guidelines recommend eating one fatty-fish meal per day (or, alternatively, taking a fish oil supplement) to achieve an intake of omega-3 fats beneficial for people with heart disease.

For the best sources of omega-3 fats, choose oilier fish: salmon, albacore tuna, lake trout, sardines, anchovies, herring and mackerel are good choices. Try the fish recipes from the Canadian Living Test Kitchen. You'll find these in my 14-Day Meal Plan on page 215.

Soy Foods

Tofu, tempeh, soy beverages, soybeans, veggie meats, soy nuts and soy flour are a great source of protein. But they also contain isoflavones, plant chemicals that may protect from a number of health problems. A growing body of research suggests that a regular intake of soy foods can protect our heart, lower blood cholesterol levels, slow bone loss and perhaps even lower the odds of getting prostate and breast cancer. Soy foods may also help ease menopausal hot flashes. Use the following tips to add soy protein to your diet.

Soy beverages This is the most popular way to introduce soy. Buy soy beverages fresh or in tetra packs and use them just like you would milk—on cereal, in smoothies, in coffee, in lattes, in soups, and in cooking and baking. To get more calcium and vitamin D, choose a fortified product.

Soybeans Look for canned soybeans in your local grocery store. Just open the can, give the beans a rinse and then add them to soups, casseroles, chili and curries. Or mash them and add them to burgers. If you have the time, buy them dried, soak overnight, then simmer them for one hour until they're cooked. (Turn to page 38 to learn how to cook dried beans.)

Soy flour Available in health food stores and some supermarkets, soy flour can be substituted for up to half of the all-purpose flour called for in bread, muffin, loaf, cookie, cake or scone recipes.

Soy meats These ready-to-eat or frozen soy foods resemble meat and can be used in place of burgers, hot dogs, deli cold cuts and ground meat. You'll find them in the freezer, deli or produce section of grocery stores.

Soy nuts This roasted snack food comes in plain, barbecue and garlic flavors. Sprinkle on salads, stir into yogurt or enjoy them on their own. Good news: these tasty munchies have less fat and more fiber than other nuts! If you're sensitive to salt, buy unsalted soy nuts.

Tempeh You'll find this soy food refrigerated or frozen in health food stores. Tempeh is a cake of fermented soybeans mixed with grain. It can be sliced and added to casseroles and stir-fries or you can grill it in kebabs and burgers.

Texturized Vegetable Protein (TVP) Made from soy flour that's been defatted and dehydrated, TVP is sold in packages as granules. Rehydrate it with an equal amount of water or broth, then use it to replace ground meat in pasta sauces, lasagna, chili and tacos.

Tofu Use soft tofu in smoothies, dips, lasagna and cheesecakes. Firm tofu is best for grilling and stir-frying. Or add cubes of firm tofu to homemade or canned soups for a vegetarian-protein boost. For recipes, information and free brochures on soy foods, visit www.soybean.ca or write to the Ontario Soybean Growers' Marketing Board, P.O. Box 1199, Chatham, Ontario, N7M 5L8.

Soy protein powders Make a morning "power shake" with 1 tablespoon (15 ml) of soy protein powder made from isolated soy protein. Buy a product that's made with Supro® brand soy protein. This extract of soy protein is manufactured by Protein Technologies International using a process that prevents isoflavone loss. It's also the soy protein isolate that's used in most of the scientific studies. Products that use Supro® include Genisoy, Twin

Lab's Vege Fuel, SoyOne, JustSoy, GNC's Challenge 95% ISP, GNC's Challenge Soy Solution, Nutrel's Soy Serenity and Soy Strategy and Naturade's Total Soy.

If you're a woman with estrogen-sensitive breast cancer, you may be concerned about adding soy to your diet. While many studies suggest that soy isoflavones offer protection from breast cancer, it is possible that isoflavones may increase the risk in certain doses and at certain stages in a woman's life. Many experts believe that it is safe to eat natural soy foods a few times a week, whereas others feel that isoflavones from any source pose a risk. Whether or not you choose to add soy foods to your diet, women with breast cancer should definitely avoid concentrated supplements of isoflavones in pills and powders.

Legumes

Kidney beans, black beans, navy beans, chickpeas and lentils are low in fat, high in fiber and packed with important nutrients and protective plant chemicals. Legumes contain soluble fiber, the type of fiber that helps lower blood cholesterol and keep blood sugar levels stable. In fact, an American study linked eating beans at least four times per week with a 22 percent lower risk of heart disease.[21]

Eat a meatless meal that features beans at least once a week. Buy dried beans, or if time is an issue, buy them canned. Just drain, rinse and add to your favorite dishes. Here are a few suggestions for adding beans to your diet:

- Enjoy a mixed-bean salad in a pita pocket for a high-protein, vegetarian sandwich.
- Add black beans to tacos and burritos. Use half the amount of lean ground meat you usually would and make up the difference with beans.
- Make a vegetarian chili with kidney beans, black beans and chickpeas.
- Sauté chickpeas with spinach and tomatoes and serve over pasta.
- Add white kidney beans to pasta sauce.
- Toss chickpeas or lentils into your next salad.
- Boost the protein content of vegetable soup by adding your favorite beans.
- Serve soup made from beans or peas: minestrone, split pea, black bean or lentil.
- Use beans as dips for vegetables or filling for sandwiches.

If you prefer to buy dried beans (they're less expensive), you'll need to soak them first. Soaking rehydrates the beans before cooking; this will reduce cooking time. Unsoaked beans take longer to cook and require more attention to ensure they don't cook dry. During soaking, beans make up their lost water, increasing up to twice their dried size. Enough water must be used to keep the beans covered while soaking. Once rehydrated, beans cook in one to three hours, depending on the type of bean.

Overnight-soak method: This takes time and some advance planning, but requires very little effort. First, cover the beans with room-temperature water (hot water may cause the beans to sour and cold water slows rehydration and the beans will take longer to cook). Soak them overnight or for eight to ten hours. Drain and cook.

Quick-soak method: This convenient shortcut rehydrates dried beans in little more than one hour. In a pot, cover the beans with water and bring to a boil. Boil for two minutes. Remove the beans from the heat and cover the pot. Let the beans stand in the soak water for one hour. At the end of the hour, discard the soak water and cook the beans in fresh water.

Cooking without soaking: Beans don't have to be soaked before they are cooked; soaking merely shortens the cooking time. To cook beans without soaking, use twice the amount of cooking water specified in the recipe. Combine the water and rinsed beans in a pot and bring to a boil. Cover the pot and reduce the heat to maintain a simmer. The beans rehydrate while cooking so watch them carefully, adding more water as necessary to keep them immersed. Cooking time for unsoaked beans can vary up to two hours. Most beans will be tender in two to three hours.

Here are some bean cookery facts:

- One pound (454 g) of beans measures about 2 cups (500 ml).

- Beans triple in volume when soaked and cooked; 1 cup (250 ml) of dry beans yields 3 cups (750 ml) cooked.

- One pound (454 g) of dry beans yields 6 cups (1.5 liters) cooked.

- Beans require a lot of water for soaking. Use 3 cups (750 ml) of water per 1 cup (250 ml) of dry beans.

- Beans should be simmered after soaking, for two hours per pound.

- One pound (454 g) of dry beans makes about 9 servings of baked beans.

- One pound (454 g) of dry beans makes about 12 servings of bean soup.

Nuts

Nuts and seeds are rich sources of vitamin E, minerals, fiber and essential fatty acids (read Chapter 5 for more on dietary fats). Nuts also contain plant sterols, special compounds that have been linked to a number of beneficial effects in the body, especially protection from heart disease.

So far, six large scientific studies have found that a regular intake of nuts protects from heart disease. The Nurses' Health Study from Harvard University discovered that women who ate more than five ounces (155 grams) of nuts each week had a 35 percent lower risk of heart attack and death from heart disease compared with women who never ate nuts or ate them less than once a month.[22] A number of studies have found that peanuts, peanut butter, walnuts, pecans, pistachios and macadamia nuts can lower LDL (bad) cholesterol levels. A few studies even suggest that nuts might protect from certain cancers.

Eat five to seven servings of nuts each week. To prevent taking in too many calories, keep your portion size to 1 ounce (30 g) or 1/4 cup (50 ml). Eating too many nuts each day can lead to weight gain—1 cup (250 ml) of nuts packs about 850 calories and 18 teaspoons (90 ml) of oil! Try these suggestions for adding a small portion of nuts to your daily diet:

- Toss a handful of peanuts into an Asian-style stir-fry.

- Stir-fry collard greens with cashews, add a teaspoon of sesame oil at the end of cooking.

- Add walnuts to a green or spinach salad.

- Mix sunflower seeds or pumpkin seeds into a bowl of hot cereal or yogurt.

- Add chopped pecans to your favorite low-fat muffin recipe.

- Snack on a small handful of almonds mixed with 1/4 cup (50 ml) of dried apricots.

- Sprinkle your casserole with a handful of mixed nuts.

10 TIPS

FOR INCORPORATING HIGH-QUALITY PROTEIN FOODS IN YOUR DIET

1. Use the table on page 21 to determine what your daily protein requirements are. Don't forget to factor in your activity level.

2. To meet your protein needs, be sure to eat at least two servings of high-protein foods per day. To help you meet these targets, make sure your plate at each meal contains some protein-rich foods. A serving is considered 3 ounces (90 grams) of lean meat, poultry or fish, 1 to 2 eggs (or 2 to 4 egg whites), 1/3 of a block of firm tofu, and 1/2 to 1 cup (125 to 250 ml) of legumes. Higher-protein breakfast foods can also include low-fat milk, yogurt and cottage cheese.

3. Adopt a plant-based diet. Incorporate more vegetarian-protein foods in your weekly menu. More often, replace meat and poultry with soy foods, nuts and beans.

4. Eat fish three times a week, or more often if you wish! For heart-healthy omega-3 fats, choose salmon, trout, sardines, herring and mackerel more often.

5. Limit your intake of swordfish, shark and fresh and frozen tuna to no more than once a week, or once a month for children, pregnant women and women of child-bearing age.

6. Choose lower-fat animal-protein foods. Lean cuts of beef (sirloin, flank steak, eye of the round, lean ground beef), pork tenderloin, chicken breast and turkey all have less saturated fat and cholesterol than their higher-fat counterparts. Avoid charring animal foods on the grill.

7. If you do eat meat, limit your intake to no more than 3 ounces (90 grams)—approximately the size of a deck of cards—per day.

8. Consider buying organically raised meat and poultry. On packaged meat and poultry, look for an organic seal that states "certified organic." Ask your local butcher about the availability of organic meat. National grocery chains may carry organic meat products in the freezer section.

9. Get to know your local organic farmers. Call the farm and ask questions about how it raises its animals. If you live close by, you might even inspect the farm yourself. Healthy looking, clean animals that are not held in a confined space are signs that the animals are treated well.

10. To prevent a bout of food poisoning, follow safe food handling practices. Always use a meat thermometer, preferably a digital one, to cook your meat and poultry thoroughly (see page 34 for a temperature guide).

ANSWERS TO LESLIE'S IQ QUIZ   PROTEIN

1. False

2. True

3. 1/2 cup (125 ml) cooked lentils has 10 grams of protein, whereas 1 ounce (30 grams) of beef and the PowerBar® both serve up 7 grams of protein, and 1 egg provides 6 grams.

4. Yogurt

5. False. Organic meat and poultry are raised without growth hormones, but antibiotics may still be used to treat an illness. (Conventional poultry is also raised without growth hormones.)

Step 3
Choose the Right
Carbohydrates

LESLIE'S NUTRITION IQ QUIZ   CARBOHYDRATES

1. True or false? Eating carbohydrate makes you gain weight.

2. Which food is rich in complex carbohydrate?
    a. pretzels   b. pasta
    c. bran flakes   d. rye crackers
    e. all of the above

3. Which carbohydrate-containing food is the best choice for long-lasting energy?
    a. unsweetened fruit juice   b. regular cola
    c. plain bagel   d. low-fat yogurt

4. Which high-fiber food *won't* help you lower your blood cholesterol?
    a. oat bran   b. wheat bran
    c. kidney beans   d. lentils
    e. psyllium

5. Which sugar is not considered an added sugar?
    a. sucrose   b. dextrose
    c. lactose   d. honey
    e. rice syrup

Carbohydrate-rich foods are often called the staff of life, and for good reason. After all, carbohydrates provide about half of all the energy your muscles, nerves and other body tissues use. And carbohydrate is your brain's preferred fuel source—it relies on a steady supply of carbohydrate to function properly. If it weren't for carbohydrate in your diet, you wouldn't have the energy to work out at the gym or concentrate at the office.

Fruit, vegetables, whole grains, legumes and nuts are all sources of energy-giving carbohydrate. The only animal foods that supply carbohydrate are dairy products (they contain a naturally occurring sugar called lactose). Plants make the carbohydrates we eat from carbon dioxide, water and the sun's energy. Carbohydrate is composed of carbon, hydrogen and oxygen. The carbohydrate family includes simple sugars, starches and dietary fiber.

What Is Carbohydrate?

Simple sugars are classified as monosaccharides ("mono" meaning one and "saccharide" meaning sugar) or disaccharides (two sugars). Monosaccharides are the simplest form of carbohydrate because they consist of only a single sugar molecule. The three monosaccharides important to nutrition are glucose (also called dextrose and blood sugar), fructose (found in fruit, honey and corn syrup) and galactose. Galactose rarely occurs by itself in foods; instead it attaches to another sugar unit to form the disaccharide lactose. The disaccharides are pairs of the monosaccharides linked together. Maltose (malt sugar), sucrose (table sugar) and lactose (milk sugar) are disaccharides we consume every day in foods.

Starches are more complex arrangements of carbohydrate. Starches in foods are long chains of hundreds or thousands of glucose units linked together. These giant molecules are stacked side by side in a grain of rice, a slice of bread or a flake of breakfast cereal. Other starchy foods are potatoes, wheat, rye, oats, corn and legumes (including chickpeas, kidney beans and lentils). You'll learn later in this chapter that starchy foods are not created equal when it comes to good nutrition and health.

Dietary fibers are the structural parts of vegetables, fruit, grains and legumes. Pectins, lignans, cellulose, gums and mucilages are different types of fibers found in these plants. Although our digestive enzymes cannot break down the chemical bonds that link the building blocks of fiber, when undigested fiber arrives in your large intestine, resident bacteria ferment these fibers and break them down. Now you know why flatulence can be a problem when you embark on a high-fiber diet (more on that later!).

A Grain of Truth about High-Carbohydrate Diets

It's hard to imagine life without bread, pasta and cereal, yet that's what many of today's popular weight-loss diets suggest we do. These weight-loss plans shun carbohydrates, claiming they promote weight gain and may even lead to heart disease and cancer. They promise that by eating a low-carbohydrate, high-protein (and in some cases high-fat) diet, you can shed pounds fast and ward off disease.

If you have tried any of these diets, you probably did lose weight and you may have even felt more energetic. There's no argument that cutting back your calories (from any food group) is an effective way to drop the pounds, but there's no evidence to suggest that low-carb, high-protein diets sustain permanent weight loss. What's more, some of these diets can be detrimental to your health (read Chapter 9 for more on fad diets).

And there may be some truth to some of the claims made by proponents of the low-carb, high-protein diet. It is certainly true that Canadians are eating more carbohydrate than ever before. Our quest for a diet full of low-fat, high-carb foods started back in the 1980s when researchers learned of the connection between a diet high in saturated (animal) fat and blood cholesterol. Nutritionists and health organizations then urged people to eat less fat. Remember all those meals of pasta and tomato sauce or skinless chicken breast?

For food manufacturers, the low-fat craze of the 1980s was a huge opportunity to market an overwhelming number of fat-reduced and fat-free products. Baked potato chips, fat-free muffins, SnackWell's cookies and bagels soon dominated our shopping carts. Don't get me wrong. Eating lower-fat foods is not a bad thing at all. In fact, these foods have helped Canadians reduce their fat intake over the past decade.

The problem is that we are eating too many of them. What's more, *the type of carbohydrate in these highly processed foods may actually be encouraging you to overeat.* And the very fact that the label says "fat free" may help you justify eating a larger portion. The take home message is clear: *fat free does not mean calorie free.* Calories add up—even calories from low-fat carbohydrate foods. If you compare the nutrition labels on some of your favorite low-fat foods with those on the cartons of the regular fat versions, you might be surprised to find that the calorie savings are relatively small, often because sugar is added to replace the fat!

We're also eating more because restaurants and fast food outlets are serving larger portions than ever before. For example, back in 1916, a serving of Coke at a restaurant was 7 ounces (207 ml). Today, some single size servings are 20 ounces (590 ml) (that's almost 17 teaspoons' worth of sugar!). In 1955, a serving of McDonald's French fries weighed about 2 ounces (60 grams). Today, an order of fries weighs as much as 6 ounces (180 grams)!

Fat-free foods are also getting bigger. Large bagels are equivalent to five slices of bread, and store-bought low-fat muffins are three times the size of a typical homemade muffin.

Many of us think that bigger is better—it means we're getting our money's worth. In this age of super-sized portions, we've lost touch with what an appropriate portion size is. Add to this an alarming rate of inactivity and the end result is an increasing number of over-weight Canadians, not to mention an epidemic of type 2 (adult onset) diabetes. (Diabetes results when the body does not produce enough insulin or does not use it properly. Glucose builds up in the blood and passes out of the body as urine, causing the cells to lose their main source of fuel.)

Advocates of a low-carb, high-protein diet claim that the high-carbohydrate, low-fat diet we've been munching away on can increase the risk of developing heart disease. And studies have found that *some* high-carbohydrate, low-fat diets can increase blood fats called triglycerides and lower HDL (good) cholesterol, two risk factors for heart disease. Popular diet books tell us that eating a high-carbohydrate diet causes the body to release large amounts of the hormone insulin and that this inhibits fat burning and leads to weight gain, diabetes and heart disease. But there's more to the story that these diets neglect to mention.

The Whole Truth about High-Carbohydrate Diets

So yes, it's true—too much carbohydrate can make you fat. Just like too much fat and too much protein can pack on the pounds. But not *all* carbohydrates make you fat, nor do they all increase your risk for health problems like diabetes and heart disease. Indeed, we are learning that not all carbohydrates are created equal. What appears to be most important is the *quality* of carbohydrate-rich foods you eat.

Populations around the world that enjoy the lowest rates of disease eat a high-carbohydrate, low-fat diet. Mediterranean, Asian and vegetarian diets all provide at least 55 percent of calories from carbohydrate in foods such as grains, beans, fruits and vegetables. These high-carb diets certainly differ from the low-fat, convenience-food diets many North Americans eat. The hallmark foods of the North American high-carb, low-fat diet include refined and processed foods—low-fat cookies, baked tortilla chips, bagels with fat-free cream cheese and so on. That's certainly a far cry from a high-carb diet that's packed with whole grains, legumes, fruits and vegetables.

Research shows that such a vegetarian-style high-carb, low-fat diet does not raise cholesterol or triglycerides. In fact, it actually tends to lower blood fats and promote weight loss. Nor do these diets depress your level of HDL cholesterol. This type of high-carb, low-fat diet is loaded with fiber, vitamins, minerals, antioxidants and protective plant chemicals, all of which can keep you healthy and trim. On the other hand, *refined* carbohydrates can affect your desire to keep on eating, promote weight gain and raise your blood fats—and perhaps even increase your risk for heart disease, diabetes and cancer.

The Whole-Grain Story

A common thread in the healthy high-carb, low-fat diets is that they all contain plenty of whole-grain foods. Eating foods made from whole grains means you're getting *all* parts of the grain: the outer bran layer where nearly all the fiber is, the germ layer that's rich in nutrients like vitamin E and the endosperm that contains the starch. When whole grains are milled, scraped, refined and heat processed into flakes, puffs or white flour, all that's left is the starchy endosperm. That means you get significantly less vitamin E, B6, magnesium, potassium, zinc, fiber … the list goes on.

A number of studies have found that a steady diet of whole grains protects from diabetes, heart disease and possibly even stroke:

- Contrary to popular belief, eating the right carbohydrates may actually lower the odds of developing type 2 diabetes. Two large American studies conducted in women revealed that, compared with those who ate very few whole grains, women who ate the most each day had a much lower risk of diabetes.[1,2] One study determined that refined-grain eaters had a 57 percent greater chance of getting diabetes and that whole grains seemed to offer the most protection for overweight women.

- The Iowa Women's Health Study followed almost 35,000 women aged 55 to 69 years and found that the more whole grains eaten, the lower the risk of dying from heart disease.[3] Those who ate at least three servings of whole grains each day had a 30 percent lower risk compared with women who ate less than one.

- The Nurses' Health Study from Harvard University found similar protection from whole grains. Compared with women who ate the least amount of whole grains, those who enjoyed the most were 33 percent less likely to have heart disease.[4] Women who never smoked and ate the most whole grains realized an even bigger benefit—a 51 percent lower risk.

- Eating plenty of whole grains may also help prevent a stroke caused by an interruption of blood flow to the brain. The Nurses' Health Study reported a 43 percent lower risk of stroke among whole-grain eaters.[5]

And there's mounting evidence that eating whole grains, instead of refined and processed carbohydrate foods, can reduce your risk of cancer:

- Italian researchers found that whole grains offered significant protection from colon cancer.[6] What's more, they reported that eating one additional serving of refined grains each day led to a 32 percent higher risk of colon cancer.

- More evidence from Italy speaks to the anticancer properties of whole grains. Studies have found not only that whole grains lower the risk of cancers of the colon and upper digestive tract but also that eating plenty of refined flour products significantly increases the risk.[7,8]

- Postmenopausal women who eat plenty of whole grains may have a lower risk of dying from cancer. The Iowa Women's Health Study reported that the risk of dying from the disease was lower in women who ate more whole grains and higher in women whose diets contained mostly refined grains.[9]

Until recently, the health benefits of whole grains were attributed to their fiber content. While fiber may play an important role in protecting the heart, scientists have identified other protective ingredients in whole grains. Antioxidant compounds such as vitamin E, tocotrienols and flavonoids may discourage the formation of blood clots and may prevent LDL (bad) cholesterol from sticking to artery walls. These same antioxidants in whole grains, along with naturally occurring plant estrogens, may also protect from cancer. As well, whole grains are important sources of minerals such as zinc, selenium, copper and iron, which may protect our health.

Eating More Whole-Grain Foods

Faced with these research findings, it seems foolish to not include whole grains in your daily diet. *Eat at least three servings of whole grain each day.*

What's a serving? One serving of grain is equivalent to:

- 1 slice whole-grain bread

- 1/4 bagel

- 1/2 pita pocket

- 3/4 cup (175 ml) ready-to-eat breakfast cereal

- 1/2 cup (125 ml) 100% bran cereal

- 1/2 cup (125 ml) cooked hot cereal

- 1/2 cup (125 ml) cooked rice

- 1/2 cup (125 ml) cooked grains

- 1/2 cup (125 ml) cooked pasta

Knowing what's whole grain and what's not can be a challenge because you won't always find this information on the nutrition labels of food packaging. Here's a listing of selected grains to help you out:

Whole Grain	Refined Grain
Barley	Cornmeal
Brown rice	Pasta
Bulgur	Pearled barley
Flaxseed	Unbleached flour
Kamut	White rice
Kasha (buckwheat groats)	
Millet	
Oat bran	
Oatmeal	
Quinoa	
Hulled barley (barley groats)	
Spelt	
Whole-rye bread	
Whole-wheat bread (100%)	
Wild rice	

When buying a loaf of bread or a box of crackers, look for the words "whole-wheat flour" or "whole-rye flour" on the list of ingredients. The words "wheat flour" and "unbleached wheat flour" mean it's a refined food. Don't be fooled: some of the healthiest-sounding breads list unbleached wheat flour as the first ingredient.

Whole grains add variety and flavor to meals. Take a break from the usual side of rice; be adventurous and try the following (you'll find more whole-grain recipes on page 199).

Buckwheat Kasha, also sold as roasted buckwheat groats, is quick cooking and very versatile. Simmer one part kasha in two parts water for 15 minutes. Try it in soups, stews, stuffing, pilafs and stir-fries. It has a nutty taste that boosts the flavor of any meal.

Bulgur If you've eaten Middle Eastern cuisine, chances are you've met bulgur in tabouli salad. Like buckwheat, it's a quick-cooking grain. Simmer two parts bulgur in five parts liquid over low heat for about 25 minutes. Remove from the heat and let stand, covered, for about 10 minutes. Bulgur is high in iron, calcium and fiber and great in pilafs, soups and stuffings.

Cracked wheat This grain takes a little longer to cook, but it's worth the effort. Simmer one part cracked wheat in two parts water for about 40 minutes. Enjoy as a side dish or add to quick-bread recipes.

Kamut This grain is related to the wheat family, but it has less potential for causing an allergic reaction. It's about two or three times the size of wheat berries and has more fiber and protein than most grains. Its chewy texture and buttery flavor make it great for salads. Kamut is also ground into flour and used for baked goods, cereals and pasta.

Quinoa Sacred to the Incas, this fluffy grain is sold as whole grain or as pasta. Try it in pilafs, salads, casseroles and stir-fries. Rinse, then cook one part quinoa in two parts water or stock. Bring to a boil, then cook over medium-low heat for 12 to 15 minutes. Quinoa is lower in carbohydrate and higher in protein than most grains.

Spelt Like kamut, spelt is touted as a grain well tolerated by people with a wheat allergy. You'll find this age-old staple sold as whole grain, flour, bread, breakfast cereal and pasta. Try using spelt flour in baking and cooking: it adds a delicious nutty taste to pizza crusts and multigrain breads.

The Carbohydrate–Insulin Connection and the Glycemic Index

Researchers are learning that there's more to whole grains than dietary fiber, antioxidant nutrients and protective plant chemicals. Their health benefits may also stem from the rate at which these carbohydrate-rich foods are digested and absorbed into the bloodstream.

Whole grains are digested and absorbed into the bloodstream more slowly than refined grains such as white bread and rice. Once carbohydrate is digested, regardless of its source, it is converted to glucose in the blood. The rise in blood sugar signals your pancreas to release insulin into the bloodstream. Insulin's job is to move glucose from the blood into your cells, where it's needed for energy. Slowly digested carbohydrate foods lead to a gradual rise in blood glucose. This means that your body's pancreas secretes less insulin and your blood sugar level remains stable. A smooth, steady rise in blood sugar level leads to more consistent energy levels.

Foods that are rapidly digested and converted to blood glucose, such as white bread, lead to excessive amounts of insulin being released. This surge of insulin causes your blood glucose to drop more quickly. The net result: you'll feel sluggish and tired, not to mention hungry, sooner. High insulin levels are also thought to contribute to the development of heart disease, diabetes and cancer.

The rate at which a food causes your blood sugar to rise can be measured and assigned a value. This measure is referred to as the food's glycemic index (GI) value. The GI is a ranking from 0 to 100. The number indicates whether a food raises your blood glucose rapidly, moderately or slowly. Foods that are digested quickly and cause your blood sugar to rise rapidly have high GI values. Foods that are digested slowly, leading to a gradual rise in blood sugar and less insulin being released, are assigned low GI values. All foods are compared with pure glucose, which is given a value of 100 (fast acting).

The Glycemic Index and Your Health

A number of studies support the notion that diets with a low GI are healthier for you. In a recent study, American investigators measured levels of blood triglycerides and HDL (good) cholesterol in 280 women. They found that women whose diets had the lowest glycemic score also had the lowest triglyceride and the highest HDL (good) cholesterol levels.[10] In a subsequent study, these researchers also linked a low glycemic diet with a lower level of inflammatory blood proteins, compounds that are linked to heart disease.[11]

Adjusting the GI of your diet might also be an important way to prevent type 2 diabetes, the type of diabetes that usually affects people after the age of 40. Two large studies from Harvard University, one of men and the other of women, showed that diets with a high GI actually increased the risk for developing diabetes.[12,13]

The effect of high glycemic carbohydrates on your insulin may also increase the risk of colon cancer. Scientists think that insulin can trigger the rapid growth of colon cells. New research from Italy suggests that a daily fare of low GI foods may protect from the disease.[14] The researchers studied the diets of 4000 people with colon cancer and compared them with healthy controls. They found that the colon cancer patients were twice as likely as other people to regularly eat high GI foods such as white bread, sweets, cakes and table sugar, putting a high insulin demand on the body. What's more, the effects of a high GI diet were more harmful in people who were overweight and ate few fruits and vegetables.

Choosing foods that minimize the amount of insulin your body secretes also may help you lose weight. Short-term studies indicate that eating fast-acting, high GI carbohydrate foods may increase hunger and trigger overeating. Researchers from the Children's Hospital in Boston fed overweight teenage boys either a low, medium or high GI lunch.[15] The boys were then given access to snack foods for five hours. Compared with the boys who ate the low GI lunch, those who were given the high GI meal ate a whopping 81 percent more calories over the course of the afternoon!

In another study, researchers prescribed either a low GI or a standard low-fat diet to 107 obese children for a four-month period.[16] At the end of the study, the children on the low GI regime dropped more weight and had a lower body mass index than those on the standard high-carb, low-fat diet. The reason for the weight-loss success? It seems that slowly digested carbohydrate can keep you feeling full longer. The prolonged presence of food in your stomach can stimulate receptors that tell your brain you're full. You stop eating and feel satisfied longer. Think about it: doesn't a bowl of oatmeal (low GI) keep your hunger at bay much longer than two slices of white toast (high GI)?

Using the Glycemic Index to Choose Carbohydrate-Rich Foods

To choose carbohydrate foods that do *not* cause large increases in blood sugar and insulin, practice the following:

- Use the table below to include at least one low GI carbohydrate choice per meal, or base two of your meals each day on low GI choices.

- Keep in mind that not all high GI foods are unhealthy, nor should they be avoided. Carrots have a high GI but are an excellent source of beta-carotene, an antioxidant that may protect from lung cancer.

- Keep in mind, too, that by the same token, not all low GI foods are good for you. Ice cream may have a low GI, but it's full of saturated fat and calories.

- Pay special attention when you choose breads and breakfast cereals, since these foods can contribute the most to the high glycemic load of your diet.

- Avoid eating high GI foods as snacks, since they can trigger a low blood sugar reaction and hunger.

- Include acidic fruits in your diet. Fruits that are more acidic have a low GI and will help lower the overall GI of your meal.

- Use salad dressings that contain vinegar or lemon juice; the acidity will help reduce the GI of your meal.

- Combine a high GI food with a low GI food to get a meal with a medium GI value.

Here's a list of foods ranked by their GI value; < 55 = low GI; 55–70 = medium GI; >70 = high GI. Use this table to plan your meals.

GLYCEMIC INDEX VALUES OF FOODS

Food	GI Value	Food	GI Value
Bread and Crackers		**Bread and Crackers (continued)**	
Baguette, French	95	Rye bread	65
Kaiser roll	73	Soda crackers	74
Melba toast	70	Sourdough bread	52
Pita bread, whole-wheat	57	Stoned Wheat Thins	67
Pumpernickel, whole-grain	51	White bread, white bagel	70–72
Rice cakes	82	Whole-wheat bread	69

GLYCEMIC INDEX VALUES OF FOODS (continued)

Food	GI Value
Breakfast Cereals	
All Bran, Kellogg's	51
All Bran Buds with Psyllium, Kellogg's	45
Bran flakes	74
Corn Bran, Quaker	75
Corn flakes	84
Oat bran	50
Oatmeal, quick or instant	66
Porridge from rolled oats	49
Shredded Wheat, spoon size	58
Special K	69
Cookies, Cakes and Muffins	
Angelfood cake	67
Arrowroot	69
Banana bread	47
Blueberry muffin	59
Graham crackers	74
Oat bran muffin	60
Oatmeal cookies	55
Social Tea biscuits	55
Sponge cake	46
Pasta, Grains and Potato	
Barley	25
Bulgur	48
Corn, sweet	55
Couscous	65
Fettuccine, egg	32
Potato, French fries	75
Potato, instant, mashed	86
Potato, new, unpeeled, boiled	62
Potato, red-skinned, mashed	91
Potato, red-skinned, boiled	88
Potato, sweet, mashed	54
Potato, white-skinned, baked	85
Rice, basmati	58
Rice, brown	55

Food	GI Value
Pasta, Grains and Potato (continued)	
Rice, converted, Uncle Ben's	44
Rice, instant	87
Rice, long-grain, white	56
Rice, short-grain	72
Spaghetti, whole-wheat	37
Spaghetti, white	41
Legumes	
Baked beans	48
Black beans	31
Black bean soup	64
Chickpeas, canned	42
Kidney beans	27
Lentils	30
Lentil soup, canned	34
Soy beans	18
Split pea soup	66
Fruit	
Apple	38
Apricot, dried	31
Banana	55
Cantaloupe	65
Cherries	22
Dates, dried	103
Grapefruit	25
Grapes	46
Mango	55
Orange	44
Peach, canned	30
Pear	38
Raisins	64
Watermelon	72
Dairy Products and Alternatives	
Milk, skim	32
Milk, whole	27

Food	GI Value	Food	GI Value
Dairy Products and Alternatives (continued)		**Snack Foods (continued)**	
Milk, chocolate	34	Pretzels	83
Ice cream, low-fat	50	Sports Bar, PowerBar™, chocolate	58
Soy beverage	31	**Sugars**	
Yogurt, flavored, low-fat	33	Fructose (fruit sugar)	19
Snack Foods		Glucose	100
Corn chips	72	Honey	55
Peanuts	14	Lactose (milk sugar)	46
Popcorn	55	Sucrose (table sugar)	68
Potato chips	54		

Foster-Powell K et al. "International table of glycemic index and glycemic load values: 2002," *Am J Clin Nutr* 2002; 76(1): 5–56. Reprinted with permission.

Don't Forget about Fiber!

With all this talk about the health benefits of whole grains, including the fact that they have a low GI, you might think I've given a back seat to fiber. Not so! After all, whole grains are good sources of fiber. By absorbing water and adding bulk, fiber in whole grains helps move food through the digestive tract faster. Not only does this bulking action keep you regular (very important I know!), but it can also reduce the exposure of cells in your colon to cancer-causing substances. Fiber may also inactivate these harmful compounds before they can do harm to your colon. And certain types of fiber can act to help keep your heart healthy, too.

Fiber is classified according to the physical properties it exerts in the body. Foods are made up of two types of fiber, *soluble* and *insoluble*. Both are always present in varying proportions in plant foods, but some foods will be rich in one or the other. For instance, dried peas, beans and lentils, oats, barley, psyllium husks, apples and citrus fruits are good sources of soluble fiber. Soluble fiber, which dissolves in water, forms a gel in the stomach and slows the rate of digestion and absorption. As soluble fiber passes through the digestive tract, its gel-like property can trap substances related to high cholesterol. Indeed, there's plenty of evidence that supports the cholesterol-lowering effect of oats, beans and psyllium.

Diets rich in soluble fiber may also be helpful for people with diabetes. By delaying the rate at which food empties from the stomach into the intestine, the rise in blood sugar after a meal is blunted. Not only does this put less wear and tear on your pancreas, but insulin requirements may be reduced in people with type 1 diabetes.

Foods such as wheat bran, whole grains and certain vegetables contain mainly insoluble fiber. This fiber has a significant capacity for retaining water and acts to increase stool bulk and promote regularity. By reducing constipation, a diet high in fiber may also prevent a condition called diverticulosis. Since high-fiber diets are usually lower in fat and calories, they may help people achieve and maintain a healthy weight.

To reap its health benefits, *ensure you get 25 to 35 grams of fiber each day*. Children over the age of two should have a daily fiber intake of 5 grams plus their age (e.g., a seven-year-old should be getting 12 (5 + 7) grams of fiber each day). Increase fiber intake gradually to prevent bloating and gas. Remember that fiber needs fluid to work, so be sure to drink at least one glass of water with each high-fiber meal and snack. Use the list of fiber-rich foods to plan your meals (you'll notice that high-fiber food choices also tend to have a low glycemic index).

FIBER CONTENT OF FOODS

Food	Fiber (grams)
Legumes	
Beans and tomato sauce, canned, 1 cup (250 ml)	20.7 g
Black beans, cooked, 1 cup (250 ml)	13.0 g
Chickpeas, cooked, 1 cup (250 ml)	6.1 g
Kidney beans, cooked, 1 cup (250 ml)	6.7 g
Lentils, cooked, 1 cup (250 ml)	9.0 g
Nuts	
Almonds, 1/2 cup (125 ml)	8.2 g
Peanuts, dry roasted, 1/2 cup (125 ml)	6.9 g
Cereals	
All Bran Buds with Psyllium, Kellogg's, 1/3 cup (75 ml)	13.0 g
Bran flakes, 3/4 cup (175 ml)	6.3 g
100% bran cereal, 1/2 cup (125 ml)	10.0 g
Corn Bran, Quaker, 1 cup (250 ml)	6.3 g
Grape Nuts, Post, 1/2 cup (125 ml)	6.0 g
Oat bran, cooked, 1 cup (250 ml)	4.5 g
Oatmeal, cooked, 1 cup (250 ml)	3.6 g
Red River Cereal, cooked, 1 cup (250 ml)	4.8 g
Shreddies, 3/4 cup (175 ml)	4.4 g

Food	Fiber (grams)
Bread and Other Grain Foods	
Bread, whole-wheat, 2 slices	4.0 g
Flaxseed, ground, 2 tbsp (25 ml)	4.5 g
Pita bread, whole-wheat, 1 pocket	4.8 g
Rice, brown, cooked, 1 cup (250 ml)	3.1 g
Spaghetti, whole-wheat, cooked, 1 cup (250 ml)	4.8 g
Wheat bran, 2 tbsp (25 ml)	2.4 g
Fruit	
Apple, 1 medium with skin	2.6 g
Apricots, dried, 1/4 cup (50 ml)	2.6 g
Banana, 1 medium	1.9 g
Blueberries, 1/2 cup (125 ml)	2.0 g
Figs, dried, 5	8.5 g
Orange, 1 medium	2.4 g
Pear, 1 medium with skin	5.1 g
Prunes, dried, 3	3.0 g
Raisins, seedless, 1/2 cup (125 ml)	2.8 g
Strawberries, 1 cup (250 ml)	3.8 g
Vegetables	
Broccoli, 1/2 cup (125 ml)	2.0 g

FIBER CONTENT OF FOODS (continued)

Food	Fiber (grams)	Food	Fiber (grams)
Vegetables (continued)		**Vegetables (continued)**	
Brussels sprouts, 1/2 cup (125 ml)	2.6 g	Lima beans, 1/2 cup (125 ml)	3.8 g
Carrots, 1/2 cup (125 ml)	2.2 g	Potato, 1 medium, baked with skin	5.0 g
Corn niblets, 1/2 cup (125 ml)	2.3 g	Sweet potato, mashed, 1/2 cup (125 ml)	3.9 g
Green peas, 1/2 cup (125 ml)	3.7 g		

Here are a few tips to help you add more fiber to your meals:

- Strive to eat five or more servings of fruits and vegetables each day.
- Leave the peel on fruits and vegetables whenever possible (but wash thoroughly).
- Eat at least three servings of whole-grain foods each day.
- Buy higher-fiber breakfast cereals. Aim for a minimum of 4 to 5 grams of fiber per serving (check the nutrition information panel).
- If you're looking for a real fiber boost at breakfast, choose a 100 percent bran cereal, which packs 10 to 13 grams of fiber per 1/2 cup (125 ml) serving.
- Top your breakfast cereal with berries, dried cranberries or raisins.
- Add 1 to 2 tablespoons (15 to 25 ml) of natural wheat bran, oat bran or ground flaxseed to cereals, yogurt, applesauce, casseroles and soup.
- Eat legumes more often. Add white kidney beans to pasta sauce, black beans to tacos, chickpeas to salads, lentils to soup (for more bean tips, see page 37, Chapter 2).
- Add a handful of seeds, nuts or raisins to salads.
- Add nuts to a vegetable stir-fry.
- Reach for high-fiber snacks like air-popped popcorn, dried apricots or dates.

What about Added Sugars?

Many of us are afraid that added sugars will put on weight, cause diabetes and make our kids hyperactive. The truth is, when eaten in moderation, sugar has not been found to cause any of these health problems. It's when you eat too much sugar along with too much fat and too little fiber that health problems occur.

Sugar is usually added to foods to make them taste better. I don't think I could eat my morning bowl of All Bran without the sugar that has been added by the manufacturers. But in the scheme of things, this is only a little bit of sugar added to a healthy diet.

You can't determine the amount of added sugar in a food by looking at the grams of carbohydrate on the package's nutrition label. This information gives you the total amount of carbohydrate, from starch, fiber, naturally occurring milk and fruit sugars and added sugars. Mandatory nutrition labeling for packaged foods is expected to become law in Canada by the end of 2002. With this change you'll see improved nutrition labels that will declare grams of sugar. In the meantime, you'll find added sugars on a food's ingredients list as brown sugar, granulated sugar, cane sugar, honey, rice syrup, maple syrup, corn syrup, corn sweeteners, high-fructose corn syrup, dextrose and molasses. Here's the lowdown on sugar and health.

Sugar and Weight Control

Sure, too much sugar can make you gain weight. Just think what would happen if you drank a can of Coke each day. That's 10 teaspoons of sugar and 150 calories each day from just one drink. Now let's say you add to this a package of Twizzlers™. There's another 18 teaspoons of sugar and 280 calories. You've just swallowed a grand total of 430 calories from pure sugar! When you consider that all it takes is to eat an extra 500 calories each day for a week to gain one pound, cutting back on sugar can make a difference. You needn't worry about the teaspoon of sugar or honey you add to your coffee—a measly 4 grams of sugar, or 16 calories, won't do much damage to your waistline.

I realize that most people probably don't consume this many added sugars each day. Most people get their calorie hits from sugar–fat combinations, or "sweetened fats" as I like to call them. You know, those tasty breakfast treats at your local coffee shop. Or the donut you pick up on the way in to the office. Even those homemade oatmeal cookies pack a fair amount of sugar and fat. Take a look at how the calories add up from these sugar–fat mixes:

FOOD	CALORIES (CAL)
Ben & Jerry's Cherry Garcia® ice cream, 1 cup (250 ml)	520 cal
Saint Cinnamon's cinnamon bun	700 cal
Starbucks butterscotch coffee cake	680 cal
Starbucks cinnamon chip scone	540 cal
Starbucks chocolate brownie Frappaccino, grande	488 cal
Krispy Kreme's glazed cruller	239 cal
Pecan pie, 1/6 of a pie	452 cal
Snickers peanut butter bar	270 cal
Tim Hortons cherry cheese Danish	380 cal

Sugar and Diabetes

Eating candy or drinking the occasional soda pop won't give you diabetes. However, if your regular diet is high in sugar *and* low in fiber, you may be at greater risk for developing type 2 diabetes. It is true, however, that people with diabetes have to carefully manage their carbohydrate intake. Meals must be regularly scheduled and contain measured portions of carbohydrate foods. It might surprise you to learn that people with diabetes are allowed to eat a little bit of added sugar.

Sugar and Dental Caries

Here's where sugar *is* a culprit. In the mouth, starches begin breaking down into sugars. Bacteria in the mouth then ferment these sugars and in the process produce an acid that erodes tooth enamel. The longer carbohydrate foods stay in the mouth, the greater the opportunity for cavities to form. Sticky foods like candy adhere to the teeth and will keep acid-yielding bacteria in action longer. If you snack on carbohydrate-rich foods regularly throughout the day, this keeps the bacteria working, too.

Eating nonsugary foods can help remove carbohydrate from the surface of your teeth. This is why, as you may have heard, eating cheese helps prevents cavities. Rinsing your mouth and brushing your teeth after eating are important strategies to help prevent dental caries.

Sugar and Kids

The amount of sugar in a child's diet and its effect on behavior remain controversial. Evidence does not support the notion that sugar causes hyperactivity. In studies in which children are given high amounts of refined sugar, behavior has not been negatively affected. Despite the fact that sugar does not seem to trigger or worsen symptoms, there may be a small number of children who react to sugary foods. One study did find that sugar worsened inattention, but not aggressive behavior, in children with attention deficit hyperactivity disorder.[16]

A steady diet of candy, pop and other sugary foods can, however, impact the nutritional quality of a child's diet. One study looked at the diets of 568 ten-year-old children and found that as sugar intake increased, there was a significant decrease in the amount of protein, vitamins and minerals a child consumed.[17] Foods high in added sugar tend to be low in other nutrients. If kids are getting a fair share of their daily calories from sugar, it becomes more difficult for them to meet their nutrient needs.

A healthy diet should minimize the consumption of table sugar, soft drinks, fruit drinks, fruit leather, candy and other sweets. Parents should help children understand that these foods are considered treats and, as such, they should not be eaten on a regular basis.

Are Artificial Sweeteners Safe?

Artificial sweeteners are often used by people trying to lose weight. Diet pop, sugar-free yogurts and little pink packets of fake sugar are thought to save calories. It's true that artificial sweeteners don't add calories, but sometimes the savings aren't that large. For instance, a teaspoon of sugar added to your coffee or tea supplies only 16 calories. If that's all you use artificial sweeteners for, the calories you save won't make much of a dent in your day. If you're watching your calorie intake, you're much better off forgoing the cream cheese on your bagel (which can run you 300 calories!) or limiting your portion of salad dressing. But if you regularly down a 12-ounce can of soda laden with 10 teaspoons of sugar, the calories you bank by switching to diet pop can really add up.

Sugar substitutes are also used by people with diabetes in an effort to avoid taking in too much sugar. Diabetes results when the body does not produce enough insulin or does not use it properly. Glucose builds up in the blood and passes out of the body as urine, causing the cells to lose their main source of fuel. Because sugar substitutes do not contain sugar and don't put demand on insulin, they can be effective sweeteners for people with diabetes.

When it comes to your health, artificial sweeteners are the subject of much controversy. Before you reach for that packet of nonsugar, read the following.

One of the first artificial sweeteners to receive Health Canada's attention was *saccharin*, a sweetener derived from coal tar (mmm, mmm). In 1977, the government released a study linking saccharin use to bladder cancer in rats. Since that time, manufacturers have not been allowed to add saccharin to foods. It's available only in pharmacies, where it's sold over the counter as a tabletop sweetener. Although several studies have suggested that large quantities of saccharin can cause cancer in laboratory rats, no harmful effects have been shown in humans, which is why this artificial sweetener has not been banned in the United States.

Cyclamate is another controversial sweetener. Like saccharin, this compound is made from coal tar, and its use has been associated with bladder cancer in animals. Although cyclamate is banned south of the border, it is available in Canada as a tabletop sweetener (Sucryl®, Sweet N' Low®, Sugar Twin®, and Weight Watchers®).

One of the most popular artificial sweeteners is *aspartame,* better known as Nutrasweet® or Equal®. Aspartame is made up of two amino acids (phenylalanine and aspartic acid) and has had the approval of Health Canada since 1981. It can be found in over 5000 different products, and, despite the controversy, there is so far no scientific evidence to show that it causes cancer. However, aspartame use has been reported to cause headaches and other reactions in sensitive people. And because aspartame contains phenylalanine, individuals with the metabolic disorder phenylketonuria (PKU) should avoid using it. PKU is an inherited disease in which the body cannot dispose of excess phenylalanine.

Sucralose, or Splenda®, is another artificial sweetener found in many diet foods and sold as a tabletop sweetener. This sweetener is made from real sugar. Sucralose is relatively new to Canada, having made its debut in 1991. So far, it has not been associated with cancer in laboratory studies.

A recent sugar substitute to come into the market is *acesulfame K*. This Health Canada–approved sweetener is sold under the brand name Sunett®, and it's found in drinks, fruit spreads, baked goods, candies, chewing gum and tabletop sweeteners. Although our government has deemed it safe for human consumption, some experts argue that the data are inadequate to assess its cancer causing potential.

While scientific studies have not proven a clear link between artificial sweeteners and human cancer, they don't rule it out either. I don't want you to think that sipping the occasional diet soda will harm your health, because it won't. But I do believe that you are entitled to know the facts before you make your decision to use these products. If you choose the artificial route to sweetness, don't overdo it.

10 TIPS
FOR INCORPORATING HEALTHY CARBOHYDRATES IN YOUR DIET

1. To keep you healthy and energetic, 55 percent of your daily calories should come from carbohydrate-containing foods. To help you achieve this, aim to eat 5 to 12 grain servings per day. If you are trying to lose weight, stick to 5 servings per day. (You'll find serving sizes listed on page 157.) Whole grains, vegetables, legumes and fruit should take up two-thirds to three-quarters of your plate.

2. Eat three servings of whole grains each day. Set a goal to try one new whole grain each week—pot barley, kasha, brown rice and quinoa are only a few. You'll find five tasty whole-grain recipes on page 199.

3. Gradually add low glycemic index (GI) foods to your diet so that eventually you're including one low GI food in two meals each day. The list on page 50 will help you choose low GI foods.

4. Buy bread and crackers that list "whole wheat" or "whole rye" as the first ingredient.

5. Try whole-wheat pasta for a change. You'll find many different varieties of whole-wheat pasta in supermarkets, health food stores and bulk food bins.

6. Choose a breakfast cereal that contains at least 4 to 5 grams of fiber per serving.

7. Add natural wheat bran, oat bran or ground flaxseed to hot cereal, yogurt, applesauce and baked good recipes.

8. Limit your intake of sugary foods such as candy, chocolate bars, soda pop, cookies, breakfast pastries and rich desserts to once a week.

9. Replace soda pop with water, tea, herbal tea, low-fat milk, soymilk or vegetable juice.

10. As often as possible, avoid buying products with artificial sweeteners.

ANSWERS TO LESLIE'S IQ QUIZ   CARBOHYDRATES

1. False. Read pages 43–44 to find out why!

2. e. All the foods listed are complex carbohydrates (starchy foods).

3. d. Low-fat yogurt has a low glycemic index.

4. b. Wheat bran has insoluble fiber, the type that keeps your bowels regular. The other foods listed are sources of soluble fiber, the type that helps lower blood cholesteral.

5. c. Lactose is a natural sugar found in milk.

Step 4

Eat More Fruits and Vegetables

LESLIE'S NUTRITION IQ QUIZ   FRUITS AND VEGETABLES

1. True or false? A high intake of fruits and vegetables can prevent cancer.

2. What is considered one serving of vegetables?
   a. 1 large carrot
   b. 2 cups (500 ml) green salad
   c. 1/2 cup (125 ml) green beans
   d. 1 1/2 cups (375 ml) vegetable juice

3. You're certain an orange is high in vitamin C. But which has even more?
   a. 1/2 cup (125 ml) raw red pepper
   b. 1 banana
   c. 1 cup (250 ml) green peas
   d. 1/2 cup (125 ml) carrots

4. How many carrots do you need to eat to get the 5 to 10 milligrams of beta-carotene you should consume every day?
   a. 1
   b. 2 or 3
   c. 4 or 5
   d. more than 5

5. True or false? Fresh fruits and vegetables can cause salmonella food poisoning.

Chances are you've been told since childhood to eat your fruits and vegetables. And while your mother's promise of dessert might have prompted you to finish those Brussels sprouts, it seems we need a little extra motivation today. According to recent statistics, only 36 percent of Canadians eat the recommended minimum of five servings of produce per day. And what's worse, our children are being short changed too. A survey from the Heart and Stroke Foundation revealed that only one in five kids aged 6 to 12 is eating five servings of fruits and vegetables each day.[1]

The Health Benefits of Fruits and Vegetables

It's hard to believe that we aren't filling our plates with fruits and vegetables. After all, it's impossible to argue with the fact that these foods are good for us. Study after study tells us that a diet high in fruits and vegetables wards off cancer, heart attack, stroke and high blood pressure and even preserves our eyesight. In fact, extensive reviews have concluded that eating at least five daily servings of fruits and vegetables could lower cancer rates by 20 percent, reduce coronary heart disease by 20 to 40 percent and stroke by 25 percent. That's pretty powerful stuff.

Fruits and Vegetables Can Prevent Cancer

The strongest evidence for the health benefits of fruits and vegetables relates to cancer protection, especially cancers of the lung, esophagus, stomach, colon and pancreas. The anti-cancer properties of fruits and vegetables were known a decade ago, when researchers reported their significant protection in 128 of 154 studies.[2]

Five years later, in 1997, the World Cancer Research Fund and American Institute for Cancer Research published a report that investigated the link between fruits and vegetables and cancer risk. Of the 247 studies assessed, 78 percent revealed significant protection for eating at least one type of fruit or vegetable.[3] Health Canada reviewed studies published after this report and their conclusions were the same: eating a diet high in fruits and vegetables reduces the risk of cancer.[4]

Fruits and Vegetables Can Protect the Heart

Eating fruits and vegetables can also lower your risk of heart attack and stroke. When scientists from the United Kingdom reviewed 28 studies, they found that fruits and vegetables offered strong protection from heart disease, especially stroke.[5] Harvard researchers agree. After examining the diets and health status of almost 76,000 women and 39,000 men for up to 14 years, they learned that compared with those who ate few fruits and vegetables, men and women who ate at least five servings per day lowered their risk of stroke by 31 percent.[6] Cruciferous vegetables, green leafy vegetables and citrus fruits seemed to offer the most protection.

Fruits and vegetables may prevent a heart attack, too. In a separate investigation of this large group of men, the researchers determined that those who ate at least two and a half servings of vegetables each day had a 23 percent lower risk of heart disease compared with men who ate less than one.[7] What's more, eating vegetables offered even greater protection for men who were overweight and for those who smoked.

Fruits and Vegetables Can Keep Your Blood Pressure Healthy

If you want to manage your blood pressure, you had better start boosting your intake of fruits and vegetables. The Dietary Approaches to Stop Hypertension (DASH) diet study recently determined an optimal pattern of eating that can dramatically lower elevated blood pressure. People with mild hypertension whose daily diet included four to five servings of fruits *and* four to five servings of vegetables, along with low-fat dairy products, achieved a reduction in blood pressure similar to that obtained by drugs. This diet lowered blood pressure within two weeks and, after two months, 70 percent of the participants achieved a normal blood pressure.[8,9]

Fruits and Vegetables Can Preserve Your Eyesight

You probably didn't realize that the spinach you were coaxed to eat when you were a child could help prevent blindness when you're older. The protective effect of fruits and vegetables on eyesight is an emerging area of research. Eating plenty of fruits and vegetables appears to ward off cataracts and macular degeneration, the leading causes of blindness in adults over age 65.

When a cataract develops, proteins within the lens of the eye become damaged and clump together. This obstructs the passage of light into the eye and causes vision to become blurry. Researchers from Tufts University in Boston studied 77 people with cataracts and found that those who ate less than three and a half servings of fruits and vegetables each day had a much higher risk of the eye disease.[10] Vegetables rich in compounds called carotenoids may offer the most protection. When a Harvard research team looked at the diets of women, they noticed that higher intakes of spinach and kale (both good sources of carotenoids) were linked with a lower risk of cataracts.

Macular degeneration develops when, as you get older, tissues in the eye (the macula) gradually thin out. The cells in the macula responsible for processing light slowly break down, blurring vision and making it difficult to see fine details. An American study revealed that a higher intake of green leafy vegetables, especially spinach and kale, was linked with a 43 percent lower risk of macular degeneration.[11]

What's in Fruits and Vegetables?

While we don't yet know all the reasons why fruits and vegetables keep us healthy, scientists have pinned down a number of protective compounds. These foods are excellent sources of important vitamins, antioxidants and literally thousands of protective plant chemicals known as phytochemicals. And let's not forget that they add a fair amount of dietary fiber to a diet. Here's an in-depth look at the insides of fruits and vegetables.

Folate

Reach for avocado, oranges, orange juice, artichokes, asparagus, bean sprouts, beets, Brussels sprouts, Romaine lettuce, spinach.

This B vitamin is essential for the production of DNA, the genetic material found inside each and every cell in your body. Without folate, your cells would not be able to grow and divide properly. Without folate, your DNA could not repair itself when damaged, and this could lead to cancer, in particular colon and breast cancer.

Indeed, studies have linked higher intakes of folate with a lower risk of both types of cancer. When it comes to colon cancer, folate appears to offer the most benefit to women who have a family history of the disease. A recent study from Harvard Medical School noted that, among women who had a family member with colon cancer, those who consumed at least 400 micrograms of folate each day had a 52 percent lower chance of developing the disease.[12]

A handful of studies suggest that higher intakes of folate may help prevent breast cancer. Folate may be most important for women who drink a moderate intake of alcohol, since alcohol disrupts the metabolism of folate in the body. The famous Nurses' Health Study examined the relationship between folate in the diet and breast cancer risk in women who drank alcohol. Among the women who consumed at least one drink per day, the risk of breast cancer was the highest among those with the lowest folate intake. Compared with women whose diet contained the least folate, those who got the most had a 45 percent lower risk of breast cancer.[13]

Folate may also help prevent heart disease by keeping your blood homocysteine level in check. Homocysteine is an amino acid the body produces during metabolism every day. Normally the body converts homocysteine to other harmless amino acids with the help of folate and vitamins B6 and B12. When this conversion doesn't occur, either because of a genetic defect or a deficiency of B vitamins, homocysteine can accumulate in the blood and damage vessel walls, promoting the build-up of fatty plaques. A number of studies have linked high homocysteine levels with a greater risk of heart attack. As well, researchers have documented the ability of an adequate folate intake to normalize elevated homocysteine levels.

Fruits and vegetables can contribute a fair amount of folate to your daily diet, especially if you focus on the choices I've listed above. Multivitamins are another important way to meet your daily B vitamin requirements. I discuss the use of supplements in Chapter 6.

Vitamin C

Reach for cantaloupe, grapefruit, kiwi, mango, oranges, strawberries, tomato juice, bell peppers, broccoli, Brussels sprouts, cauliflower.

Vitamin C is a potent antioxidant. That means it can protect the body from the harmful effects of unstable oxygen molecules called free radicals. While oxygen is essential for life, it also has the potential to harm. When oxygen participates in chemical reactions in the body, toxic by-products called free radicals are formed. Alcohol, cigarette smoking, air pollution and pesticides are also free radical generators and increase the free radical burden placed on the body.

If left unchecked, free radicals can destroy virtually every cell in the body. Free radical damage is thought to contribute to many disorders: heart disease, cancer, cataracts, Alzheimer's disease and arthritis, to name only a few. Fortunately, the body has its own defense system of enzymes that fight free radicals. These antioxidant enzymes scavenge and neutralize free radicals before they do harm. But scientists are learning that this built-in protection is not enough to prevent disease. Rather, we need a daily supply of dietary antioxidants from fruits and vegetables to help out.

Enter vitamin C. This antioxidant nutrient, along with vitamin E, can protect your LDL (bad) cholesterol from the wrath of free radicals. If LDL cholesterol particles become damaged by free radicals, they stick more readily to artery walls and can lead to blocked arteries and possibly a heart attack. Research findings support the notion that getting enough vitamin C in your diet is good for your heart. People with the highest levels of vitamin C in their blood and their diet appear to have a lower risk of heart attack and stroke.

Vitamin C also plays a crucial role in the lens of your eye, where it mops up free radicals that can damage proteins and cause cataracts. We are only just beginning to recognize the significant role that vitamin C–rich foods (and supplements) play in lowering the odds of cataracts.

That's not all. It looks as though vitamin C might protect from osteoporosis, the bone-thinning disease that afflicts one in four Canadian women and one in eight Canadian men over the age of 50. A number of studies in postmenopausal women have linked higher intakes of vitamin C with a higher bone density. Vitamin C might protect your bones in two ways. First, the nutrient is needed for the formation of collagen, a tissue that supports your bones. Second, the antioxidant activity of vitamin C may buffer the harmful effect of cigarette smoking on bones. (Many studies have shown that cigarette smoking reduces bone density and increases the risk of fracture.)

Beta-Carotene (Think Orange and Green!)

Reach for apricots, cantaloupe, mango, nectarines, papaya, peaches, broccoli, carrots, collard greens, kale, pumpkin, spinach, sweet potato, winter squash.

This nutrient is another powerful antioxidant that's able to protect DNA from free radical damage. But the job of beta-carotene doesn't stop here. Your body converts some of the beta-carotene you consume to vitamin A, a nutrient that helps you see, supports normal cell growth and division, builds strong bones and teeth and maintains a healthy immune system.

When it comes to cancer prevention, this is one category of fruits and vegetables you absolutely must include in your daily diet. That's right: every day, eat one orange fruit or vegetable and one dark green vegetable. If you're a smoker, take this advice very seriously. This is because there's substantial evidence that green vegetables and carrots prevent lung cancer.

If you were to review every study that looked at lung cancer risk and vegetable intake, you'd see that green vegetables lower the risk by 40 to 70 percent and carrots by 40 to 90 percent. In a large study from Harvard University, women who consumed five or more carrots per week had a 60 percent lower risk of lung cancer compared with women who never ate carrots.[14]

The antioxidant powers of vegetables and fruits loaded with beta-carotene may also prevent cataracts and macular degeneration.

Don't think you can pop a beta-carotene pill to make up for a diet that lacks fruits and vegetables. It won't work and, in fact, it may be dangerous. Studies have found that only a diet plentiful in beta-carotene-rich foods protects from lung cancer; beta-carotene supplements do not reduce the risk of lung cancer. What's more, these supplements have been shown to *increase* lung cancer risk in men who smoke. *Do not take single beta-carotene supplements if you smoke* (the small amount that's added to multivitamins is considered safe).

The message is loud and clear: fruits and vegetables, *not supplements*, protect from cancer. Whole foods contain an array of different nutrients and natural chemicals that likely work in concert to keep you healthy.

Dietary Fiber

We all know about the benefits of eating more fiber: it prevents constipation, diverticulitis, certain cancers, heart disease, type 2 diabetes and so on. When you think about fiber, you probably think about a bowl of bran cereal or whole-wheat bread. It's true that we get a good share of fiber from whole grains, but eating five to ten daily servings of fruits and vegetables can make a hefty contribution to your fiber intake. To help you meet your daily target of 25 to 35 grams of fiber, use the following list to "bulk" up your diet.

FIBER CONTENT OF FRUIT AND VEGETABLES

Fruit	Vegetables
High Fiber (5+ grams)	**High Fiber (5+ grams)**
Apple, with skin, 1	Green peas, 1/2 cup (125 ml)
Blackberries, 1/2 cup (125 ml)	Snow peas, 10
Blueberries, 1 cup (250 ml)	Swiss chard, cooked, 1 cup (250 ml)
Figs, dates, 10	
Kiwi, 2	
Mango, 1 medium	
Pear, 1 medium	
Prunes, dried, 5	
Prunes, stewed, 1/2 cup (125 ml)	
Raspberries, 1/2 cup (125 ml)	
Medium Fiber (2–4 grams)	**Medium Fiber (2–4 grams)**
Orange, 1 medium	Bean sprouts, 1/2 cup (125 ml)
Raisins, 2 tbsp (25 ml)	Beans, string, 1/2 cup (125 ml)
Rhubarb, cooked, 1/2 cup (125 ml)	Broccoli, 1/2 cup (125 ml)
Strawberries, 1 cup (250 ml)	Brussels sprouts, 1/2 cup (125 ml)
Tangerine, 1 medium	Carrots, raw, 1/2 cup (125 ml)
	Eggplant, 1/2 cup (125 ml)
	Parsnips, 1/2 cup (125 ml)
	Vegetables, mixed, 1/2 cup (125 ml)

Manual of Clinical Dietetics, 6th ed. The American Dietetic Association and Dietitians of Canada, 2000. Reprinted with permission.

Phytochemicals

There's a whole lot more to fruits and vegetables than vitamins, minerals and fiber. Loading up on antioxidants and dietary fiber is only the tip of the iceberg when it comes to preventing chronic diseases. Today the buzzword among nutritionists is *phytochemicals,* referring to the natural chemicals found in all plant foods. Since the 1990s, excited scientists have been identifying and isolating hundreds of these health-enhancing chemicals from fruits and vegetables.

Phytochemicals give plants their vibrant color and delicious flavor. They also defend plants from disease, light and pollution. Best of all, once we consume phytochemicals in a stir-fry, pasta sauce or salad, they appear to bolster our defenses against illnesses such as cancer, heart disease and osteoporosis.

Anthocyanins

Reach for blackberries, blueberries, boysenberries, cherries, cranberries, currants, grapes, plums, prunes, raspberries, strawberries.

Anthocyanins are potent antioxidants and, as such, they can protect your LDL cholesterol from free radical damage. In fact, anthocyanins are up to six times more potent as an antioxidant than vitamin C. Research conducted at Tufts University in Boston reported that blueberries scored the highest in antioxidant power when compared with popular fruits and vegetables. When it comes to the antioxidant powers of berries, blueberries lead the pack, followed by strawberries, blackberries and then raspberries.

The anthocyanins in cranberries can help treat and prevent urinary tract infections. These compounds act as natural antibiotics, preventing bacteria from adhering to the bladder wall. Instead of hanging around to multiply, bacteria are flushed out in the urine.

Anthocyanins may also keep your brain cells healthy, allowing nutrients and chemical signals to pass easily in and out of brain cells. Preliminary research found that animals fed an anthocyanin-rich diet outperformed animals on a control diet in tests of memory, balance and coordination.[15]

Berries also contain other phytochemicals that can inactivate cancer-causing substances and defend the body from the harmful effects of cigarette smoke and air pollution.

Cruciferous Compounds

Reach for bok choy, broccoli, Brussels sprouts, cabbage, cauliflower, collard greens, kale, rutabaga, turnip.

Vegetables in this group contain four phytochemicals that trigger the release of enzymes in the body that block the cancer process and reduce the size of tumors. They may also help the body convert a potent form of estrogen into a harmless one, thereby protecting from hormone-related cancers (breast, prostate, ovarian and endometrial).

Studies have revealed that higher intakes of cruciferous vegetables reduce the risk of colon, lung and prostate cancer. One large study found that men with the highest intake of these vegetables had a 39 percent lower risk of prostate cancer.[16]

Flavonoids

Reach for most fruits and vegetables but especially apples, citrus fruit, broccoli, celery, onions, and also tea leaves (black and green).

There are many, many different types of flavonoids in plant foods and, as a result, these phytochemicals have a wide range of effects in the body. Some act as antioxidants, some induce enzymes to destroy cancer-causing substances, some block estrogen action and others reduce the formation of cancerous tumors.

Specific flavonoids found in apples, onions and white grapefruits might protect from lung cancer, while those in apples may reduce the risk of stroke.[17-19] The flavonoids in green and black tea have been linked to a lower risk of heart disease and cancer.

Lutein

Reach for grapes, kiwi, beet greens, broccoli, collard greens, kale, mustard greens, okra, red peppers, spinach, Swiss chard, zucchini.

Lutein is a member of the carotenoid family. While it's found in many plant foods, the very best sources are spinach, kale and collard greens. Scientists are learning that this natural chemical may be very important to eye health. High dietary intakes of lutein are associated with up to a 40 percent lower risk of age-related macular degeneration.[20]

Lutein is concentrated in the macula of the eye, the small part of the retina that's responsible for fine, detailed vision. Here, lutein acts as a filter, protecting structures of the eye from the damaging effects of the sun's ultraviolet light. The denser, or thicker, the macula, the better it can block damaging light rays.

A handful of studies have shown that adding lutein-rich foods to your daily diet can increase the density of the macula. In one study, from the Veterans Administration Medical Center in Chicago, eating 1/2 cup (125 ml) of sautéed spinach four to seven times per week led to improved visual function in men with age-related macular degeneration.[21]

Lutein also acts as an antioxidant, protecting the retina from oxidative damage that can lead to cataracts. Two large studies from Harvard University found that men and women with the highest intakes of lutein had a 20 percent lower risk of cataract compared with those who consumed the least.[22,23] Broccoli, spinach and kale were most often associated with protection.

Lycopene

Reach for canned tomatoes, fresh tomatoes, tomato juice, tomato paste, tomato sauce, guava, pink grapefruit, watermelon.

Like lutein, lycopene is a cousin of beta-carotene. This natural chemical gives the fruits and vegetables listed above their bright red color. Lycopene is an antioxidant that seems to protect prostate cells from damage that can lead to cancer.

Back in 1995, lycopene was in the headlines when a study from Harvard Medical School reported that men who consumed ten or more weekly servings of tomato-based foods had a 35 percent lower risk of prostate cancer compared with men who ate one serving or less.[24] In 2002, after collecting an additional seven years of data on these men, the researchers reported that lycopene, and in particular tomato sauce, was protective from prostate cancer. Compared with men who consumed tomato sauce less than once per month, those who enjoyed it at least twice a week had a 23 percent lower risk of prostate cancer.[25]

Some studies suggest that consuming foods rich in lycopene protects women from cervical dysplasia, a condition in which cells lining the surface of the cervix grow abnormally. One study from the University of Pennsylvania School of Medicine found that women with the highest intake of lycopene were one-third as likely to have dysplasia compared with those who consumed the least.[26]

The best sources of lycopene are heat-processed tomato products. Foods such as tomato sauce and tomato juice contain a form of lycopene that's more available to the body than the lycopene found in fresh tomatoes. You'll absorb even more lycopene if you add a little fat to your meal, so bring on the extra-virgin olive oil! (This holds true for all carotenoids.)

Sulfur Compounds

Reach for chives, garlic, leeks, onions, scallions, shallots.

Onions and garlic contain many sulfur compounds, some of which are responsible for bad breath and others that seem to protect the heart and prevent cancer. The Iowa Women's Health Study, which followed 42,000 postmenopausal women, found that women who consumed 0.7 grams of garlic per day (less than one clove) had a 32 percent lower risk of colon cancer compared with those who ate no garlic at all.[27]

These protective sulfur compounds have been shown to lower blood cholesterol levels, help the liver detoxify carcinogens, kill certain types of disease causing bacteria and boost the body's immune system.

Strategies to Eat More Fruits and Vegetables

By now you might be saying, "Enough already! I know that fruits and vegetables are good for me!" Indeed, a whopping 70 percent of Canadians are well aware of the protective effects of fruits and vegetables.[28] Yet despite the overwhelming evidence for their health benefits, many of us still fall short of the recommended five to ten servings per day. We grab a bagel instead of an orange; we throw together pasta with pesto sauce instead of eating a salad with a baked potato; we munch on a strawberry cereal bar instead of eating a piece of fruit.

What's a Serving?

Many of us think that five to ten servings is a large amount of food. How could it be possible to eat so many fruits and vegetables in one day? In fact, a serving size isn't that large. You're probably eating two servings when you think you're only getting one. Take a look:

One serving of fruit or vegetables is equivalent to:

- 1 medium-sized whole fruit (apple, orange, banana, pear, peach, nectarine)
- 1/2 grapefruit
- 1 cup (250 ml) cubed fruit
- 1/2 cup (125 ml) berries or grapes

- 1/4 cup (50 ml) dried fruit

- 2 tbsp (25 ml) raisins

- 3/4 cup (175 ml) unsweetened fruit juice

- 1/2 cup (125 ml) cooked vegetables

- 1 cup (250 ml) salad

- 3/4 cup (175 ml) vegetable juice

Planning Ahead

Some of us think that adding fruits and vegetables to our diet is time-consuming. Not so! With a little planning and the help of pre-prepped produce in the grocery store, eating your five to ten is a breeze! If you forgo eating fruits and vegetables until the end of the day, you aren't going to come close to getting your five to ten servings. The key is mapping out a plan to incorporate fruits and vegetables in all your meals and snacks.

Remember I told you that the very first step is getting organized? Well, that applies to eating fruits and vegetables, too. You've got to plan ahead. Use the "road map" below to ensure you're getting enough.

BREAKFAST

Include one to two fruit servings
(e.g., a small glass of citrus juice and chopped fruit on your cereal)

SNACKS

Carry fruit in your bag for midday snacks
(e.g., a box of raisins, an apple or single-serving cans of unsweetened fruit or applesauce)

LUNCH

Include one to two vegetable servings
(e.g., a can of tomato juice, extra veggies in your sandwich, a handful of baby carrots, a cup of vegetable soup)

DINNER

Include two different vegetable servings
(e.g., carrots and broccoli, vegetable stir-fry, tomato pasta sauce with zucchini and peppers)

DAILY TOTAL

Five to Eight Fruit and Vegetable Servings
(two to four fruit servings and three to four vegetable servings)

You can easily bump up your vegetable intake by eating larger servings—why stop at 1/2 cup (125 ml) of stir-fried vegetables when you can enjoy 1 cup (250 ml) and get two veggie servings?

Think Convenience—and Safety

If scrubbing, peeling and chopping isn't your thing, take advantage of convenient pre-prepped produce sold in the grocery store. You'll find ready-to-eat salads, carrot sticks, broccoli florets, chopped celery, sliced onions, chopped garlic, stir-fry vegetables, shredded cabbage, grated carrot, triple-washed fresh spinach, cubed turnip and squash.

And that's just the vegetables. In the convenient fruit category you'll find fresh fruit salad, peeled and cored fresh pineapple and individual serving sizes of raisins, dried fruit bars, canned fruit, applesauce and unsweetened fruit juice.

Ready-to-eat pre-packaged fruits and veggies can be huge time savers. But they are also potential sources of food poisoning since they are subject to more handling before they make it into your fridge. Add to that the fact they're often eaten raw. Seeds used for sprouting are a likely source of salmonella contamination. Bacteria can lodge in tiny cracks in the seed and multiply during warm, humid sprouting conditions. Recent reports of disease-causing bacteria in sprouts, cabbage and raspberries remind us of the need for vigilance in the kitchen. Keep in mind the following:

- Adhere to the use-by dates on packaged ready-to-eat vegetables.

- When buying fresh-cut produce, be sure it is refrigerated or surrounded by ice.

- Don't eat raw sprouts (alfalfa, broccoli, radish, clover). Instead, cook them in stir-fries or soups. Heating to high temperatures kills harmful bacteria.

- Wash and scrub the outer rind of cantaloupe and other melons before cutting.

- After purchase, put produce that needs refrigeration away promptly. Fresh produce should be chilled within two hours of peeling or cutting.

- Wash your hands before and after handling fresh produce.

- Wash all fresh vegetables and fruits with cool running water before eating.

- Wash cutting surfaces often. Use clean cutting boards when handling produce.

- Use a cooler or ice packs when transporting or storing food outdoors.

Don't think you have to rely on fresh fruits and vegetables to get your five to ten daily servings. Frozen produce may be a better choice when the lettuce is wilted, the green beans aren't available or the wild blueberries (my favorite!) aren't in season. In some cases, frozen produce is more nutritious than their fresh counterparts that have been imported from our southern neighbors. That's because the food is processed soon after it's been picked in the field, locking in nutrients and flavor.

In the freezer section of your supermarket you'll find different medleys of frozen veggies ready to throw into a stir-fry or soup. You'll find frozen chopped spinach that, once defrosted, is ready to add to pasta sauce or lasagna. I recommend avoiding any frozen vegetables with sauce, as they often add too much fat and sodium to your diet. Frozen blueberries, cranberries, strawberries, mixed berries and mixed fruits are also readily available—all great for throwing into a smoothie or muffin batter.

Should You Worry about Pesticide Residues?

Approximately 6000 types of pesticides are currently used in Canada. These products are used in agriculture, on lawns and on golf courses to combat weeds, insects and fungi that destroy plant life. The use of pesticides in fruit and vegetable farming allows us to enjoy a wide variety of foods at a relatively low cost. According to the Crop Protection Institute of Canada, without pesticides, our ability to produce food would decrease by 40 percent.[29] It also says that Canada uses only a fraction of the volume of pesticides used in many other parts of the world, including the United States and Europe.

Pesticide residues on food are monitored by Health Canada's Pest Management Regulatory Agency (PMRA). The PMRA sets maximum residue limits for all pesticides. These limits have built-in safety margins that set the final level at a minimum of 100 times below the limit that could cause health problems. The PMRA and the Canadian Food Inspection Agency test thousands of produce samples each year to ensure that maximum residue limits are not exceeded.

Despite this, some Canadians are worried about the possible ill effects of pesticide residues that linger on the surface of fruits and vegetables. Some pesticides can disrupt hormone function, some cause nerve damage and some are carcinogenic. Other pesticides don't break down in the environment and can accumulate in fatty tissues.

Some scientists and watchdog groups worry that certain people may be more vulnerable to the effects of toxic pesticide residues than others. Pregnant women, breastfeeding moms and children may be more at risk. From conception to puberty, children's bodies are developing and are more sensitive to disruption. And because they eat more food per unit of body weight, they are more exposed to these residues than adults. And let's not forget that infants and young children eat a steady diet of apples, peaches, applesauce and apple juice.

Pesticide Residues and Cancer

Can consuming many different pesticide residues over a lifetime affect our health? Unfortunately, the studies that address this question are few and far between. Some research does suggest that people whose occupations involve being exposed to pesticides may suffer more health problems than those who are not regularly exposed to pesticides. A study from North Carolina discovered that women who farm and are present on the field during or shortly after application of a pesticide are at greater risk of breast cancer.[30]

But what about the rest of us, whose only exposure to pesticides is from residues on the food we eat? To date, the majority of research has focused on cancer risk. In 1997, the experts from the National Cancer Institute of Canada reviewed a number of studies and concluded that pesticide residues from fruits and vegetables did not pose any increased risk of cancer.[31]

Much of the research has addressed breast cancer risk from DDT, an insecticide that's been banned in Canada and the United States for nearly two decades. Why study the effects of DDT if it's been banned for so long? For one, DDT is a persistent pesticide. That means that DDT and its metabolites, the chemicals it breaks down into (DDE and DDD), can remain in the environment for years and years, and DDT can also leak into the environment from contaminated sites and spills, which means it may still be present even in those countries that have now banned DDT.

Another reason for concern is that DDT accumulates in fat stores of animals and humans, becoming concentrated as it moves up the food chain. As a result, DDT is more present in fat-containing foods such as meat, fish, milk, cheese and oil than in fruit, vegetables and grains. DDT can act like estrogen in the body, binding to estrogen receptors and potentially increasing the risk of breast cancer. However, recent studies, including the Nurses' Health Study, have found no evidence that exposure to DDT increases the risk of breast cancer.[32-34]

Best and Worst Fruits and Vegetables

While pesticides are hazardous at high doses, there's no evidence to suggest that pesticide residues cause cancer (but there's plenty of evidence to say that fruits and vegetables *prevent* cancer). Yet some people still prefer to avoid them. And certainly I agree with this. You can start by knowing which fruits and vegetables are the worst culprits for containing pesticide residues.

American researchers examined the pesticide residues found on 38 popular fresh produce items. They looked at the number of different residues found on produce as well as the quantity of residues present. Here's what they found:

CONTAMINATED FRUITS AND VEGETABLES

12 Most Contaminated	12 Least Contaminated
Strawberries	Avocados
Bell peppers (U.S. and Mexico)	Corn
Spinach	Onions
Cherries	Sweet potatoes
Peaches	Cauliflower
Cantaloupe (Mexico)	Brussels sprouts
Celery	Grapes (U.S.)
Apples	Bananas
Apricots	Plums
Green beans	Green onions
Grapes (Chile)	Watermelon
Cucumbers	Broccoli

Keep in mind that this study did not test Canadian-grown fruits and vegetables. But it is a useful guide when buying imported produce. It's important to know that none of the worst offenders were so contaminated with pesticide residues that they should never be eaten. There are simple measures you can take at home to minimize your exposure:

- Rinse produce with running water to remove most trace residues. Produce washes are unnecessary.

- Avoid using detergents to wash produce, since these may leave trace residues of chemicals that have not been tested for human consumption.

- Remove and discard outer leaves of lettuce and cabbage.

- Scrub thick-skinned produce such as potatoes, carrots and parsnips.

Going Organic

Many people are turning to organically grown fruits and vegetables to minimize their intake of pesticide residues. Finding organic produce has become increasingly easy. Once available only in health food stores, these fruits and vegetables are now found in the produce section of most grocery stores, right next to their nonorganic counterparts. And many can also be found in the freezer case.

Organic fruits and vegetables are grown and processed without the use of genetic engineering (see below), synthetic or artificial fertilizers, pesticides, growth regulators, antibiotics, preservatives, dyes or additives. However, most processed organic foods (e.g., organic frozen food meals, canned chili con carne) are allowed to contain a small percentage of nonorganic ingredients.

Organic produce is more expensive, but this is not because it's more nutritious than nonorganic fruits and vegetables. There is no difference in the nutrient content between organically grown and conventional farm produce. It is more expensive because organic farmers produce smaller amounts—insects and weeds compete more effectively with the crops. Nevertheless, many people do say that organic produce tastes better. For some, this is worth the extra cost.

Third-party organizations, called certification bodies, have been established to assure you that the produce you're buying is organic. However, because there are about 45 certifiers in Canada, certification logos come in all shapes and sizes. Some "Certified Organic" logos to look for include Organic Crop Improvement Association (OCIA), Demeter, Organic Crop Producers and Processors, Quality Assurance International and Canadian Organic Producers Association.

While there are many certification bodies, they all use similar national standards. And organic farms have to reapply for certification each year. It is anticipated that one day there will be a common "Canada Organic" seal. Such a national organic standard has been developed, but it awaits support of the federal government.

What about Genetically Modified Foods?

If you think genetically modified tomatoes sound like something cooked up in a test tube, you're not far off the mark. The biotechnology industry is revolutionizing agriculture—and your dinner plate. Ever since these foods made their way into the supermarket in mid-1995, you've likely been savoring a firmer baked potato, tofu made from pesticide-resistant soybeans and sweeter tasting tomatoes. What's more, you probably didn't even realize you were filling your grocery cart with these "biotech" foods.

Biotech 101

Simply put, biotechnology is the application of living organisms to develop new products. When it comes to food production, this process is not altogether unfamiliar. Ever since 1800 B.C., yeast has been used to make wine, beer and leavened bread. It's when we start hearing phrases like "genetically modified," "genetically engineered" or "gene spliced" that many of us start taking a closer look at the food we're eating.

Genetically modified food, one aspect of biotechnology, is not a brand-new concept. Traditional plant breeding, called hybridization, involves combining all the genetic traits of the two plants by grafting them together. Since the resulting plant may have some undesirable traits, it can take years of breeding to achieve the desired result. By 1973 scientists had the ability to isolate the genetic material of cells (DNA), and by the 1980s it was possible to transfer these genes from one organism to another. So rather than spending 10 to 12 years breeding a plant, scientists are now, through biotechnology, able to select one desired trait from a plant, bacterium or animal and move it into the genetic code of the other plant.

Plant biotechnology is often heralded as the means by which an exploding global population will achieve an abundant, safe and sustainable food supply. And it's estimated to become an industry worth over US$60 billion by the year 2010. Supporters of biotechnology point out many potential benefits, including reduced reliance on chemical pesticides, disease resistance, rapid crop growth, improved nutrition, improved food quality and longer storage life.

Biotech Foods in the Marketplace

A number of genetically modified foods have been approved for sale in both the United States and Canada. Here's a rundown of some foods that have likely made their way into your shopping cart:

- *Corn, soybeans and potatoes modified to require fewer applications of herbicides and pesticides.* Almost 20 percent of the soybeans grown in North America have been genetically manipulated so that they are tolerant to the herbicide glyphosate, commonly known as Roundup. Roundup Ready soybeans have been modified by introducing a gene from a soil bacterium that enables the plant to resist the herbicide. In a nutshell, farmers growing the bean can treat the crop with glyphosate to kill the weeds, without destroying the crop. If you want to avoid genetically modified soybeans, it won't be easy. Soy products and soy lecithin are in 60 percent of our processed foods, everything from breakfast cereal to baby food.

- *NewLeaf™ potatoes* that resist the Colorado Potato Beetle, a pest that has caused huge losses in fields. These insect-resistant spuds were developed by introducing the gene from a soil bacterium called *Bacillus thuringiensis (Bt)* into the plant. This gene enables the potato plant to produce its own pesticide, the Bt toxin. Corn also has an added gene that kills insects. That genetically modified cob of corn in the field is used to make corn syrup, cornstarch and other products that are estimated to be used in 25 percent of processed foods.

- *Flavr Savr™ tomatoes that soften slower* and remain on the vine longer, resulting in better flavor and color. The genetically modified tomatoes are able to suppress an enzyme that degrades its cell walls. (These tomatoes are in the fresh produce section of the grocery store but are unlabeled as such.)

- *Canola oil with a higher monounsaturated fat content.* In addition to its heart-healthy benefits, this biotech oil lasts longer on the shelf. The Canadian oilseed is also used in food products, animal feed and detergents.

- Other biotech crops include squash, sugarbeet, flax and cottonseed oil.

Concerns about Biotech Foods

With biotechnology, we assume control over the genetic codes of plants to achieve goals of efficiency and production. In *The Biotech Century,* author Jeremy Rifkin asks how "any reasonable person can believe for a moment that such unprecedented power is without substantial risk." Indeed, the profound implications of genetic engineering have roused much debate, for and against. Much of the debate against biotechnology has focused on the following areas of concern.

Super Bugs, Super Weeds and Super Viruses

Scientists and organic farmers worry that the widespread use of pest-resistant crops will build resistance among affected insects. And it appears there may be cause for concern. Over the past decade, at least eight species of pests have developed resistance to the Bt toxin. Ecologists fear the potential for herbicide resistance to spread from a genetically modified crop to a weed, a process called gene flow. Scientists also worry that virus-resistant crops offer a mechanism for creating new viruses. It is possible that a plant's gene could combine with genes of a related virus that finds its way naturally into the biotech plant, creating a virus with new features.

Resistance to Antibiotics

When developing plants through biotechnology, researchers use marker genes to determine whether the gene transfer was successful. Antibiotic proteins are often used for this purpose. Will eating plants with antibiotic-resistance marker genes increase our resistance to antibiotics? Biotech experts argue that this is not a possibility. They say the marker genes cannot function in the human body because the proteins they produce are broken down in the digestive tract.

Increased Food Allergies

Critics voice concern that food allergies will increase if genetically modified foods become a regular part of our diet. The worry is that the new proteins in the modified plants could produce a whole new class of allergenic foods. It has also been argued that foreign proteins introduced into plants, such as genes from deep-soil bacteria, may be unfamiliar to the human immune system and cause an allergic reaction.

Biotech companies argue that genetically modified foods approved for sale have been extensively tested for allergenic potential and that so far there have been no reports of allergies attributable to such foods. A biotech company must demonstrate by scientific testing that an allergen is not present in the new food if common allergens such as milk, eggs, wheat, fish, shellfish, nuts or legumes are added through genetic engineering. If an allergen is introduced into the new food, the manufacturer must label the product to alert allergy-prone people.

Lack of Labeling

Currently there's no way for consumers to tell if the food they purchase has been genetically altered. Consumer groups promoting informed consumption believe that individuals have the right to know and are lobbying for genetically modified foods to be labeled as such. In Canada and the United States, special labeling of foods derived from genetically modified plants is not required. In Canada, only products that involve a health or safety issue, such as allergenicity or change in nutritional value, must be labeled. Food companies are allowed to voluntarily label their products to meet consumer demands. In fact, you can find a number of soy products in grocery stores labeled as "non GMO," meaning the food is made from soybeans that were not genetically modified.

Knowing whether a food is a product of genetic engineering has become an important issue for Canadians. The government is currently working to develop a labeling standard for foods derived from biotechnology. This standard is expected to be ready by the fall of 2002.

Labeling might seem straightforward—until highly processed foods made with soy, corn and canola enter the picture. Many processed foods are made from a multitude of ingredients obtained from a variety of sources. At this time, no tracking systems are in place to grow, harvest and process modified and nonmodified crops in separate streams.

The Future of Biotech Foods

It seems that genetically altered foods are here to stay. It's clear that the mixing of genes from different species is not completely understood. As author Jeremy Rifkin points out, it's a "high risk venture with few ground rules and benchmarks to guide the journey." Like all new technologies, bioengineering holds both promise and potential danger. As new foods enter the marketplace, it may take decades to identify the ramifications of a genetically modified food supply. Until that time, we all have the choice to become as informed as possible. Only by becoming watchdogs of the biotech revolution can we continue our fight for safe and nutritious foods.

30 TIPS
FOR EATING MORE FRUITS AND VEGETABLES

(I JUST COULDN'T STOP AT MY USUAL 10 TIPS HERE!)
PRACTICE TWO OR THREE OF THESE SUGGESTIONS NOW, AND TRY MORE LATER.

BREAKFAST

1. Throw chopped banana, raisins or dried cranberries into a bowl of whole-grain cereal.

2. Purée frozen mixed berries with low-fat milk or soy beverage to make a refreshing breakfast shake.

3. Add dried berries to muffin mixes and cookie batters. Try dried cherries, currants, cranberries and blueberries.

4. Drink a 6-ounce (175-ml) glass of unsweetened citrus juice with your morning meal—an especially great idea for menstruating women since the vitamin C enhances iron absorption.

5. Enjoy a bowl of precut fresh fruit salad purchased from the grocery store's salad bar.

6. Fill half a cantaloupe with low-fat cottage cheese (wash the outer rind before cutting!).

7. Enjoy a bowl of low-fat yogurt mixed with cut-up fruit. Use canned unsweetened fruit when you're in a hurry.

8. If you're running out the door, grab an apple, banana or pear to eat in the car or on the bus.

9. Fill an omelet with diced tomatoes, spinach leaves and grated cheddar cheese.

10. Replace that cereal bar with two pieces of fruit.

LUNCH

11. Grab a can of vegetable juice instead of diet Coke.

12. When dining out for lunch, order a green salad (and ask for dressing on the side).

13. Add sliced tomatoes, cucumbers and lettuce to your sandwich. Try spinach leaves as a change from lettuce. Other tasty sandwich additions include grated carrot.

14. Pack leftover roasted vegetables in your lunch. Red peppers, zucchini, onion and Portobello mushrooms all make a delicious sandwich—just add a little goat cheese and you're set!

15. If you frequent the deli, order a small vegetable soup to have with your sandwich.

16. Add a handful of baby carrots or strips of red and green peppers to your brown-bag lunch.

17. Add shredded cabbage mixed with low-fat coleslaw dressing to a turkey sandwich.

DINNER

18. Use romaine and other dark-green lettuces in your salads (they're high in beta-carotene).

19. Add quick-cooking greens such as spinach, kale, rapini or Swiss chard to soups and pasta sauces.

20. Fortify your next soup, pasta sauce or casserole with grated zucchini and grated carrot.

21. Top a homemade pizza with a variety of fresh or grilled vegetables.

22. Fill whole-wheat flour tortillas with chopped tomato, green and red pepper strips and minced green onion. Just add beans or browned ground turkey and you've got a Mexican meal.

23. Bake, microwave or boil a sweet potato for a change from the usual spud. I enjoy mine mashed with a little orange juice.

24. For dessert, try strawberries marinated with balsamic vinegar and a sprinkle of sugar. Or drizzle sliced bananas or pineapple with lemon juice and brown sugar and broil until golden.

SNACKS

25. Snack on a washed apple, pear or nectarine. Keep a bowl of fresh fruit on your kitchen counter and in your office.

26. Pack snack-size cans of unsweetened fruit or applesauce in your briefcase.

27. Prepare individual snack bags of dried apricots, raisins and almonds.

28. Munch on carrot sticks, cherry tomatoes, red or green pepper strips, broccoli florets and mushroom caps with a low-fat creamy dip.

29. Slice up bananas, apples and pears and dip in low-fat vanilla yogurt.

30. Boost your energy with a glass of spicy tomato or vegetable juice.

ANSWERS TO LESLIE'S IQ QUIZ   FRUITS AND VEGETABLES

1. True!

2. c. 1/2 cup (125 ml) green beans is considered one vegetable serving. All the others are considered two servings.

3. a. 1/2 cup (125 ml) raw red pepper has 95 milligrams of vitamin C (a medium orange has 70 milligrams).

4. a. One medium carrot has 11 milligrams of beta-carotene.

5. True. Read page 72 to find out why.

Step 5

Choose Healthier Fats and Oils

LESLIE'S NUTRITION IQ QUIZ   FATS AND OILS

1. You know that fast food is loaded with fat. But can you pick the item with the least?
    a. single-patty hamburger
    b. fillet of fish sandwich
    c. 6 chicken nuggets
    d. 2 slices pepperoni pizza

2. You know it's important to start the day off with breakfast. Do you know which breakfast is the lowest in fat?
    a. 1/2 cup (125 ml) granola with 2 percent milk
    b. 1 large bran muffin
    c. 1 poached egg on toast, with 2 tsp (10 ml) butter
    d. 3 medium pancakes, syrup and 2 strips of side bacon

3. True or false? Margarine has more calories than butter.

4. True or false? All vegetable oils are free of cholesterol.

5. You know that frying adds fat to an otherwise healthy food. One vegetable absorbs oil like a sponge; which is it?
    a. potato
    b. eggplant
    c. zucchini

You might be surprised to learn that, when it comes to health, dietary fat has some virtues. In fact, some types of fat may ward off heart disease and cancer; others may ease the symptoms of rheumatoid arthritis, inflammatory bowel disease and depression. It's only when we consume too little or too much fat that ill health occurs.

Today, Canadians continue to overeat unhealthy fats and consume too little of the healthy fats. The good news is that we are doing better than we did 20 years ago. As news reports continue to bombard us with messages about the link between fat and heart disease, our intake of fatty foods has decreased over the years.

Fat Chemistry 101

Molecules of fat in food and in the body are called *triglycerides*. Each triglyceride is made up of individual building blocks called *fatty acids*. Once we eat fat in a meal, digestive enzymes in our intestine break down food fats into their individual fatty acids. These fatty acids are then absorbed into the bloodstream, where they make their way to the liver.

In the liver, fatty acids are repackaged into larger triglyceride molecules so they can be transported to different tissues in the body. Every cell in your body has enzymes that dismantle these circulating triglycerides into their fatty-acid building blocks. By doing so, fatty acids can enter your cells, where some will be used immediately for energy. Fatty acids that aren't needed right away are repackaged into triglycerides and stored as body fat.

Why You Need Some Fat in Your Diet

Fat has many important roles in your body. Body fat stores provide an important source of energy for daily activity. In fact, about half of your daily energy requirements are supplied by stored fat. The fat that's stored in your muscles provides most of the fuel used during light exercise such as walking or climbing a flight of stairs. Our ability to store fat is pretty much unlimited, since our fat cells can increase in size if we consume more than we need. And we can always form new fat cells if we've filled up our existing fat cells to the point that they can't expand anymore.

Your body fat serves another important purpose. It acts as a layer of insulation protecting your major organs. Although we all need a little body fat, storing too much can increase your risk of heart disease, diabetes and certain cancers.

Dietary fat is necessary, too. It's not healthy to completely eliminate fat from your diet. Most of us agree that fat in foods enhances flavor, adds "mouth feel" and helps us feel satisfied after a meal. That's because dietary fat empties from the stomach slowly, imparting satiety, or a feeling of fullness. From a health perspective, dietary fat supplies your body with fat-soluble vitamins A, D, E and K, nutrients that you can't live without.

There's yet another reason why you must include some fat in your diet. Consuming fat in your meals is the only way your body can get *alpha-linolenic acid* and *linoleic acid,* two essential fatty acids that form cell membranes, aid in immune function and vision and produce immune compounds called eicosanoids. Without these essential fatty acids, we would not be able to maintain good health.

Eating Fat Can Make You Fat

But eating too much fat is not a good thing. There's no question that a steady diet of greasy foods and high-fat spreads can pack on the pounds. Gram per gram, fat delivers double the calories than either protein or carbohydrate. This means that fat calories add up fast! Fat can pack a lot of calories into even small portions of food. A typical side of French fries has 350 calories and 17 grams of fat. For the same amount of calories you can eat four apples, five slices of whole-wheat bread or 1 1/2 cups of spaghetti with tomato sauce. You get a lot more volume for the same calories when you go low fat.

That's why cutting back on fat can help people lose weight: you save calories. People who eat low-fat diets fill up on a larger volume of food for fewer calories. If you skip the side of fries and have a baked potato with salsa instead, you save 130 calories. Or, if you substitute a green salad with 4 teaspoons of dressing, you save close to 300 calories. I'm sure you get the idea. Don't get me wrong—I am not saying that eating too much fat is the only reason we're witnessing an epidemic of overweight and obese Canadians. It's only part of the reason. If you need to lose weight, start skimming calories from your diet by eliminating excess fat.

Cutting Back on Dietary Fat

Based on years of scientific study investigating the link between dietary fat and disease, Canadians are recommended to aim for a fat intake of *no more than 30 percent of daily calories*. Right now, we're getting about 38 percent of our calories from fat. Lower-fat intakes are associated with lower rates of heart disease, obesity and cancer. Here's how the 30 percent rule translates into grams of fat.

DAILY UPPER LIMIT OF FAT

Daily Calorie (cal) Intake	Daily Upper Limit (grams)	Daily Calorie (cal) Intake	Daily Upper Limit (grams)
1200 cal	40 g	2000 cal	65 g
1400 cal	47 g	2200 cal	73 g
1600 cal	53 g	2500 cal	80 g
1800 cal	60 g	2800 cal	93 g

The average Canadian woman needs to cut about 20 grams of fat from her diet; the average man, about 30 grams. We get most of our daily fat from added fats and oils. These are the visible fats that we add to our foods in the form of cooking oils, high-fat spreads and salad dressings. Added fats and oils are also the hidden fats added to commercial foods during the manufacturing process. It's the hidden fats that are tricky—since you can't see them, you may not realize they are present in a food.

If you've already flipped to the answers for this chapter's Nutrition IQ Quiz, you might have been surprised to learn the amount of hidden fat in certain foods. Most Canadians don't realize that a typical bran muffin contains 4 teaspoons' worth of oil. Learning where fat lurks in foods is the first step to cutting back your daily fat intake.

To help you consume no more than 30 percent fat calories, limit your intake of added fats and oils to a total of four to eight servings per day. If you are trying to lose weight, stick to four servings per day. *One* serving is:

- 1 tsp (5 ml) vegetable oil, margarine or butter

- 2 tsp (10 ml) diet margarine

- 2 tsp (10 ml) regular mayonnaise

- 2 tsp (10 ml) salad dressing

- 1 tbsp (15 ml) nuts or seeds

- 1 1/2 tsp (7 ml) peanut butter

- 1/8 medium-sized avocado

- 10 small or 5 large olives

The next step is learning where hidden fat lurks in foods. Most of us realize that greasy fast food is loaded with the stuff. A McDonald's Big Mac packs 32 grams of fat. Add the super-size fries and a large chocolate milkshake and you've hit (or exceeded) your fat quota for the day—a whopping 78 grams in just one meal!

There are other fast foods that can deliver a lot of fat to your plate, despite their healthier-sounding names. For instance, a typical taco salad from a Mexican fast food joint can pack as many as 900 calories and 12 teaspoons of hidden fat. The deep-fried shell that holds the salad and higher-fat toppings such as cheese and sour cream are the culprits here. Even a chef's salad with dressing can be upward of 650 calories by the time the high-fat dressing is added. Some of those packets of creamy dressing served at fast food outlets are 400 calories alone—each one of those calories coming from fat!

Decoding Nutrition Labels

I love to grocery shop in the United States. That's because every package of food carries a nutrition label that allows me to compare brands on grams of fat, sugar, fiber and so on.

With one quick glance I can easily choose the lower-fat version of cracker, or the higher-fiber brand of breakfast cereal. There's little doubt that nutrition labels allow me to make quick, informed food choices that help me eat healthier.

At the time of writing this book, Canada is still operating under a voluntary system of nutrition labeling. Only if a food carries a claim such as "low in fat" or "good source of fiber" or "light" does the manufacturer have to declare nutrition information on the package. Otherwise, it's the manufacturer's decision whether to add this useful information or not. However, even if the information is present, it's often difficult to find, inconsistent in its presentation and sometimes hard to read.

Soon this will change. By fall 2002, *all* pre-packaged foods sold in Canada will be required by law to carry a new and improved nutrition label; consumers can expect to start seeing the new labels on packages by late 2002 or early 2003. This nutrition facts panel will list detailed information about the nutrient content in one serving of the food.

The move to new and improved nutrition labeling includes:

- A new title: Nutrition Facts.

- The serving size on which nutrient information is based; this will be consistent for like products.

- An expanded list of nutrients.

- A standardized format that is bold, clear and easy to read. Also, nutrient information is more clearly identified.

- The daily value gives a context to the actual amount. It indicates if there is a lot or a little of the nutrient in a serving of food.

Nutrition Facts		
Per 1 cup (264g)		
Amount		**% Daily Value**
Calories 260		
Fat 13g		20%
Saturated Fat 3g + Trans Fat 2g		25%
Cholesterol 30mg		
Sodium 660mg		28%
Carbohydrate 31g		10%
Fibre 0g		0%
Sugars 5g		
Protein 5g		
Vitamin A 4%	•	Vitamin C 2%
Calcium 15%	•	Iron 4%

To help you choose a lower-fat food, look at the grams of total fat listed on the nutrition facts panel. This information is listed after the calories per serving. In the example shown here, a 1-cup (250-ml) serving provides 13 grams of fat. Is this amount more or less than you usually eat? If you eat twice as much, then you're getting 26 grams of fat. Once you find the grams of total fat per serving, you can use this information to choose between different brands. If possible, choose a brand that provides less than 13 grams of fat for the same serving size.

If nutrition information is not available, read ingredients lists. Manufacturers are required to list all ingredients in a product, beginning with the ingredient present in the largest quantity. To search out hidden fat, look for ingredients such as lard, shortening, palm oil, coconut oil, vegetable oil, hydrogenated oil, monoglycerides, diglycerides and tallow.

Of course, not all the foods you eat need to be low in fat. I fully expect you are going to splurge on the occasional burger and fries or decadent dessert. It's the overall picture that counts. If you eat one high-fat meal, simply return to your low-fat eating style at the next meal. Every single food, or meal, does not need to conform to the 30 percent fat calories rule. It's what you eat over the course of a day that matters.

Fat Intakes for Children

The recommendation to consume no more than 30 percent of calories from fat applies to children two years of age and older. It does not apply to infants and toddlers, who need more fat to support growth and development. But once children start eating with the rest of the family, usually at age two, they should be encouraged to eat a lower-fat diet. Older children and teenagers may need to make some dietary changes to gradually work toward a lower-fat diet.

Fat and Your Blood Cholesterol

In order to understand how different types of fat affect our cholesterol levels, we first need to know about blood cholesterol. Here's a short primer. You may have heard these terms used by your doctor but never been sure what they meant.

Cholesterol can't dissolve in your blood. This means it has to be piggybacked on protein carriers throughout your bloodstream.

LDL cholesterol This cholesterol is transported to the arteries on low-density lipoproteins. LDLs packed with cholesterol are referred to as "bad" cholesterol because they are directly linked to the process of hardening and narrowing of the arteries. The higher your level of LDL cholesterol, the greater your risk of heart disease.

HDL cholesterol High-density lipoproteins carry cholesterol away from the arteries toward the liver for degradation, meaning that HDL cholesterol does not accumulate on your artery walls. The higher your HDL level, the lower your risk of heart disease. That's why it's called the "good" cholesterol.

Triglycerides These fat particles are made in the liver from the food you eat and are transported in your blood on very low-density lipoproteins. High levels of triglycerides are associated with a greater risk of heart disease.

Get to Know the Different Types of Fat

When it comes to weight control, all types of fat are considered equal. Whether it's from butter, lard, margarine or olive oil, 1 gram of fat packs 9 calories. As you learned earlier, fat calories from any source add up fast and can quickly lead to a few extra pounds around your waistline. But when it comes to health, not all fats and oils are created equal. It is important that you reduce the total amount of fat you eat, but there are certain fats that you need to focus on when doing so.

Let's begin with another chemistry lesson. Fatty acids in food consist of long chains of carbon molecules linked together, which in turn are attached to hydrogen atoms. Each fatty acid has a different chemical structure that determines how it will behave in the body. For instance, when a fatty acid is completely full of hydrogen atoms, it is considered a *saturated fatty acid*. Animal fat in meat, poultry and dairy products contains mostly saturated fatty acids. Fatty acids that are not saturated with hydrogen atoms are called *unsaturated fats*. These include *monounsaturated* (found in olive and canola oils) or *polyunsaturated* (found in corn, sunflower and safflower oils).

Fat in food almost always contains a mixture of saturated and unsaturated fatty acids. We classify fats as saturated, monounsaturated or polyunsaturated based on what fatty acids are present in the greatest concentration.

Saturated Fats

This type of fat is found in all animal foods; meat, poultry, eggs and dairy products all have saturated fat. Some vegetable oils, such as coconut, palm kernel oil and palm oil, are also saturated. Diets that contain a lot of saturated fat raise your risk of heart disease by increasing your blood cholesterol level. In particular, saturated fat raises your LDL cholesterol. Saturated fat blocks the ability of your cells to clear cholesterol from your bloodstream.

There are many different types of saturated fats in foods, and researchers are learning that they don't all influence our blood cholesterol to the same degree. For instance, the saturated fat in dairy products is more cholesterol-raising than the saturated fat in meat. And the type of saturated fat in chocolate does not seem to raise blood cholesterol levels at all (thank goodness for that!).

Don't worry, you certainly don't need to know the different types of saturated fats in foods. What's most important is to just *eat less saturated fat*. No more than 10 percent of your daily calories should come from saturated fat (if you eat 2000 calories per day, that means no more than 20 grams of saturated fat).

TOTAL FAT AND SATURATED FAT CONTENT OF FOODS

Food	Total Fat (grams)	Saturated Fat (grams)
Dairy Products		
Cheddar cheese, regular fat, 31% milk fat (MF), 1 oz (30 g)	9.4 g	6.0 g
Cheddar cheese, low-fat, 7% MF, 1 oz (30 g)	2.0 g	1.2 g
Cottage cheese, 1% MF, 1/2 cup (125 ml)	1.1 g	0.8 g
Milk, homogenized, 3.3% MF, 1 cup (250 ml)	8.1 g	5.1 g
Milk, 2% MF, 1 cup (250 ml)	4.7 g	2.9 g
Milk, skim, 0.1% MF, 1 cup (250 ml)	0.5 g	0.3 g
Meat and Poultry		
Beef, flank steak, broiled, 3 oz (90 g)	9.3 g	4.0 g
Beef, rib roast, roasted, 3 oz (90 g)	9.7 g	3.8 g
Beef, short ribs, simmered, 3 oz (90 g)	14.3 g	6.1 g
Beef, strip loin steak, broiled, 3 oz (90 g)	8.2 g	3.1 g
Ground beef patty, extra-lean, broiled, 3 oz (90 g)	12.2 g	5.2 g
Ground beef patty, lean, broiled, 3 oz (90 g)	14.7 g	6.0 g
Ground beef patty, medium, broiled, 3 oz (90 g)	17.2 g	7.3 g
Pork, back ribs, broiled, 3 oz (90 g)	13.5 g	5.0 g
Pork, side bacon, fried, 5 slices, 1 oz (32 g)	16.0 g	5.6 g
Pork tenderloin, roasted, 3 oz (90 g)	3.2 g	1.0 g
Chicken breast, skinless, cooked, 3 oz (90 g)	1.8 g	0.6 g
Desserts		
Ice cream, vanilla, 11% MF, 1/2 cup (125 ml)	7.3 g	4.5 g
Frozen yogurt, vanilla, 5.6% MF, 1/2 cup (125 ml)	4.0 g	2.5 g
Fruit ices, 1/2 cup (125 ml)	0 g	0 g
Fats and Oils		
Butter, 2 tsp (10 ml)	7.7 g	4.8 g
Margarine, soft tub, corn, 2 tsp (10 ml)	7.5 g	1.4 g

Canadian Nutrient File. Health Canada, Ottawa, 1997.

U.S. Department of Agriculture, Agricultural Research Service, 2001. USDA Nutrient Database for Standard Reference, Release 14. Nutrient Laboratory Home Page, http://www.nal.usda.gov/fnic/fooddomp

Trans Fats

If you haven't heard of trans fat, you may have heard the term "hydrogenated fat." Trans fats are formed when vegetable oils are processed into margarine or shortening. This chemical process, called hydrogenation, adds hydrogen atoms to liquid vegetable oils, making them more solid and useful to food manufacturers. Cookies, crackers, pastries and muffins made with hydrogenated vegetable oils are more palatable and have a longer shelf life. A margarine that's made by hydrogenating a vegetable oil is firmer, like butter.

Hydrogenation makes a fat become saturated *and* it forms a new type of fat called *trans fat.* Hydrogenation also destroys essential fatty acids that your body needs from unprocessed vegetable oils. Consuming too much trans fat can increase your risk of heart disease by raising LDL cholesterol, lowering HDL cholesterol and impairing blood vessel function.

Studies have linked diets containing trans fat to coronary heart disease. Scientists from the Netherlands collected detailed information on the dietary habits of almost 700 elderly men. They learned that heart disease turned up more often in the men who had eaten more trans fats. For every additional 2 percent of trans fats consumed, a man was almost 25 percent more likely to develop heart disease.[1]

The Nurses' Health Study from Harvard University revealed that women who ate the most trans fat had a 50 percent higher risk of heart disease compared with women who ate the least. Foods that contributed the most trans fat were margarine, cookies, cake and white bread.[2] Other studies have revealed that eating margarine is linked with a higher risk of heart disease in men and women.[3,4]

The harmful effects of trans fats aren't limited to heart disease. Findings from the Nurses' Health Study determined that a woman's risk of developing type 2 (adult onset) diabetes increased with a greater intake of trans fat.[5]

It's important to read ingredients lists if you want less trans fat. Look for the term "hydrogenated vegetable oils," "partially hydrogenated vegetable oils" or "shortening." Eat less often foods that contain these. As much as 40 percent of the fat in foods such as French fries, fried fast food, donuts, pastries, snack foods and store-bought cookies and crackers is trans fat.

If you eat margarine, choose a soft-tub brand that's made with nonhydrogenated fat. Many brands state this right on the label. If "nonhydrogenated" isn't printed on the tub of margarine, look at the nutrition facts panel and add the values for polyunsaturated and monounsaturated fats. For a 10 g (2 tsp.) serving they should add up to at least 6 grams for a regular margarine and 3 grams for a light margarine. If the values don't add up to these numbers, that means there are more saturated and trans fats present.

When the new and improved food labels become law, prepackaged foods will list the grams of trans fat on the nutrition facts panel. In the meantime, check the ingredients lists.

Polyunsaturated Fats

There are two types of polyunsaturated fats in foods: omega-6s and omega-3s. Omega-6 polyunsaturated fats are found in all vegetable oils, including soybean, sunflower, safflower, corn and sesame. Our bodies need omega-6 oils because they contain linoleic acid, an essential fatty acid that the body can't make on its own. The problem is, our modern diet is overwhelmed with linoleic acid from vegetable oils used in processed and fast foods. In the body, some of this linoleic acid is used to fuel agents that contribute to inflammation and pain.

Meanwhile, we're not eating enough of the healthy omega-3 fats. Omega-3 polyunsaturated fats are plentiful in cold-water fish such as salmon, sardines, trout and mackerel. These omega-3 fats are called DHA (docosahexanaenoic acid) and EPA (eicosapentaenoic acid). You'll find another type of omega-3 fat in plant foods such as soybeans, flaxseed and nuts. This is called alpha linolenic acid, or ALA.

Eating polyunsaturated fat in place of saturated fat can help you lower LDL (bad) cholesterol levels. And there's a growing body of evidence indicating that there are other reasons why you should increase your intake of omega-3 fats.

Omega-3 Fats in Fish

Plenty of studies show that eating more fatty fish can lower your risk of heart disease. Researchers have known for some time that populations, such as the Greenland Inuit and the Japanese, that consume fish a few times per week have lower rates of heart disease. Scientists from Seattle, Washington, recently learned that eating one fatty fish meal per week was linked with significant protection from having a first heart attack.[6]

A recent analysis of the Nurses' Health Study from Harvard School of Public Health adds further evidence that fish oils are heart healthy. After studying almost 85,000 women for 16 years, the researchers found that eating fish as infrequently as a few times a month protected from heart disease. However, the women who ate fish five or more times a week had the lowest risk of heart disease—a 34 percent reduced risk. While eating fish protected these women from having a heart attack, it offered the most protection from dying of heart disease.[7]

There's more evidence that omega-3 fats in fish might prevent dying from a heart attack. A large study recently examined the link between fish consumption and heart disease in almost 3000 men living in Finland, Italy and the Netherlands. When the results were analyzed, fatty-fish eaters had a 34 percent lower risk of dying from heart disease.[8] American researchers found similar protective effects in men who ate fish at least once a week.[9]

DHA and EPA, the two omega-3 fats in fish, can lower high levels of blood fats called triglycerides and reduce the stickiness of platelets, the cells that form blood clots in arteries. Omega-3 fats in fish may also increase the flexibility of red blood cells so they can pass more readily through tiny blood vessels. Recent studies have found that omega-3 fats in fish lower the risk of heart rhythm disturbances, the cause of many sudden deaths from heart disease.

Omega-3 fats in fish may also protect from cancer, most notably breast, colon and perhaps prostate cancer. Laboratory studies have shown fish oil can enhance the immune system and suppress cancer cell growth. Remember that at the beginning of this chapter I told you that your body needs dietary fat to make eicosanoids? Eicosanoids are powerful hormone-like compounds that regulate our blood, immune system and hormones. The type of fat you eat determines what kind of eicosanoids your body produces. For instance, omega-6 oils are used to synthesize so-called "unfriendly" eicosanoids that cause inflammation and pain. The omega-3 fats in fish, on the other hand, produce "friendly" eicosanoids that tend to decrease inflammation and improve circulation.

These omega-3 and omega-6 fats compete with each other for the same metabolic pathways. So if you eat a diet packed with processed and fried foods that contain primarily omega-6 oils, the unfriendly eicosanoids win out. On the other hand, if most of the fat you eat is rich in omega-3s, more friendly, health-enhancing eicosanoids will be formed. Eicosanoids derived from omega-3 fats are believed to help prevent cancer, ease the symptoms of rheumatoid arthritis and prevent flare-ups of colitis.

The best way to get plenty of DHA and EPA is by eating cold-water fish such as salmon, trout and sardines. The colder the water fish live in, the more omega-3 oil they contain. Farm-raised fish are fed commercial feed that results in lower omega-3 fat levels, though farm-raised salmon is still a good source of omega-3 fat.

Alpha-Linolenic Acid (ALA)

If you don't like fish, this omega-3 fat found in plant foods may help protect your heart. Research conducted on men and women has found that higher intakes of alpha-linolenic acid are linked with protection from heart disease.[10] The Nurses' Health Study revealed that women who consumed the most ALA had a 45 percent lower risk of dying from heart disease.[11] The women in the study got most of their ALA by using oil and vinegar salad dressings at least five times per week. There's also preliminary research to suggest that ALA might protect women from breast cancer.[12]

You'll find alpha-linolenic acid in flaxseed oil, canola oil, nuts (especially walnuts), soybeans, tofu, omega-3 eggs, whole grains and leafy greens. Based on the research findings, it seems wise to include 2 grams of alpha-linolenic acid per day. That's the amount found in 14 walnut halves, 1 tablespoon (15 ml) of flaxseeds or 4 1/2 teaspoons (22 ml) of canola oil.

Monounsaturated Fats and the Mediterranean Diet

Chances are you already know that these unsaturated fatty acids are considered to be healthy fats. After all, who doesn't think of heart health when they hear the words "olive oil"? Monounsaturated fats found in olive oil, canola oil, peanuts and peanut oil, avocado and some nuts (filberts, almonds, pistachios, pecans and cashews) are a large part of the Mediterranean diet, a pattern of eating that's associated with less heart disease and cancer.

Eating a diet that gets most of its fat from monounsaturated oils may not only prevent heart disease in the first place, but might also dramatically lower the risk of suffering a second heart attack. That's what researchers from France found when they studied 600 men and women who had survived a first heart attack. Men and women enrolled in the Lyon Diet Heart Study were told to follow either a Mediterranean-style diet or a typical Western diet. The study was actually stopped early when the researchers saw the huge benefits of the Mediterranean-style diet. The group eating the Mediterranean diet had a 50 to 70 percent lower risk of recurrent heart attack![13]

The Mediterranean diet in the Lyon Study averaged 30 percent calories from fat, 8 percent from saturated fat, 13 percent from monounsaturated fat and 5 percent from polyunsaturated fat. The sources of monounsaturated fat included olive oil, canola oil, margarine with alpha-linolenic acid and nuts.

There's no one typical Mediterranean diet. At least 16 countries border the Mediterranean Sea, countries with different cultures, ethnic backgrounds and dietary practices. But there is a common pattern to the Mediterranean diet:

- Fruits, vegetables, grains, beans, nuts and seeds are eaten daily.

- Extra-virgin olive oil is the predominant source of added fat.

- Dairy products, fish and poultry are eaten in moderate amounts.

- Eggs are eaten zero to four times weekly.

- Red meat is seldom eaten.

- Wine is consumed with meals, in low to moderate amounts.

How can this pattern of eating protect your heart? Aside from the fact that it is high in plant foods that contain antioxidants and fiber, its monounsaturated fat content can take some credit. Research shows that when you substitute monounsaturated fat for saturated fat in your diet, you can lower high levels of blood cholesterol, in particular LDL cholesterol. Some studies suggest that extra-virgin olive oil helps prevent blood clots from forming and acts as an antioxidant to help protect from heart disease.

When buying olive oil, be sure to choose *extra-virgin* olive oil. It has been processed the least (that's why it's a dark-green color) and contains more protective compounds than regular or light olive oil.

Dietary Cholesterol

A discussion about dietary fat would not be complete without mentioning dietary cholesterol. This wax-like fatty substance is found in meat, poultry, eggs, dairy products, fish and shellfish. It's particularly plentiful in shrimp, liver and egg yolks. While high-cholesterol diets cause high blood cholesterol in animals, this effect is not seen in humans.

It seems we overstated the link between cholesterol in foods and blood cholesterol. Back in the 1980s we thought dietary cholesterol contributed to higher blood cholesterol levels.

But now we know that dietary cholesterol has little or no effect on most people's blood cholesterol. One reason is that our intestines absorb only one-half of the cholesterol we eat; the rest is excreted in our stool. Our bodies are also very efficient at turning cholesterol into digestive juices that are stored in the gallbladder. This means there is less cholesterol available for transport in the blood.

In spite of these built-in protective mechanisms, too much dietary cholesterol can raise levels of LDL cholesterol in some people, especially people with hereditary forms of high cholesterol. Health Canada recommends that we consume *no more than 300 milligrams of cholesterol each day*. If you have heart disease, aim for no more than 200 milligrams per day.

Choosing animal foods that are lower in saturated fat will automatically cut dietary cholesterol from your diet. Here's how foods stack up when it comes to cholesterol content.

CHOLESTEROL CONTENT OF FOODS

Food	Cholesterol (milligrams)
Meat, Poultry, Fish and Eggs	
1 egg, whole	190 mg
1 egg, white only	0 mg
Beef sirloin, lean, 3 oz (90 g)	64 mg
Calf's liver, fried, 3 oz (90 g)	416 mg
Pork loin, lean, 3 oz (90 g)	71 mg
Chicken breast, skinless, 3 oz (90 g)	73 mg
Salmon, 3 oz (90 g)	54 mg
Shrimp, 3 oz (90 g)	135 mg
Dairy Products	
Milk, skim, 1 cup (250 ml)	5 mg

Food	Cholesterol (milligrams)
Dairy Products (continued)	
Milk, 2% milk fat (MF), 1 cup (250 ml)	19 mg
Cheese, cheddar, 31% MF, 1 oz (30 g)	31 mg
Cheese, mozzarella, part skim, 1 oz (30 g)	18 mg
Cream, half and half, 12% MF, 2 tbsp (25 ml)	12 mg
Yogurt, 1.5% MF, 3/4 cup (175 ml)	11 mg
Butter, 2 tsp (10 ml)	10 mg

Putting It All Together: How Much and What Type of Fat Should You Eat?

Our current nutrition guidelines emphasize the importance of cutting back on total fat and saturated fat. But it is also important to ensure you are getting essential fatty acids and omega-3 oils found in fish. Here's what you should be striving for:

- *Consume no more than 30 percent of your daily calories from fat.* If you read nutrition labels, that means there should be no more than 3 grams of fat for every 100 calories. But this doesn't mean that every food you eat must be low in fat. It's the overall picture that counts. You can make up for eating one higher-fat food by including plenty of low-fat foods in the rest of your meals.

- *Focus on reducing your intake of saturated fat.* This fat should contribute no more than 10 percent of your daily calories. Don't worry too much about numbers and percentages. All you have to do is make a habit of choosing lower-fat animal foods. Vegetarian protein foods such as legumes (dried peas, beans and lentils) and soy foods have very little saturated fat. Try eating more vegetarian meals during the week (but I know you're already doing that if you've been following Step 2!).

- *Reduce your intake of trans fat.* As often as possible, avoid products that list "hydrogenated fat" or "shortening" as an ingredient.

- To get heart-protective omega-3 fats, *eat fatty fish three times a week.* The oilier the fish the better.

- To ensure you're meeting your daily requirements for essential fatty acids, *include 1 or 2 tablespoons (15 to 25 ml) of an oil rich in alpha-linoleic acid.* Use flaxseed oil, walnut oil and canola oil. Because linoleic acid is so widespread in processed foods, most of us don't have a problem getting enough of this essential fatty acid. It's our intake of alpha-linolenic acid that we must pay attention to.

- *Use extra-virgin olive oil* in salad dressings.

- *Limit your intake of dietary cholesterol to no more than 300 milligrams per day.* If you have heart disease, limit your intake to 200 milligrams.

35 TIPS
FOR CHOOSING HEALTHIER FATS AND OILS

TO LIMIT *ADDED* FATS AND OILS
IN YOUR KITCHEN

1. Use added fats and oils sparingly. Use cooking methods that add little or no fat to foods. Grilling, broiling, baking, steaming, lightly stir-frying and poaching are good choices.

2. When sautéing or stir-frying, use vegetable or chicken stock or water instead of heaps of oil.

3. Cook and bake food in nonstick pans.

4. Use high-fat spreads such as butter, margarine, mayonnaise and cream cheese sparingly. Choose fat-reduced versions when possible. Avoid doubling up on your spreads—do you really need butter *and* peanut butter on your toast? Margarine *and* mayonnaise in your sandwich?

5. Replace oil in quick-bread recipes with an equal amount of applesauce or other puréed fruit.

6. Top baked potatoes with plain, low-fat yogurt or 1 percent cottage cheese. Add a few tablespoons of salsa or chili powder for a flavor boost.

WHEN DINING OUT

7. Don't be shy—ask that foods be prepared without added oil or butter (did you realize that steakhouses often add butter to your steak?).

8. At fast food restaurants, search the menu for grilled chicken sandwiches, veggie burgers, grilled chicken salad or chili.

9. Save French fries and other fried foods for special occasions; order a small portion or share with a friend.

10. If you ask, most fast food outlets will provide a nutrition information pamphlet that identifies the fat grams and calories of each menu item.

11. Order salad dressings on the side—and don't use all of it. With creamy dressings, use the fork method: dip your fork in the dressing, then grab a bite of salad. You'll enjoy great taste with every bite while using only a fraction of the dressing.

12. Limit your intake of rich pasta dishes covered with cream sauce, pesto sauce or olive oil. Order pastas in broth (al brodo) or tomato sauce more often.

AT THE GROCERY STORE

13. When buying packaged foods, read ingredients lists. Fat can be listed as lard, shortening, palm oil, coconut oil, vegetable oil, hydrogenated oil, monoglycerides, diglycerides and tallow.

TO EAT LESS *SATURATED* FAT

MEAT AND POULTRY

14. Choose leaner cuts of meat and poultry: flank steak, inside round, sirloin, eye of the round, extra-lean ground beef, pork tenderloin, center-cut pork chops, poultry breast and lean ground chicken are all lower-fat choices.

15. Trim all visible fat from meat and poultry before cooking.

16. Limit your portion of meat or poultry to 3 ounces (90 grams)—that's the size of a deck of cards.

17. Limit your intake of high-fat processed meats such as bacon, sausage, salami, pepperoni, bologna and other cold cuts. Lower-fat deli choices include turkey or chicken breast, lean ham, roast beef and pastrami.

DAIRY PRODUCTS

18. Choose skim or 1 percent milk.

19. Buy yogurt with less than 2 percent milk fat (MF).

20. Try lower-fat cheeses, such as those with less than 20 percent MF content.

21. Replace full-fat sour cream with products that contain 7 percent MF or less.

22. Substitute evaporated 2 percent or evaporated skim milk for cream in your coffee.

23. Choose low-fat frozen yogurt or sorbet instead of ice cream.

FATS AND OILS

24. Choose vegetable oils rather than solid fats.

25. If you use butter, use it sparingly. And if you're a margarine user, read the next section to make sure you're using the healthiest one!

TO AVOID *TRANS* FAT

26. Avoid foods that mention "hydrogenated vegetable oil" or "shortening" on the ingredients list.

27. Buy a margarine whose label says it is made from "nonhydrogenated fat."

28. Limit your intake of fried fast food, commercial bakery goods, packaged snack foods and store-bought cookies and crackers containing trans fat.

TO EAT *MORE* HEALTHY *POLYUNSATURATED* FATS

29. Eat fatty fish three times per week. The best sources of omega-3 fat are salmon, trout, herring, mackerel, sardines, anchovies and albacore tuna. Frozen and canned fish are fine, too.

30. If you have heart disease, aim to eat one fatty-fish meal per day. Try salmon sandwiches at lunch, grilled tuna for dinner or tinned sardines on a salad. If you're averse to eating this much fish, consider taking mixed fish oil capsules to achieve a combined intake of 900 milligrams of EPA and DHA per day. Avoid fish *liver* oil capsules since these can contain large amounts of vitamins A and D, two nutrients that can have toxic effects if consumed in high doses for a prolonged period.

31. Use canola oil when cooking and baking. Not only does this oil contain alpha-linolenic acid, but it's also better suited for high-heat cooking. And it's a source of heart-healthy monounsaturated fat.

32. Toss a little walnut oil into your next salad dressing. For every tablespoon of extra-virgin olive oil you use, add one teaspoon of walnut oil. Store walnut oil in the fridge.

33. Try flaxseed oil in salad dressings and dips. You can't heat this oil, but you can add a little to hot foods once they've finished cooking. Store flaxseed oil and flaxseed in the fridge.

34. Add ground flaxseed to hot cereal, yogurt, smoothies and baking recipes.

35. Buy omega-3 eggs. These eggs are a good source of alpha-linolenic acid because they were laid by hens fed a diet high in flaxseed.

ANSWERS TO LESLIE'S IQ QUIZ   FATS AND OILS

1. a. The single patty burger has on average 10 grams of fat. The fillet of fish sandwich has 23 grams; 6 chicken nuggets, 18 grams; and 2 slices of pepperoni pizza, 14 grams.

2. d. The pancake breakfast is the lower-fat winner, at 9 grams of fat. The granola with 2 percent milk has 13 grams, the large bran muffin has 16 grams and the poached egg on buttered toast has 13 grams.

3. False. A teaspoon of margarine has 45 calories—the same as butter.

4. True. Cholesterol is found only in animal foods.

5. b. eggplant

Step 6

Boost Your
Vitamins and Minerals

LESLIE'S NUTRITION IQ QUIZ   VITAMINS AND MINERALS

1. You're well aware that calcium helps to ward off osteoporosis. Which food contains the most?
    a. 1/4 cup (50 ml) almonds
    b. 1/2 cup (125 ml) fruit-bottom yogurt
    c. 1 cup (250 ml) cooked broccoli
    d. 1/2 can salmon with bones, drained

2. True or false? A supplement made from calcium carbonate is better absorbed by the body than one made from calcium citrate.

3. Which food will *not* help you boost your vitamin D intake?
    a. chocolate milk   c. tinned sardines
    b. poached egg   d. plain yogurt

4. True or false? A vegetarian's daily iron requirement is almost double that of a meat eater.

5. You're trying to eat more folate-rich foods in an effort to prevent a heart attack. Which food contains the most?
    a. 1 cup (250 ml) cooked pasta   c. 1 cup (250 ml) orange juice
    b. 1/2 cup (125 ml) cooked lentils d. 1/2 cup (125 ml) cooked spinach

ongratulations! If you've been following Steps 1 to 5, you're by now practicing many of my tips to help you achieve a truly healthy diet. You're eating enough protein and you're experimenting with vegetarian protein foods such as beans and soy. Mastering Steps 1 to 5 on the road to healthy eating also means that you're no longer afraid of carbohydrates. You're eating plenty of the good carbohydrates—nutritious whole grains—and limiting your intake of refined, processed starchy foods. Chances are, you've also noticed a big difference in your fruit and vegetable intake. And finally, you're more selective about the types of fats you include in your diet.

Now it's time to fine-tune your diet. It's time to focus on your food choices to ensure you're meeting your daily requirements for important nutrients. When I meet with clients, the first question I ask is, "What do you want to achieve by coming to see me?" Inevitably, my clients' goals include getting the right nutrients in the proper amounts. People want to make sure they're choosing the healthiest foods that supply enough vitamins and minerals. Besides fat and cholesterol, the top concerns among my clients are getting enough calcium, iron and antioxidants through their diets.

It seems that most of us share these nutrition concerns. According to a survey from the National Institute of Nutrition, today we are as concerned about vitamins as we are about fat. Eighty-two percent of Canadians say they are very or somewhat concerned about their vitamin intake, with women expressing more interest in certain nutrients than men.[1]

Can Supplements Replace Food?

There's a growing desire among Canadians to learn about nutrition supplements. Whenever I give a seminar, I am bombarded with questions about vitamins, minerals, antioxidants and other natural health products: How do I know if I need a calcium supplement? What's the best brand to take? Is it safe to take my multivitamin with my medication? Is it best to buy a time-released vitamin C? I could spend literally hours answering questions about supplements. Having spent the better part of my career researching this very topic, I am very happy that I am able to offer people sound, credible advice.

I hear the same questions from clients in my private practice. My clients want to know if they need to add special vitamin or mineral supplements to their usual diet. They want to know if higher amounts of certain nutrients will ward off disease. If you've read my other books, or watched me on television, you probably already know that I do believe that supplements can be an important way for people to get key nutrients. If your diet lacks certain vitamins or minerals, or if you're at risk for certain health problems, chances are good that I will recommend you take at least one supplement.

In most cases, I teach my clients how to eat as best they can before I recommend any one particular supplement. I show them how to choose foods based on their vitamin and mineral contents. The meal plans I develop for people include nutrient-dense foods—foods that are low in fat and packed with calcium, iron, folate or vitamin C. Once I am confident that my clients are eating healthy, we then address the supplement issue.

This is an important first step because no vitamin pill can make up for a diet that's high in fat and salt and low in fiber, fruit and vegetables. When it comes to cancer prevention, it's nutrient-rich foods that count, not vitamin pills. Hundreds of studies have found that eating a diet packed with antioxidant-rich foods helps prevent cancer. But not one single study has found that individual supplements of these antioxidants can lower your cancer risk. Whole foods contain vitamins, minerals, fiber and protective plant chemicals that work together to keep you healthy.

The following sections will tell you what nutrients you need to focus on, how to get them from the foods you eat and, if you need to supplement, how to do so safely.

Focus on Calcium

Most of us know we need to get plenty of calcium to keep our bones healthy. During childhood, calcium helps bones grow longer and become denser and stronger. Once children have finished their growth spurt, their bones continue to increase in density but at a slower rate. For girls, most bone density is achieved between the ages of 8 and 16. Then, sometime in our 20s, our bones achieve what's called their *peak mass*. Once this occurs, they stop building density; at this point, you have all the bone mass you're ever going to have.

After you achieve your peak bone mass, natural bone loss begins. Before menopause, women lose bone at a rate of 1 percent per year, the same rate as men. Within the first five years after menopause, women lose bone two to six times faster than premenopausal women do. Then, ten years after menopause, bone loss returns to 1 percent per year. During this ten-year period, women have the potential to lose bone very quickly.

So, as you can see, calcium is vital to bone health at all ages: it helps bones grow when we're young, and it helps slow down natural bone loss when we're older.

There's no doubt that meeting calcium requirements throughout life can help prevent osteoporosis, a painful bone disease characterized by thinner, weaker bones that are more likely to break. It's estimated that 1.4 million Canadians suffer from this debilitating bone disease.[2] Osteoporosis has always been considered to be a woman's health concern. It's true that one in four women over the age of 50 has osteoporosis, but older men are also affected. In fact, among men over 50, one in eight has the disease. And although osteoporosis usually affects adults over 50, it can strike at any age.

Calcium keeps you healthy in other ways, too. The mineral helps your muscles contract and relax, supports nerve function and aids in blood clotting. New research also shows that high-calcium diets may ease symptoms of premenstrual syndrome, lower high blood pressure and prevent colon cancer.

RECOMMENDED DIETARY ALLOWANCE (RDA) FOR CALCIUM

Age	RDA (milligrams)
1–3 years	500 mg
4–8 years	800 mg
9–13 years	1300 mg
14–18 years	1300 mg
19–50 years	1000 mg
51+ years	1200 mg
Pregnancy	1000 mg
Breastfeeding	1000 mg
Daily upper limit	*2500 mg*

Standing Committee on the Scientific Evaluation of Dietary Reference Intakes, Food and Nutrition Board, Institute of Medicine, National Academy Press, Washington, D.C., 2001.

Calcium in Foods

You'll get the most calcium per serving from dairy products and calcium-fortified beverages like soymilk or orange juice. Just 1 cup (250 ml) packs a good 300 milligrams of calcium. Here's how foods stack up in terms of their calcium content.

CALCIUM CONTENT OF FOODS

	Calcium (milligrams)
Dairy Products	
Milk, Lactaid, 1 cup (250 ml)	300 mg
Milk (Neilson TruTaste), 1 cup (250 ml)	360 mg
Milk (Neilson TruCalcium), 1 cup (250 ml)	420 mg
Carnation Instant Breakfast, with 1 cup (250 ml) milk	540 mg
Chocolate milk, 1 cup (250 ml)	285 mg
Cheese, cheddar, 1 1/2 oz (45 g)	300 mg
Cheese, Swiss or Gruyère, 1 1/2 oz (45 g)	480 mg
Cheese, mozzarella, 1 1/2 oz (45 g)	228 mg
Cheese, cottage, 1/2 cup (125 ml)	75 mg
Cheese, ricotta, 1/2 cup (125 ml)	255 mg
Pudding, low-fat Healthy Choice, 1/2 cup (125 ml)	110 mg

	Calcium (milligrams)
Dairy Products (continued)	
Evaporated milk, 1/2 cup (125 ml)	350 mg
Skim milk powder, dry, 3 tbsp (45 ml)	155 mg
Yogurt, plain, 3/4 cup (175 ml)	300 mg
Yogurt, fruit, 3/4 cup (175 ml)	250 mg
Sour cream, low-fat, 1/4 cup (50 ml)	120 mg
Nondairy Products	
Soy and Legumes	
Soybeans, cooked, 1 cup (250 ml)	175 mg
Soybeans, roasted, 1/4 cup (50 ml)	60 mg
Soy beverage, 1 cup (250 ml)	100 mg
Soy beverage, fortified, 1 cup (250 ml)	330 mg

CALCIUM CONTENT OF FOODS (continued)

	Calcium (milligrams)		Calcium (milligrams)
Nondairy Products (continued)		**Vegetables** (continued)	
		Kale, cooked, 1 cup (250 ml)	179 mg
Soy and Legumes		Okra, cooked, 1 cup (250 ml)	176 mg
Baked beans, 1 cup (250 ml)	150 mg	Rutabaga, cooked, 1/2 cup (125 ml)	57 mg
Black beans, cooked, 1 cup (250 ml)	102 mg	Swiss chard, raw, 1 cup (250 ml)	21 mg
Kidney beans, cooked, 1 cup (250 ml)	69 mg	Swiss chard, cooked, 1 cup (250 ml)	102 mg
Lentils, cooked, 1 cup (250 ml)	37 mg	**Fruit**	
Tempeh, cooked, 1 cup (250 ml)	154 mg	Currants, 1/2 cup (125 ml)	60 mg
Tofu, raw, firm, with calcium sulphate, 4 oz (120 g)	260 mg	Figs, 5 medium	135 mg
Tofu, raw, regular, with calcium sulphate, 4 oz (120 g)	130 mg	Orange, 1 medium	50 mg
Fish		**Nuts**	
Sardines, 8 small (with bones)	165 mg	Almonds, 1/4 cup (50 ml)	100 mg
Salmon, 1/2 can (with bones), drained	225 mg	Brazil nuts, 1/4 cup (50 ml)	65 mg
		Hazelnuts, 1/4 cup (50 ml)	65 mg
Vegetables		**Other Foods**	
Bok choy, cooked, 1 cup (250 ml)	158 mg	Blackstrap molasses, 2 tbsp (25 ml)	288 mg
Broccoli, raw, 1 cup (250 ml)	42 mg	Orange or grapefruit juice, calcium-fortified, 1 cup (250 ml)	300–360 mg
Broccoli, cooked, 1 cup (250 ml)	94 mg		
Collard greens, cooked, 1 cup (250 ml)	357 mg		

Your body does not absorb calcium from all foods equally well. It's true that foods such as broccoli and almonds supply you with calcium, but natural compounds in plant foods bind some of this calcium and prevent it from being absorbed by your body. Studies show that dairy products contain the most absorbable form of calcium. Follow these strategies to enhance your body's absorption of calcium:

• Eat green vegetables cooked, rather than raw, to boost their calcium content. Cooking releases some of the calcium that's bound to a compound called oxalic acid.

• Don't take iron supplements with calcium-rich foods, since these two minerals compete with each other for absorption.

• Drink tea and coffee between, rather than during, meals. Natural compounds in these beverages inhibit calcium absorption.

Calcium Supplements

Many of my clients find it challenging to meet their daily calcium requirements. They may be lactose intolerant, follow a vegetarian diet or have poor eating habits. Often, taking supplements is the only way many of my clients can ensure they are meeting their calcium needs.

To help you decide if you need a calcium supplement, use my 300 Milligram Rule. Remember that one serving of dairy or calcium-fortified beverage gives you approximately 300 milligrams of calcium. This means that most of you need to get three to four servings per day to meet your calcium requirements. For each serving you miss without replacing it with other calcium-rich foods, you need to supplement with 300 milligrams of elemental calcium. Here's a list to help you decide which kind of supplement to take, along with some tips for taking it:

Calcium carbonate This form of calcium requires a fair amount of stomach acid in order to be absorbed. Because of this, calcium carbonate is not the best choice for older adults or people on medications that block stomach acid production. The advantage is that this is the least expensive type of calcium supplement, usually providing 500 milligrams of elemental calcium per tablet. If you do take calcium carbonate, take it with meals to increase absorption. Calcium carbonate can cause bloating, gas and constipation.

Calcium citrate I often prefer this type of calcium supplement to calcium carbonate because it is more absorbable. Calcium citrate can be taken with meals or on an empty stomach. Most calcium citrate pills offer 300 milligrams of elemental calcium, so it's a cinch to replace your missing dairy servings. If you need 1000 milligrams of calcium each day but you're only getting two dairy servings (600 milligrams), you need only take one calcium citrate supplement.

Effervescent calcium Supplements in tablet or powder form are made from calcium carbonate and often other forms of more absorbable calcium. Because it gets a head start on disintegrating, it may be absorbed in your intestinal tract more quickly. Dissolve in water or orange juice.

Bone meal, dolomite or oyster shell calcium I do not recommend calcium supplements made from these sources, as some products have been found to contain trace amounts of toxic contaminants such as lead and mercury.

Whether you take calcium carbonate or citrate, be sure to choose a formula with vitamin D and magnesium added. These nutrients work in tandem with calcium to promote optimal bone health. If you need to take more than one calcium pill to meet your daily requirements, split larger doses throughout the day. Don't take more than 500 milligrams of calcium at one time.

Focus on Vitamin D

When it comes to preventing osteoporosis, vitamin D is one nutrient you must not neglect. Vitamin D promotes bone-building by making calcium available in the blood that bathes your bones. It does this by helping your intestine absorb more calcium from the foods you eat and by telling your kidneys to stop excreting calcium in the urine. A lack of vitamin D can speed up bone loss and increase the risk of bone fracture at a younger age. In fact, many experts believe that a silent epidemic of vitamin D deficiency contributes to osteoporosis.

We meet most of our requirements for vitamin D by being exposed to sunshine during the spring, summer and fall. When ultraviolet light hits your skin, a vitamin D precursor is formed. This compound makes its way to your kidneys, where it's transformed into active vitamin D. But the long Canadian winter means that your skin produces little or no vitamin D from October through March. Even in the summer, you might be producing less vitamin D than you think. If you wear sunscreen, its sun protection factor (SPF) may block your skin's production of vitamin D by as much as 95 percent! I am certainly not advising that you regularly avoid using sunscreen. I wouldn't walk out of the house without first applying sunscreen to protect me from skin cancer, not to mention wrinkles. But it doesn't take much sun to get vitamin D pulsing through your bloodstream. All you have to do is expose your hands, face and arms with no sunscreen to sunlight for 10 to 15 minutes, two or three times a week. Just be sure to avoid the strong sunlight hours of 10 a.m. to 2 p.m. to prevent sunburn.

The elderly are at greatest risk of vitamin D deficiency. As we get older, our skin becomes less efficient at producing vitamin D. By the age of 70, there's a three- to fourfold decrease in the ability of the skin to synthesize vitamin D. That's why our vitamin D needs increase as we age.

ADEQUATE INTAKES (AI) FOR VITAMIN D

Age	AI (International Units)
1–3 years	200 IU
4–8 years	200 IU
9–30 years	200 IU
31–50 years	200 IU
51–70 years	400 IU
71+ years	600 IU
Pregnancy	200 IU
Breastfeeding	200 IU
Daily upper limit	*2000 IU*

Standing Committee on the Scientific Evaluation of Dietary Reference Intakes, Food and Nutrition Board, Institute of Medicine, National Academy Press, Washington, D.C., 2001.

The Osteoporosis Society of Canada recommends that Canadian adults receive 400 IU of vitamin D per day, and adults over the age of 50 should receive between 400 and 800 IU of the vitamin.

Getting enough vitamin D may also be important for preventing prostate cancer and multiple sclerosis. Some researchers believe that a vitamin D deficiency caused by a lack of sunlight may predispose the body to both diseases.

Vitamin D in Foods

By now it's clear that it's very important to rely on foods for your vitamin D, especially during the winter months. The best food sources are fluid milk (yogurt and cheese don't have any vitamin D), fortified soy and rice beverages, fatty fish, egg yolks, butter and margarine. Here's a look at amounts of vitamin D in selected foods:

VITAMIN D IN FOODS

Food	Vitamin D (International Units)
Cod liver oil, 1 tsp (5 ml)	450 IU
Herring, 3 1/2 oz (100 g)	680 IU
Salmon, canned, 3 1/2 oz (100 g)	600–860 IU
Sardines, Atlantic, 3 1/2 oz (100 g)	290 IU
Milk, fluid, 1 cup (250 ml)	100 IU
Rice beverage, fortified, 1 cup (250 ml)	100 IU
Soy beverage, fortified, 1 cup (250 ml)	100 IU
Egg, 1 whole	24 IU
Butter, 1 tsp (5 ml)	3 IU
Margarine, 1 tsp (5 ml)	15 IU

U.S. Department of Agriculture, Agricultural Research Service, 2001. USDA Nutrient Database for Standard Reference, Release 14. Nutrient Laboratory Home Page, http://www.nal.usda.gov/fnic/fooddomp

Vitamin D Supplements

Single vitamin D supplements should be taken only under the supervision of your doctor. Taking too much vitamin D can cause toxic effects in the body and will do more harm than good. Your doctor may prescribe extra vitamin D if a blood test reveals a deficiency or you're at risk for osteoporosis.

Most of us can rely on a little sunshine and a steady diet of foods rich in vitamin D to meet our requirements. As well, most multivitamin and mineral supplements supply 400 IU of vitamin D. If you take calcium supplements, choose a product with vitamin D added. Most calcium products offer 100 to 200 IU of the vitamin. Single vitamin D supplements are available in doses of 400, 800 and 1000 IU.

Focus on Iron

If you're a menstruating woman, read this section carefully! A lack of iron is the most common nutrient deficiency among women. Women who diet to lose weight, shy away from red meat and animal foods, engage in heavy exercise or who are pregnant are all at risk of missing out on this important mineral. In fact, it's been estimated that up to 39 percent of teenage girls are iron deficient.[3,4]

Your body needs iron to make hemoglobin, the component of red blood cells that carries oxygen to all your tissues. In your muscles, oxygen is stored in a pigment called myoglobin, which is also made from iron. If your diet does not provide the amount of iron your body needs, your iron stores will become depleted. Iron deficiency eventually leads to anemia, a condition in which the hemoglobin level in the blood is low.

One doesn't become anemic overnight. Iron deficiency is a progressive condition that develops in stages, though you will feel its effects along the way. Early symptoms of iron deficiency include tiredness, headache, irritability and depression. You may also look pale, lack motivation to exercise, experience breathlessness and fatigue during a workout and have difficulty concentrating. In young children and teens, iron deficiency can impair attention span, cognitive function and learning ability.

All women of reproductive age are at risk of developing iron deficiency, especially if their diet lacks iron-rich foods. Because of the regular blood loss that occurs during menstruation, women have higher iron requirements than men. Pregnancy also depletes a woman's iron stores at a much faster rate than normal, because the growing fetus and placenta require a higher blood volume and a larger supply of iron. Pregnant women need additional iron and are very likely to develop iron deficiency unless they take a prenatal supplement that provides extra iron.

Female runners or triathletes are another high-risk group for developing anemia. During heavy exercise, iron is lost through sweat. If these losses are not replaced through eating iron-rich foods, iron deficiency can result. Any woman who reduces her calorie intake to lose weight or follows a vegetarian diet is also at risk. It is near impossible for women to meet their daily iron requirements from a 1200-calorie weight-loss diet.

RECOMMENDED DIETARY ALLOWANCE (RDA) FOR IRON

Age	RDA (milligrams)	Age	RDA (milligrams)
1–3 years	7 mg	Men, 19+ years	8 mg
4–8 years	10 mg	Women, 19–50 years	18 mg
9–13 years	8 mg	Women, 51+ years	8 mg
Boys, 14–18 years	11 mg	Pregnancy	27 mg
Girls, 14–18 years	15 mg	Breastfeeding	9 mg

RECOMMENDED DIETARY ALLOWANCE (RDA) FOR IRON (continued)

Age	RDA (milligrams)	Age	RDA (milligrams)
Daily upper limit, 1–13 years	*40 mg*	*Daily upper limit, 19+ years*	*45 mg*
Daily upper limit, 14–18 years	*45 mg*		

Standing Committee on the Scientific Evaluation of Dietary Reference Intakes, Food and Nutrition Board, Institute of Medicine, National Academy Press, Washington, D.C., 2001.

Iron in Foods

The richest sources of iron come from beef, fish, poultry, pork and lamb. These are known as *heme* sources of iron, the type that can be absorbed and utilized the most efficiently by your body. Heme sources of iron contribute about 10 percent of the iron we consume each day. Even though heme iron accounts for such a small proportion of our intake, it is so well absorbed that it actually contributes a significant amount of iron.

The rest of our iron comes from plant foods such as dried fruits, whole grains, leafy green vegetables, nuts, seeds and legumes. These are called *nonheme* sources of iron. The body is much less efficient at absorbing and using this type of iron. Vegetarians may have difficulty maintaining healthy iron stores because their diet relies exclusively on nonheme sources. *If you are a vegetarian who does not eat meat, poultry or fish, your RDA of iron is 1.8 times greater than the RDA listed in the table above for your age and sex.* For instance, if you're a 35-year-old female eating a meat-free diet, you need 32 milligrams of iron each day (1.8 × 18 = 32 mg).

Practice the following strategies to enhance your body's absorption of nonheme iron:

- *Add a little animal food to your meal if you're not vegetarian.* Meat, poultry and fish contain MFP factor, a special compound that promotes the absorption of nonheme iron from other foods.

- *Add a source of vitamin C.* Including a little vitamin C in your plant-based meal can enhance the body's absorption of nonheme iron fourfold. The acidity of the vitamin converts iron to a form that's ready for absorption (your stomach acid enhances iron absorption in the same way). Here are some winning combinations:

  - Whole-wheat pasta with tomato sauce

  - Brown rice stir-fry with broccoli and red pepper

  - Whole-grain breakfast cereal topped with strawberries

  - Whole-grain toast with a small glass of orange juice

  - Spinach salad tossed with orange or grapefruit segments

- *Don't take your calcium supplements with an iron-rich meal,* since these two minerals compete with each other for absorption.

- *Drink tea and coffee between, rather than during, meals.* These beverages contain polyphenols, compounds that bind to nonheme iron and cause it to be excreted from the gut.

- *Cook your vegetables.* Phytic acid (phytate), found in plant foods, can attach to iron and hamper its absorption. Cooking vegetables like spinach releases some of the iron that's bound to phytates.

IRON CONTENT OF FOODS

Food	Iron (milligrams)
Meat, Poultry and Fish	
Beef, lean, cooked, 3 oz (90 g)	3.0 mg
Chicken breast, cooked, 3 oz (90 g)	0.6 mg
Liver, beef, cooked, 3 oz (90 g)	5.3 mg
Liver, chicken, cooked, 3 oz (90 g)	7.6 mg
Oysters, cooked, 5 medium	7.2 mg
Shrimp, cooked, 10 large	1.7 mg
Tuna, light, canned, 1/2 cup (125 ml)	1.2 mg
Legumes	
Beans in tomato sauce, 1 cup (250 ml)	5.0 mg
Kidney beans, 1/2 cup (125 ml)	2.5 mg
Fruits and Vegetables	
Apricots, dried, 6	2.8 mg
Prune juice, 1/2 cup (125 ml)	5.0 mg
Spinach, cooked, 1 cup (250 ml)	4.0 mg

Food	Iron (milligrams)
Cereals	
All Bran, Kellogg's, 1/2 cup (125 ml)	4.7 mg
All Bran Buds, Kellogg's, 1/2 cup (125 ml)	5.9 mg
Bran Flakes, 3/4 cup (175 ml)	4.9 mg
Just Right, Kellogg's, 1 cup (250 ml)	6.0 mg
Raisin Bran, 3/4 cup (175 ml)	5.5 mg
Shreddies, 3/4 cup (175 ml)	5.9 mg
Cream of Wheat, 1/2 cup (125 ml)	8.0 mg
Oatmeal, instant, 1 pouch	3.8 mg
Other Foods	
Blackstrap molasses, 1 tbsp (15 ml)	3.2 mg
Wheat germ, 1 tbsp (15 ml)	2.5 mg

Iron Supplements

To help you meet your daily iron requirements, taking a multivitamin and mineral supplement is a wise idea, especially if you're a menstruating woman. Most formulas provide 10 milligrams, but you can find multivitamins that provide up to 18 milligrams of the mineral (read the multivitamin section below).

If you are diagnosed with iron-deficiency anemia, your doctor will prescribe single iron pills. Depending on the extent of your iron deficiency, you will be advised to take 50 to 100 milligrams of elemental iron, one to three times per day. Iron supplements are best absorbed if taken on an empty stomach. Iron can be constipating, so I recommend you make a real effort to boost your fiber and water intake to help prevent this side effect.

A supplementation period of 6 to 12 weeks is usually sufficient to treat anemia. However, you may need to take the supplements for up to six months in order to completely restore your body's iron reserves. Once your iron stores improve and your blood test shows that you have a healthy level of iron, stop taking the iron pills. Continue with your multivitamin and an iron-rich diet.

When it comes to iron supplements, more is *not* better. Excessive doses of iron can be toxic, causing damage to your liver and intestines. An iron overload can even result in death. Do not take iron supplements without having a blood test to confirm that you are suffering from an iron deficiency.

Focus on Folate (Folic Acid)

Folate is a B vitamin that occurs naturally in foods. When a synthetic version of this vitamin is being added to food or supplements, it's called folic acid.

Folate and Pregnancy

Many women already understand the importance of getting enough folate. If you've had a baby, you might remember taking a daily supplement of this B vitamin before and during your pregnancy. It's well accepted that an adequate intake of folate reduces the risk of neural tube defects, birth defects that involve the spinal cord and brain. Neural tube defects can occur in a fetus before a woman realizes she's pregnant. This is why it is so important for *all* women of childbearing age to pay attention to their folate intake. But since the body absorbs folic acid much better than it does folate, women planning to become pregnant are advised to meet their daily requirements from a supplement.

Folate and Heart Disease

Folate can protect our health at all stages in life—from preconception to old age. A growing body of evidence suggests that eating folate-rich foods can help reduce risk of heart disease by keeping blood homocysteine levels in check. Homocysteine is an amino acid that's produced by the body's cells during metabolism. Normally we convert homocysteine to other harmless amino acids with the help of folate and vitamins B6 and B12. When this conversion doesn't occur, because of a genetic defect or a lack of B vitamins, homocysteine accumulates and damages blood vessel walls, promoting the build-up of fatty plaques.

Researchers are indeed finding that folate-rich diets are linked with less heart disease. Harvard University researchers studied 80,000 women for 14 years and found that those who consumed the most folate (and vitamin B6) had a 45 percent lower risk of heart disease compared with women who consumed the least.[5] Finnish researchers found similar results in men. After following a large group of middle-aged men, they learned that those whose diets had the most folate were 55 percent less likely to suffer a heart attack.[6]

Folate and Cancer

You also need folate to make DNA, the genetic blueprint inside every single cell. Without folate, your cells would not be able to properly grow and divide. It's thought that a deficiency of folate can cause damaged DNA and that this may lead to cancer, especially breast and colon cancer.

If you're a woman, chances are you've heard that drinking alcohol can increase your risk of breast cancer. Alcohol may harm breast cells in a number of ways, including disrupting folate metabolism. It seems that boosting your folate intake can offset some of alcohol's harmful effects. The Nurses' Health Study revealed that women who consumed one drink per day *and* had the highest daily intake of folate were 45 percent less likely to have breast cancer compared with women who drank but consumed much less folate.[7] Mayo Clinic researchers found similar results in almost 35,000 postmenopausal women. Among those women who drank, those who consumed the least folate had a higher risk of breast cancer. And the more alcohol consumed, the greater the risk.[8]

When it comes to colon cancer, folate seems to offer protection for both men and women. An American study that examined the diets and health of over 14,000 adults learned that men who consumed more than 249 micrograms of folate per day were 60 percent less likely to have colon cancer compared with those who got less folate. And the more folate these men consumed, the lower their risk of colon cancer.[9]

The Nurses' Health Study showed that getting at least 400 micrograms of folate per day offered significant protection from colon cancer in women.[10] Folate might offer the most protection for women with a family history of colon cancer. A recent analysis of the ongoing Nurses' Health Study found that getting more than 400 micrograms of folate per day reduced the risk of colon cancer by 20 percent in women without a family history of the disease. But when the researchers looked at women with a family history, they found that this same amount of folate reduced the risk of colon cancer by 52 percent![11]

RECOMMENDED DIETARY ALLOWANCE (RDA) FOR FOLATE

Age	RDA (micrograms)	Age	RDA (micrograms)
1–3 years	150 mcg	51+ years	400 mcg
4–8 years	200 mcg	Pregnancy	600 mcg
9–13 years	300 mcg	Breastfeeding	500 mcg
14–18 years	400 mcg	*Daily upper limit, 19+ years*	*1000 mcg*
19–50 years	400 mcg		

Standing Committee on the Scientific Evaluation of Dietary Reference Intakes, Food and Nutrition Board, Institute of Medicine, National Academy Press, Washington, D.C., 2001.

Folate in Foods

The top foods for folate include spinach, lentils, orange juice, asparagus, artichoke, avocado and seeds. You'll also find some in bread and pasta, since flour is fortified with this B vitamin. Here's a look at amounts of folate in selected foods.

FOLATE CONTENT OF FOODS

Food	Folate (micrograms)	Food	Folate (micrograms)
Artichoke, 1 medium	64 mcg	Black beans, cooked, 1/2 cup (125 ml)	135 mcg
Asparagus, 5 spears	110 mcg	Chickpeas, cooked, 1/2 cup (125 ml)	85 mcg
Avocado, California, 1/2	113 mcg	Kidney beans, cooked, 1/2 cup (125 ml)	120 mcg
Avocado, Florida, 1/2	81 mcg		
Bean sprouts, 1 cup (250 ml)	91 mcg	Lentils, cooked, 1/2 cup (125 ml)	189 mcg
Beets, 1/2 cup (125 ml)	72 mcg	Peanuts, 1/2 cup (125 ml)	96 mcg
Brussels sprouts, 1/2 cup (125 ml)	83 mcg	Sunflower seeds, 1/3 cup (75 ml)	96 mcg
Romaine lettuce, 1 cup (250 ml)	80 mcg		
Spinach, raw, 1 cup (250 ml)	115 mcg	Pasta, cooked, 1 cup (250 ml)	100 mcg
Spinach, cooked, 1/2 cup (125 ml)	139 mcg		
Orange, 1 medium	40 mcg	Liver, chicken, 3 1/2 oz (100 g)	770 mcg
Orange juice, frozen, diluted, 1 cup (250 ml)	115 mcg		
Orange juice, freshly squeezed, 1 cup (250 ml)	79 mcg		

Folic Acid Supplements

As I mentioned earlier, it's folic acid that you'll find in vitamin pills and fortified foods. Your body absorbs folic acid much better than folate. By now you know that higher folate intakes are linked with lower risk of both heart disease and cancer. But what you probably didn't know was that most of the studies I described above revealed that people who achieved these higher folate intakes did so by eating folate-rich foods *and* taking a multivitamin. Indeed, multivitamins were a major source of the B vitamin in these studies.

If you've scanned the list of folate-rich foods above, you might think that getting your daily 400 micrograms of folate will be a challenge. To ensure you are meeting your daily folate requirements, take a multivitamin and mineral pill or a B-complex supplement. Most supplements will provide 400 to 1000 micrograms of folic acid.

If you decide to take a single supplement of folic acid (1000 micrograms), buy one that has vitamin B12 added. Supplementing with folic acid alone can mask a vitamin B12 deficiency, which may lead to irreversible nerve damage. Don't exceed 1000 micrograms of folic acid per day.

Do You Need a Multivitamin and Mineral Supplement?

Many health professionals argue that if you eat a well-balanced diet, there's no need for vitamin pills. It's true that a healthy diet is better for you than a handful of supplements, but there are a few reasons why a daily multivitamin and mineral supplement is a wise idea.

For starters, many Canadians don't get enough vitamins and minerals, despite an overload of information on the benefits of eating healthy. Indeed, the most recent national survey shows that many women's diets are falling short of folate, calcium, iron and zinc. And it seems that Canadian children need a boost of good nutrition. A national study by the Canadian Heart and Stroke Foundation found that only 20 percent of children eat the recommended daily minimum of five servings of fruits and vegetables. This means they're likely missing out on vitamin C, beta-carotene and folate.

Despite your best intentions, even after reading this book you might still find it challenging to eat healthy day after day. After all, we're busy people leading hectic lifestyles. Step 1 to healthy eating involved getting organized: planning ahead so that when your life gets a little crazy, you'll be less likely to succumb to the fast food drive-through.

But no matter how good you are at planning your family's meals, there will be times when eating right is downright difficult. Looming deadlines at work, a week packed with business travel, chauffeuring kids to an endless string of extracurricular activities or an emotionally stressful time can temporarily put the brakes on your healthy eating regime. Even if you are getting Health Canada's recommended dietary allowance (RDA) of vitamins and minerals, you might still want to consider taking a multivitamin and mineral pill. Certain vitamins, in amounts greater than the official RDAs, may reduce your risk of cancer, heart disease and other age-related illness. But it can be a challenge to consume the daily recommended intakes of some heart-protective vitamins—such as folate and vitamin E—from foods. And as we age, we absorb certain nutrients—vitamin B12, for example—less efficiently. This is why adults over the age of 50 are recommended to get their B12 from a supplement.

Who should take a multivitamin and mineral pill? Anyone who is looking for a little extra nutritional insurance. Haphazard eaters, dieters, young women wanting extra iron, adults over age 50 and seniors with a poor food intake could all benefit from a one-a-day formula.

Choosing a Supplement

For all the reasons outlined above, it is smart to take a multivitamin and mineral pill, a broad-spectrum supplement that provides 100 to 300 percent of the RDA for most vitamins and minerals (with the exception of calcium, magnesium and iron). *Mega, super and high-potency formulas* usually provide higher doses of B vitamins and antioxidants (vitamins C, E, beta-carotene, selenium). Some high-potency formulas are really a B-complex supplement and a multivitamin and mineral all rolled into one pill. They're a good choice for people looking for a higher amount of B vitamins.

Women's formulas should offer extra calcium (200–300 mg), iron (15–18 mg) and folic acid (600–1000 mcg) but do not always include all 13 minerals. This is because adding more calcium to a formula takes up space, often at the expense of other nutrients. You can find a complete woman's multivitamin and mineral supplement that contains all vitamins and minerals, but be forewarned—it's probably going to be a fairly large pill to swallow. Women's formulas with extra iron are suitable for women who are still menstruating and losing iron each month. *Men's formulas* often have less iron (4–8 mg), more zinc and more selenium. *Older adult formulas* provide less iron (4–8 mg) and more B vitamins, especially B12.

These are only guidelines; formulas will vary by manufacturer. Be sure to check the ingredients list to see what you're paying for. You can also choose between tablets, capsules and chewable multivitamins. This decision really comes down to a personal preference. I prefer capsules because I find them easier to swallow than big tablets. I take a high-potency multivitamin and mineral, and for years I always bought tablets. But for some reason, it became increasingly difficult for me to swallow these horse-sized pills and, as a result, I often skipped my multivitamin. I finally made the switch to a capsule form. If you don't like to swallow any type of pill, capsule or tablet, a chewable product is the choice for you. But check the instructions on the label. You will probably need to chew two of these tablets to meet your recommended daily nutrient intakes.

What to Look For

Buy a product that contains beta-carotene, vitamins A, D, B1, B2, B6, B12 and folic acid. Biotin and pantothenic acid aren't important since they're easily found in food. In terms of minerals, it should contain iron, copper, zinc, magnesium, iodine, selenium and chromium. Don't worry if phosphorus or potassium aren't included, since these nutrients are widely distributed in the diet.

Make no mistake: nutritional supplements are meant to *support and reinforce* your healthy diet. So eat right first, then take your multivitamin and mineral. Consult your registered dietitian, doctor or pharmacist for more advice about supplementing safely.

25 TIPS
FOR BOOSTING YOUR NUTRIENT INTAKE

TO GET MORE CALCIUM

1. Aim for 3 to 4 servings of dairy or calcium-fortified beverages each day. One serving equals 1 cup of milk, yogurt, calcium-fortified beverage or 1 1/2 ounces of low-fat cheese.

2. Cook hot cereal, rice and grains in low-fat milk.

3. Add skim-milk powder to casseroles, soups, shakes, meatloaf, French toast, muffins, breads, mashed potatoes and dips. A single tablespoon (15 ml) adds 52 milligrams of calcium, and 2 to 4 tablespoons (25 to 50 ml) can be easily added to most recipes.

4. Use evaporated 2 percent or evaporated skim milk instead of regular milk in puddings, low-fat cream soups and cream sauces.

5. In a hurry each morning? Whip up a smoothie with low-fat milk or calcium-fortified soymilk.

6. Enjoy a glass of calcium-fortified citrus juice with breakfast.

7. Eat at least one calcium-rich vegetable every day—broccoli, Swiss chard, kale and collard greens are winners!

TO GET MORE VITAMIN D

8. Include at least two servings of milk or fortified soy or rice beverage in your daily diet.

9. Eat fatty fish three times per week (you're already doing this if you're following my advice in Step 5 on choosing healthy fats).

10. Spend ten minutes in the sunshine (without wearing sunscreen), two or three times a week.

11. Take a multivitamin and mineral supplement that contains 400 international units (IU) of vitamin D.

12. If you need to take calcium pills, buy a brand with vitamin D added. If you don't take extra calcium, take a single vitamin D supplement to reach your daily target.

TO GET MORE IRON

13. If you're not a vegetarian, include lean red meat in your diet once or twice a week.

14. Start the day with a bowl of iron-fortified breakfast cereal (be sure to choose a high-fiber cereal).

15. Eat shrimp more often. Throw cooked shrimp into a stir-fry, pasta sauce or green salad. (Yes, it's true that shrimp contain cholesterol, but remember that dietary cholesterol has little or no effect on most people's blood cholesterol level.)

16. Add 1 to 2 tablespoons (15 to 25 ml) of blackstrap molasses to hot cereal or yogurt.

17. Include a food rich in vitamin C when you're eating iron-rich plant foods. Try mandarin orange segments in your next spinach salad, or red pepper strips in a brown-rice stir-fry.

18. Avoid drinking tea and coffee with iron-rich foods.

19. Take a multivitamin and mineral supplement. Menstruating women should look for a brand that supplies 10 to 18 milligrams of iron.

TO GET MORE FOLATE

20. Include at least one folate-rich vegetable in your diet each day—spinach, asparagus, broccoli, Brussels sprouts, green peas and Romaine lettuce are good choices.

21. Add a small glass of unsweetened orange juice to your morning meal (this will also help you absorb more iron from your foods).

22. Add cooked lentils to soups, pasta sauce and salads.

23. Snack on 1/3 cup (75 ml) of sunflower seeds mixed with raisins and dried apricots—a good source of both folate and iron.

24. Spread your next sandwich with hummus, a dip made from mashed chickpeas.

25. Take that multivitamin! Choose a brand that offers 400 micrograms of folic acid.

ANSWERS TO LESLIE'S IQ QUIZ   VITAMINS AND MINERALS

1.   d. 1/2 can of salmon with the bones packs 225 milligrams of calcium. The almonds offer 100 milligrams, the yogurt, 166, and the cooked broccoli, 94.

2.   False. Calcium citrate is better absorbed than calcium carbonate.

3.   d. Yogurt contains no vitamin D. The other foods all supply some of the nutrient, with the fatty fish taking the lead.

4.   True. Turn to page 110 to learn why vegetarians need to consume more iron.

5.   b. The lentils win the folate race: 1/2 cup (125 ml) of cooked lentils pack 189 milligrams, almost one-half of your daily requirement.

Step 7
Eat More Often

LESLIE'S NUTRITION IQ QUIZ   EATING TO BOOST
ENERGY AND ENHANCE YOUR HEALTH

1. True or false? Grazing means adding between-meal snacks to your diet.

2. True or false? Eating breakfast enhances your short-term memory.

3. Which breakfast will keep you feeling full longer?
    a. whole-wheat bagel with strawberry jam
    b. bowl of Corn Flakes with low-fat milk
    c. cereal bar and a glass of orange juice
    d. bowl of oatmeal with low-fat milk

4. True or false? Eating several mini-meals each day can help control your
    blood cholesterol.

5. You know you need a pick-me-up around four o'clock each afternoon.
    Pick the best choice for long-lasting energy.
    a. one medium banana
    b. Gatorade sports drink, 2 cups (500 mL)
    c. baked pretzels, 1 cup (250 mL)
    d. low fat yogurt, fruit bottom, 3/4 cup (175 mL)

"I'm tired of dragging myself through the day," groaned Susan, a client who recently came to see me for a complete overhaul of her diet. "Tell me what foods to eat so I have more energy," she said, clearly frustrated by her chronic low energy level, not to mention her creeping weight. Susan had gained ten pounds since she started her new job in downtown Toronto.

When I pressed her further, Susan complained that there wasn't a day she didn't feel tired by midafternoon. Concentrating on her work had become a real chore. And by the end of her workday, Susan lacked the energy to sneak in a quick workout. All she could do was muster up the strength to prepare a healthy dinner for her family. She was fed up with feeling sluggish and overweight. She had decided it was time, once and for all, to do something about it.

A Typical Day in a Hectic Life

Once I assessed Susan's diet and lifestyle, it became obvious where the problem areas were. Susan rose each morning at 6:30 a.m., spent a hectic hour getting the kids ready for school and feeding them breakfast—a meal she neglected to eat herself ("no time!" she exclaimed). She arrived at her office by 9:00 a.m. after commuting for almost an hour in rush-hour traffic. Fueled by coffee only, Susan would work at her desk until a growling stomach persuaded her to buy a bagel and cream cheese from the company cafeteria, around 10:30 a.m. Susan claimed she never felt very hungry when lunch hour arrived. Her usual lunch included a small soup and a package of soda crackers. Almost six hours later she'd leave the office, and by 7:00 p.m. she was sitting down with her family to eat dinner, a meal she said she always overate.

Sound familiar? Does your hectic morning schedule leave no time for breakfast? Do you find yourself grabbing a quick bite at erratic times during the day? Are you so ravenous at the end of the day that dinner becomes a feeding frenzy? If you answered yes to one of these questions, you're not alone. It's not very often that I see a client who is eating at regular intervals throughout the day. And yet, almost all my clients list "increase my energy level" as one of their goals. Busy family schedules, stressful work deadlines and taking care of *you* all require energy. The best way to have a steady stream of energy is to eat more often during the day.

Together, Susan and I revamped her diet. My first goal was to revise her eating schedule. I persuaded her to take five minutes in the morning, before she left for work, to eat a nutritious breakfast. We also added a small midmorning snack. She ate a satisfying lunch at noon every day and made sure to eat a midafternoon snack. We did not change the time she ate dinner.

When I saw Susan for her follow-up visit two weeks later, she was in much better spirits. She happily reported that she had noticed a big difference in her energy levels. She was no longer tired every afternoon. And she was thrilled that her appetite was reduced at the end of the day—she was having no problem eating smaller portions at dinner. What's more, Susan had lost three pounds in two weeks! She was surprised to learn that eating more often during the day had helped her lose weight.

Six Good Reasons to Eat More Often

Most of us know *what* foods we should be eating. We know it's important to eat less fatty foods and plenty of whole grains, fruit and vegetables. If you're following the advice I've given in the previous chapters of this book, you're well on your way to eating a healthy diet. But it's also important to know *how to eat*—how to spread out those healthy foods over the course of the day. How frequently, or infrequently, you nourish your body can have an impact on how much you eat, your energy levels and your overall health.

More Energy

An immediate benefit of eating more often is feeling more energetic. My clients always tell me how much better they feel once they start eating between-meal snacks. Your body relies on glucose, a form of sugar, as its main source of fuel for daily activities. Whenever you digest food, the breakdown of carbohydrates into glucose causes your blood sugar level to rise. This triggers your pancreas to release the hormone insulin. Insulin helps glucose enter body cells, where it supplies the energy to fuel most bodily functions. Any unused glucose is stored in your muscles and liver as glycogen. Your body draws on these sugar stores for energy when your blood sugar drops.

As glucose is absorbed into the cells, your blood sugar level gradually drops back to a normal range. But a few hours later, when most of your body's available glucose supply is used up, your blood sugar level will start to fall below normal. A low blood sugar level is one of the most common causes of afternoon fatigue. When your body lacks glucose, you may also experience headache, dizziness and shakiness. Some people become irritable and have difficulty concentrating. These symptoms are telling you that you need to eat more often! Planning to eat a midday snack is a key strategy for boosting your energy level.

Better Brain Power

I just told you that a low blood sugar level could affect your ability to concentrate. This is because your brain and nervous system rely exclusively on glucose for energy. Your brain's energy stores are very small; without constant replacement of glucose, your brain cells would become depleted in less than ten minutes. And without a steady stream of glucose nourishing your brain cells, your attention span and short-term memory are likely to diminish.

Studies have demonstrated that eating breakfast improves thinking power later in the morning and a late-afternoon snack enhances performance on tasks that involve prolonged concentration and memory. Most studies have focused on the cognitive effects of breakfast. Based on these findings, it certainly seems that breakfast-skippers are at a disadvantage when it comes to mental performance. Studies find that compared with their peers who eat breakfast, elementary school children and teenagers who skip the morning meal make more errors and have slower memory recall on psychological tests.[1-3]

Don't think that the effects of breakfast are limited to children. Not so! Australian researchers found that eating breakfast led to improved mood, better memory, more energy and feelings of calmness in overweight women.[4] Three more experiments conducted in young men and women revealed that going without breakfast impaired the ability to recall a word list and read a story aloud. This decline in test performance associated with skipping breakfast was reversed when the study participants were given a glucose drink.[5]

Breakfast foods such as cereal, whole-grain bread, fruit and milk are full of carbohydrates that supply glucose to your brain, and it's glucose that seems to be the key factor in mental tasks requiring you to rely on your memory.

Improved Nutrition

Eating at regular intervals, and especially starting the day with breakfast, has other benefits as well. Study after study shows that breakfast-skippers eat more fat and less carbohydrate and do not meet their recommended daily intakes for many vitamins and minerals.[6-9] Breakfast-eaters are more likely to meet their daily targets for calcium, iron, folate, niacin, vitamin A, vitamin D and zinc. It appears that people who skip the morning meal do not make up for these missing nutrients later in the day.

According to researchers, ready-to-eat breakfast cereals can make a real difference to your daily nutrient intake. Two studies found that kids who ate a fortified breakfast cereal each morning consumed significantly more vitamins and minerals compared with kids who ate fast food breakfasts, other breakfast foods or no breakfast at all.[10,11] The children whose breakfast did not include ready-to-eat cereal fell below the daily recommendations for many B vitamins and iron.

Skipping any meal, for that matter, can shortchange your body of important nutrients. A study conducted among almost 3000 older adults found that those who ate fewer than three meals per day consumed significantly fewer calories and nutrients, especially calcium, compared with those who ate more often.[12]

Eating at frequent intervals during the day can impact your vitamin and mineral intake, provided, of course, that you choose your snacks carefully. Your snacks should include key nutrients that you may not be getting from your meals. The two foods I find lacking in most of my clients' diets are fruit and dairy products. It's for this reason that my recommended snacks usually include some type of fruit and a good source of calcium. You'll find a list of healthy snacks on page 127.

Cholesterol Control

A number of studies have revealed that grazers, people who eat at least six times per day, have lower cholesterol levels than those who eat the same number of calories in three or fewer meals. The grazing phenomenon made headlines back in 1989 when Toronto researchers published in the *New England Journal of Medicine* results of a carefully controlled study. For two weeks, seven men ate 2500 calories as three ordinary-sized meals. For the next two weeks, these men ate 2500 calories in 17 snacks, eaten once an hour. The nibbling diet reduced total cholesterol levels by 8.5 percent and LDL (bad) cholesterol by 13.5 percent.[13] This cholesterol-lowering effect was achieved by increasing meal frequency alone: the men ate the same calories and the same foods on both regimes.

Don't worry, you don't need to eat 17 times a day to realize the cholesterol-lowering benefits of grazing. A recent study from Norfolk, England, followed almost 15,000 men and women aged 45 to 75 and found that, compared with people who ate only once or twice a day, those who ate at least six times each day had lower total and LDL cholesterol levels.[14] A smaller study conducted in healthy young men found a similar effect of eating six mini-meals each day. Compared with men who ate three square meals, the grazers had significantly lower blood cholesterol levels.[15] Scientists from California found that compared with eating once or twice per day, eating at least four times daily was linked with lower cholesterol levels in 2034 men and women aged 50 to 89.[16]

Some researchers believe that grazing is associated with a steady metabolism, whereas stockpiling a day's worth of calories into three or fewer meals may cause the body to store more food as energy. Gorging animals adapt to periodic loads of foods by absorbing more carbohydrate from a meal, making more fat from glucose, producing more cholesterol in the liver and storing more body fat.

The hormone insulin also seems to play an important role in maintaining healthy cholesterol levels. Insulin is released into the bloodstream after you eat a meal or snack. I've already told you that insulin's job is to clear sugar from the blood into your cells, where it's needed for energy. But insulin also activates an enzyme in your liver that produces cholesterol. Gorging causes *more insulin* to be secreted after eating a meal. Grazing, on the other hand, is associated with less insulin being released after eating. This makes sense, since grazers eat smaller amounts of food at one time. So less sugar arrives in the bloodstream, and less insulin is needed to transport that sugar into cells.

Appetite Reduction

If you skip meals in an effort to save calories, think again! This plan will backfire and, chances are, you'll end up overeating at the next meal. The number of calories you consume at one sitting relates to the amount of time that has elapsed since you last ate. One of the best ways to control your appetite in an effort to eat less is to eat more often during the day!

Yes, that's right—you'll consume fewer calories if you *don't* skip meals. Furthermore, if you eat more frequently, say, several small mini-meals instead of one large meal, the odds are even higher that you'll eat less at your next meal.

Researchers from Johannesburg, South Africa, proved this point when they tested different meal frequencies on appetite control and subsequent food intake in obese and normal weight men. In one study, healthy men fasted overnight and were then given breakfast. On one occasion, the meal was given as a single meal; on another occasion, it was divided into five equal-sized meals and fed at hourly intervals. On both occasions, the men were served lunch five hours after breakfast.

Compared with the men fed their breakfast in five mini-meals, those who ate the single meal consumed 27 percent more calories at lunch! Peak blood sugar and insulin levels were significantly higher after the men ate the single meal versus the multi-meals. What's more, the men who ate more often in the five-hour period rated their hunger level before lunch dramatically lower than did the men who ate the single meals.[17,18]

What's at work here? Researchers believe that insulin is somehow responsible for appetite control. Eating smaller quantities of food more often results in a prolonged elevated, but not maximal, insulin level, and this seems to reduce appetite. On the other hand, when the breakfast was given as one single meal, insulin rose to a much higher level after eating. And, five hours later, insulin levels of these men had returned to the fasting level. Eating frequently may keep your insulin level just high enough to ward off hunger.

Weight Management

If eating smaller meals more often can control your appetite, can it help you lose weight? It certainly sounds logical: if you consistently eat less at meal times, you're bound to save enough calories to gradually shed a few pounds. Eating several small meals per day, instead of one or two big meals, helps the body burn fuel more efficiently. Gorging on one or two calorie-laden meals makes it easy for your body to store energy as fat.

Researchers first demonstrated a strong relationship between eating frequency and body weight back in the 1960s. Studies conducted in men and schoolchildren found that infrequent eaters were more likely to be overweight and have more body fat.[19,20] Since then, a few studies have linked eating frequently with leanness. Japanese researchers gave 12 competitive boxers a 1200-calorie weight-loss diet either as two meals per day or as six meals per day. After two weeks, they found that while there was no difference in the amount of weight loss between the two groups, the frequent eaters lost more body fat and preserved more muscle mass.[21]

Although some researchers have found that dieters lose more weight when given several mini-meals rather than three meals daily,[22] most studies have demonstrated that grazing does not speed up weight loss. However, it is true that low-calorie weight-loss diets may be easier to follow if those calories are divided into several small meals. This brings us back to the point about eating frequent small meals to control your appetite. And let's face it: diets usually fail because they make you hungry. Feeling hungry on a diet, not to mention feeling deprived, often triggers overeating and bingeing.

If you want to be successful at losing and maintaining a weight loss, *do not skip breakfast!* Although many dieters intentionally skip this meal in an effort to save calories, this is a mistake. People who skip breakfast are actually more likely to be overweight.[23-25] Breakfast-skippers tend to make up for the calories they have saved by eating more later on in the day. What's more, skipping breakfast slows down metabolism, the rate at which your body burns calories. After a night of sleeping, your metabolism normally slows down. Eating breakfast in the morning revs it back up as your body burns calories to digest, absorb, transport and store the nutrients you eat at breakfast.

Eating breakfast also seems to keep the pounds off. American researchers recently surveyed close to 3000 people who had successfully maintained a weight loss of 30 pounds (14 kg) for one year. When asked what strategies they employed to maintain their weight, a whopping 78 percent said they ate breakfast every day.[26] You can't argue with that!

How Often Should You Eat?

Now comes the real question: Just how often should you eat? Should you eat every hour? Six times a day? Four times a day? To be honest, there's no right answer. Your eating routine will depend to a large extent on your day's activity and work schedule. Here are a few rules I follow whenever I map out a meal plan for a client. Follow these guidelines to boost your energy level, improve your nutrient intake and control your appetite.

Eat Breakfast Every Day Before Leaving Home

Don't wait until you arrive at the office to eat breakfast. For starters, the time between waking up and getting to work can be hours for many people. I have many clients who rise by 5:30 a.m. but don't get to work until 9:00 a.m. That's more than three hours without food! But more importantly, if you wait to pick up breakfast on the road, your choices are few. Unless, of course, you plan to eat fast food, a bagel with cream cheese or a super-sized muffin. You'll be hard-pressed to find whole-grain cereal and fresh fruit at your local coffee shop.

Of course, you can always bring your breakfast with you to work. Many of my clients do this because they literally have no time to sit down before they have to catch a commuter train or bus to work. If you do bring a healthy breakfast to work, that's great. Just be sure to rev up your metabolism by eating something small at home or on the way to work—a piece of fruit, a single serving of yogurt or a small low-fat latte will do the trick.

Your breakfast should always include whole grains, a source of calcium and fruit. These foods are a must to boost your intake of dietary fiber, iron, B vitamins and, of course, calcium. When choosing whole-grain foods, whether it be cereal or toast, *choose a food that has a low glycemic index.* These carbohydrate foods are digested more slowly and lead to a *gradual* rise in blood sugar. This gives you sustained energy and keeps you feeling full longer. You'll find a list of foods with a low glycemic index on page 50, Chapter 3.

Some people like to add a bit of protein or fat to breakfast. A hardboiled egg, cottage cheese or a tablespoon of peanut butter can give your breakfast additional staying power.

BEST BREAKFASTS	WORST BREAKFASTS
Whole-grain cereal with low-fat milk or calcium-fortified soymilk, 1 fruit serving	Fast food sandwiches (McDonald's Western Omelette Bagel packs 680 calories and 39 grams of fat!)
Whole-grain pumpernickel toast, 1 tablespoon (15 ml) nut butter, 1 fruit serving, 3/4 cup (175 ml) low-fat yogurt	Fatty sweets such as store-bought muffins, Danish pastries, cinnamon buns, scones, donuts and coffee cake (Most muffins and donuts pack 4 teaspoons (20 ml) worth of fat, much of it artery-clogging trans fat. And large cinnamon buns can tip the scale at 700 calories! Even a Starbucks scone provides a good 500 calories.)
Small homemade low-fat bran muffin, 1 oz (30 g) low-fat cheese, 1 fruit serving	Store bought breakfast cereal bars (Sure these are low-fat, and they do have some vitamins and minerals, but they lack fiber and real fruit, and they'll leave you hungry.)
Whole-grain toast, 1 poached egg, 1 small skim-milk or 1 percent milk latte, 1 fruit serving	Bagel with cream cheese (No doubt one of the easiest breakfasts to grab on the go. The problem is that large bagels are just that—large. One bagel is equal to four or five slices of bread. The cream cheese is loaded with saturated fat and offers little calcium.
Bowl of oatmeal with raisins, low-fat milk or calcium-fortified soymilk, 1/2 grapefruit	No breakfast at all (No comment needed!)

Breakfast Ideas to Go

- Spread 2 tablespoons (25 ml) of hummus on half a whole-grain bagel.

- Stuff half a whole-wheat pita pocket with cottage cheese and fruit.

- Whip up a smoothie with low-fat milk or soymilk, frozen berries, half a banana and 1 tablespoon (15 ml) wheat germ or ground flaxseed.

- Enjoy 3/4 cup (175 ml) low-fat yogurt, a piece of fruit and a low-fat granola bar.

- Enjoy a package of instant plain oatmeal, a small box of raisins and 3/4 cup (175 ml) low-fat yogurt.

- Combine spoon-size shredded wheat, whole-grain flakes, raisins, dried cranberries and nuts for homemade trail mix. Add a yogurt or a small latte for calcium.

- Spread 1 tablespoon (15 ml) of nut butter or tahini on a whole-wheat tortilla and then wrap around a small banana.

Eat Every Three or Four Hours

For optimal energy levels, aim to eat every three hours. For most of us, this means planning for midday snacks. If you eat breakfast at 7 a.m. and don't sit down to lunch until 1 p.m., you'll need a snack around 10 a.m. If you eat breakfast by 7 a.m., have an early lunch at noon but don't have dinner until 7 p.m., you will need to eat a midafternoon snack by 4 p.m.

Listen to your body and use common sense when deciding when to eat. Snacks should not be eaten too close to meal times. I suggest to my clients that they eat them two to three hours apart from meals. For those of you who exercise during the day, snacks provide a source of fuel for your working muscles. Snack 45 to 60 minutes before exercising.

Leslie's Guidelines for Choosing Snacks

- Plan ahead. Foods eaten on impulse tend to be high in fat and sugar. Bring your snacks to work or buy them when you buy your lunch (you may not have time to leave the office in the afternoon to buy a snack).

- Snacks should provide 100 to 200 calories. If your next meal is only an hour away but you need a pick-me-up, choose a 100-calorie snack. Most often, I recommend snacks in the calorie range of 150 for women, 200 for men.

- When possible, include fruit, vegetables and calcium-rich foods as part of your snack. You'll find a list of calcium-rich foods on page 104, Chapter 6.

- Always include some carbohydrate for brain energy and protein for staying power.

- Choose carbohydrate foods with a low glycemic index (see page 50, Chapter 3).

Now let's put this principles into practice. Here's a look at some of the most, and least, nutritious snacks.

BEST SNACKS	WORST SNACKS
3/4 cup (175 ml) low-fat yogurt and 1 serving of fruit	Cookies, cakes and rich desserts
Medium-sized low-fat skim or soy latte and 1 serving of fruit	Coffee and a chocolate bar
1/4 cup (50 ml) dried fruit and 2 tablespoons (25 ml) nuts	Potato chips or tortilla chips (baked or fried)

BEST SNACKS	WORST SNACKS
1 slice whole-grain bread with 1 tbsp (15 ml) nut butter or tahini	Pretzels or baked potato chips (Yes, these are fat-free but they have a high glycemic index so they won't put much of a dent in your appetite.)
Energy Bar with 14–18 grams protein and no more than 200–250 calories (Balance Bar, The Zone Bar, Protein Blast, Genisoy, SoyOne)	Energy bars with less than 10 grams protein (These high-carb bars are great for people who need the extra fuel for long workouts, but if you're looking for a between-meal snack, stick to bars that have 20–25 grams of carbohydrate.)
Whole-wheat or whole-rye crackers with 1 ounce (30 g) low-fat cheese	Bagels, bread or crackers (Once again, these are high glycemic index foods.)
Homemade smoothie made with milk or soymilk, and your choice of fruit	Smoothie made from frozen yogurt (These store-bought frozen treats contain more sugar, more fat and less calcium than your homemade version.)

Avoid Large Meals after 8 P.M.

Unless you work a night shift, I recommend that you set a cut-off time for dinner. I usually tell my weight-conscious clients to avoid eating a big meal after 8 p.m. That is, if they walk in the door from work after eight o'clock at night, it's too late for dinner. I tell my clients to instead have a small meal or snack—a bowl of soup, a small sandwich or fruit and yogurt.

While there is no scientific evidence that eating late in the evening can make you gain weight, my clinical experience tells me differently. In my private practice, people who make a habit of eating their main meal late have more difficulty controlling their weight. And when they break this habit, losing weight becomes easier. It only makes sense that eating 500 to 700 calories and going to bed a short while later can trigger the body to store fat.

Nighttime-eaters *do* seem to have more difficulty losing weight. To have what scientists call *night eating syndrome,* you must 1) skip breakfast at least four times per week (due to lack of appetite), 2) consume more than 50 percent of your daily calories after 7 p.m. and 3) have difficulty falling asleep or staying asleep at least four nights per week. American researchers recently studied a group of overweight men and women embarking on a weight-loss program. The men and women with night eating syndrome were more depressed, had lower self-esteem, ate more food later in the day and were more likely to feel full in the morning. What's more, they lost less weight than their peers who did not eat at night.[27]

Even if you don't have night eating syndrome, eating late at night can predispose you to weight gain. Some research suggests that your body burns calories less efficiently later in the day. French scientists reported that the body burns more calories to digest a morning and afternoon meal than it does an evening meal.[28] So it does seem to make sense to eat a lighter meal if it's late in the evening.

Eating at night also may cause weight gain because most of us are less active at this time. A large meal eaten in the middle of the day is less likely to be stored as fat since it is usually followed by several hours of activity. Our body is busy using up these calories and nutrients to fuel daily activities. But after a large evening meal, most of us are sedentary, watching television, reading or sleeping. This practice increases the likelihood that a late meal will be stored as body fat.

When my clients follow my advice about sticking to the 8 p.m. rule, they report sleeping better, waking up with an appetite for breakfast and feeling less bloated in the morning. These are reasons enough to cut back the late-night meals and snacks.

Should You Become a Grazer?

The tips I have provided here will help you eat more often during the day to keep your energy levels up. But this advice will not convert you into a true grazer. If you want to graze, you must divide your day's worth of calories into several small meals of equal size. If you just add more mini-meals to your current intake, you will gain weight.

For a woman who needs 1800 calories per day, this means eating six 300-calorie meals. For a man who requires 2400 calories to maintain his weight, he would have to graze on either six 400-calorie mini-meals or eight 300-calorie meals. Not only should these mini-meals contain the same number of calories, but they should also be equally spaced throughout the day.

For most people, this pattern of eating is impractical. It requires careful planning of meals, eating according to a rigid schedule and carrying foods with you. As healthy as grazing might be, I find it just doesn't lend itself to our busy lifestyle. In my opinion, you are much better off eating four or five times a day—three meals plus one or two snacks.

10 TIPS
FOR EATING MORE OFTEN

1. Always start the day with breakfast, preferably before you leave home.

2. To boost your nutrient intake, make sure your breakfast includes whole grains, fruit and a good source of calcium.

3. If you don't have time to eat breakfast before you leave home, pack one to take with you to eat en route or at your desk. This will save you from giving in to those readily available high-fat muffins and breakfast pastries.

4. Use the list on page 50, Chapter 3, to choose carbohydrate breakfast foods that have a low glycemic index.

5. Take a moment to map out your day's schedule. When you write down when you eat, you might see gaps that need to be filled with a healthy snack.

6. Go no longer than four hours during the day without eating. If the span between your meals is longer, plan for a snack.

7. Choose fruit, vegetables and calcium-rich foods for snacks.

8. If you want to eat a starchy food for a snack, be sure to choose a low glycemic index carbohydrate to keep you feeling full and energetic longer.

9. When you're away from home or traveling, carry portable snacks in your purse or briefcase. Energy bars, dried fruit and nuts or a piece of fruit work well.

10. Plan your dinners to help you eat before 8 p.m. (Refer to my tips for planning ahead in Chapter 1.) You'll find suggestions for tasty dinners in my 14-Day Meal Plan, on page 182. The recipes, from the Canadian Living Test Kitchen, start on page 184.

ANSWERS TO LESLIE'S IQ QUIZ   EATING TO BOOST ENERGY AND ENHANCE YOUR HEALTH

1. False. Grazing means dividing your daily calorie intake into several small meals of equal size.

2. True. Breakfast foods provide glucose to brain cells. Glucose appears to be particularly important for mental tasks that require memory.

3. d. The bowl of oatmeal with low-fat milk. Both foods have a low glycemic index and contribute to feeling full, not to mention sustained energy levels.

4. True. Read page 123 to find out more!

5. d. The low-fat yogurt is your best snack choice because it is a low glycemic index food. That means it is digested slowly, leading to a more consistent energy level.

Step 8

Don't Forget about Fluids

Water is the most abundant compound in the human body—it makes up 50 to 80 percent of our body weight—yet we tend to take it for granted. Water is an essential nutrient, just like vitamins and minerals, because our bodies can't make enough of it on their own to meet daily requirements. Believe it or not, you can survive only a few days without water, but a deficiency of other nutrients can take weeks, months or even years to develop.

Water lives inside and around every single cell in the body. In fact, there is not one system in your body that does not rely on a steady supply of water. Every biochemical reaction that takes place in your body does so with the help of water. Water in saliva and digestive juices helps break down the food you eat into smaller nutrients that can be absorbed into your bloodstream. These nutrients are then transported to your cells and tissues via water in your blood. And your cells would not get the oxygen they need to survive if it weren't for water in your bloodstream. Fluid in your blood, urine and stool also helps remove toxic waste products from your body.

Your body's ability to regulate its temperature is also dependent on water. The fluid in your sweat allows your muscles to release heat that builds up during exercise. The amount of water in your bloodstream also regulates your blood pressure and heart function. And finally, water acts as your body's central lubricant. It cushions your joints, moistens your eyes and protects your brain and spinal cord.

The Health Benefits of Drinking Water

It's clear that life would not exist without water. You need to drink water every day to help your body function properly. If you drink too little fluid, or lose too much through sweat, your body can't perform at its peak. But you may not realize that your hydration status can affect your health in other ways too. If your body is continually compensating for an inadequate fluid intake, your risk for certain diseases may be higher. New research suggests that water plays an important role in the development of cancer, heart disease, kidney stones and obesity.

Water and Cancer

Several studies have discovered a direct relationship between the amount of water you drink and your risk for certain cancers. Harvard researchers learned that drinking more water helps protect men from bladder cancer. In their study of 47,909 men, those who drank at least 6 cups (1.5 liters) of water each day were half as likely to get bladder cancer compared with men who drank less.[1]

Studies also show that people who drink too little fluid have a higher risk of developing cancer of the lower urinary tract (bladder, kidney, prostate, testicle and ureter). A study conducted in Hawaii revealed that total fluid intake, especially tap water, lowered the risk for urinary tract cancer in women. Compared with those women who drank the least fluid, those who consumed the most had a 70 percent lower risk. High fluid intakes appeared to offer even more protection against cancer for smokers.[2]

Drinking plenty of water may also help ward off colon cancer. Studies have found that frequent water drinkers have a lower risk of developing precancerous polyps and also colon cancer.[3-5] American researchers from Seattle, Washington, found that women who drank more than five glasses of water each day had a 45 percent lower risk of the cancer versus those who consumed two glasses or less. Among men, drinking at least four glasses of water each day was linked with a 32 percent reduced risk, but this finding was not statistically significant (meaning the results could have occurred by chance).[6]

One study even suggests that an adequate intake of water might help prevent breast cancer. The authors reported that the risk for developing breast cancer was reduced by 79 percent among water drinkers. When the researchers looked at the effects of water drinking in premenopausal and postmenopausal women separately, the risk for breast cancer was reduced by 33 percent in premenopausal women and 79 percent in postmenopausal women.[7]

Scientists speculate that chronic mild dehydration can impair the activity of metabolic reactions that take place inside your cells. An inadequate fluid intake might affect the action of important enzymes and, as a result, impede the removal of cancer-causing substances from your cells.

Water and Heart Disease

You probably didn't think that boosting your water intake could prevent a heart attack. But that's exactly what researchers from Loma Linda University in California recently learned. The study followed over 20,000 men and women who were Seventh-Day Adventists and found that people who drank at least five glasses of water each day were less likely to die from heart disease. Women who drank more than five 8-ounce (250-ml) glasses of water were 41 percent less likely to die from a heart attack, and the risk was reduced by 54 percent in water-drinking men.

When the researchers looked at other fluids, such as coffee, tea, juice, milk and alcohol, the risk was reversed. Women who drank plenty of these types of fluids were more than twice as likely to die from a heart attack, and in men there was a 46 percent higher risk.[8]

When you drink water, it becomes absorbed into the bloodstream and acts to "thin the blood." Researchers believe that this might prevent the formation of blood clots that could trigger a heart attack. Other fluids, however, are thought to "thicken the blood" because they need water in order to be digested. During the process of digestion, water gets pulled into the gut from the bloodstream.

Water and Kidney Stones

If you have ever suffered from kidney stones, drinking plenty of fluids each day is a key strategy to prevent their recurrence. Drinking more fluids helps flush away substances that can cause crystals to form in the kidneys. In fact, chronic dehydration is a common cause of kidney stones.[9,10] When the urine is less dilute from a lack of water, it becomes more concentrated with chemicals that can crystallize into stones.

Certain beverages might help lower the risk of kidney stone recurrence. Coffee, decaffeinated coffee, tea, beer and wine have been shown to prevent stone formation, presumably by increasing the flow of a more dilute urine.[11,12] Grapefruit juice and apple juice may increase the risk of stones, for reasons that remain unknown.[13] Some research suggests that lemonade made from 4 ounces (125 ml) of reconstituted lemon juice is beneficial for people with calcium kidney stones.[14]

Water and Weight Control

Many of my clients say that drinking water helps them fill up, so they eat less food at a meal. Unfortunately, studies have not found that drinking water before or with a meal reduces food intake. Yet the practice of drinking at least 8 cups of water every day is recommended by many weight-loss programs. I always recommend that my clients drink plenty of water each day, if not to stave off hunger then to stay healthy.

It's also possible that people confuse thirst with hunger. They reach for food when what their body really needs is water. Again, there's little proof that thirst causes feelings of hunger. In fact, your body regulates thirst and hunger by completely different mechanisms. But there are reasons why some people might confuse thirst with hunger. For one, these sensations tend to occur together, around meal times, especially since most people drink fluids with their meals. Your best bet is to drink a calorie-free beverage like water at meals, and fill up on low-fat, high-fiber foods. In some cases, people just want to satisfy an oral craving. And instead of reaching for water, many people gravitate toward snack foods.

When it comes to treating and preventing childhood obesity, kids should be encouraged to replace calorie-laden drinks like fruit juice and soda pop with water. Overweight older children and teenagers who quench their thirst with these beverages can be taking in as many as 500 calories per day. So while drinking water might not make you thin, drinking other liquids can certainly lead to weight gain.

How Much Fluid Do You Need Each Day?

Fluid needs vary considerably among people. How much water you need to drink will depend on your size, your diet (high-fiber diets increase fluid needs), your activity level and the weather. High temperatures and low humidity increase your fluid needs.

The National Research Council recommends that we consume 4 cups (1 liter) of water for every 1000 calories we expend in daily activities. That means that the average woman—burning 2200 calories each day—needs to drink 9 cups (2.2 liters) of fluid each day, and the average man—burning 2900 calories each day—12 cups (2.9 liters). Children actually need more water per pound of body weight than do adults. That's because children have a larger surface area per unit of body weight. Children should drink at least 8 cups (2 liters) of fluid per day.

When You Need Even More Fluid

Pregnancy

If you're pregnant, you need to drink more fluid than the amount recommended above. During pregnancy, the fluid spaces between your cells enlarge, demanding more fluid. The growing fetus and the amniotic fluid that surrounds your baby also require more fluid. Pregnant women should drink an additional 1 cup (250 ml) of water each day.

Breastfeeding

Nursing moms can lose a considerable amount of fluid—up to 3 cups (750 mL) per day. Since the majority of breast milk is water, this fluid must be replaced by drinking more water each day. Breastfeeding moms need to drink an additional 2 to 3 cups (500 to 750 mL) of water daily.

Exercise

When you exercise, your muscles generate heat. This heat must be released from your body as sweat or your performance will be impaired. If you lose too much sweat during exercise and become dehydrated, the fluid in your bloodstream can't circulate efficiently to your working muscles and your skin. As a result, you'll produce less sweat, causing your muscles to build up heat. Dehydration is one of the most common causes of early fatigue during exercise. Use the following guide to stay well hydrated before, during and after exercise.

Fluid Requirements for Exercise[15]

24 Hours Before Exercise

- Follow a nutritionally balanced diet and drink adequate fluids.

Two Hours Before Exercise:

- Drink 2 cups (500 ml) of fluid.

During Exercise

- Start drinking cool fluids early, at a rate of 1/2 to 1 cup (125 to 250 ml) every 15 to 20 minutes.

- For exercise lasting less than one hour, plain water is the best fluid for hydration.

- For exercise lasting longer than one hour, sports drinks (such as Gatorade, PowerAde or All Sport) that contain 4 to 8 percent carbohydrate and electrolytes (sodium, chloride, potassium) may improve hydration and performance.

After Exercise

- Drink 2 cups (500 ml) of fluid for every pound you lose during exercise.

- A sports drink that contains sodium may improve recovery, but it's not necessary as long as sodium is in the foods you eat.

Illness

When you're sick, your body loses higher amounts of fluid than it normally does. Vomiting and diarrhea drain your body of water and important salts. When you have a fever, your body loses extra water through perspiration. In fact, any disruption to the body's normal state, such as trauma, shock and emotional stress, can increase your risk for mild dehydration. Be sure to drink extra fluids during these times. If you're taking prescription medications, ask your pharmacist if they increase your need for fluid.

How Do You Know if You Are Dehydrated?

Unfortunately, there aren't any surveys that tell us how well Canadians are doing when it comes to drinking water. But if we are anything like our neighbors across the border, many of us may be walking around in a state of dehydration. Researchers have estimated that up to one-half of the American population is mildly dehydrated. Among women, the average intake for water and water-based beverages was less than five cups per day.[16]

Dehydration can be acute, from a bout of heavy exercise, or chronic, resulting from a poor fluid intake day after day. Dehydration is defined as losing at least 1 percent of your body weight from fluids. For a 170-pound man, that means losing almost 2 pounds because of fluid loss. It may not sound like a lot, but losing as little as 1 percent of your body weight can impair your physical performance.

Early symptoms of dehydration include headache, early fatigue during exercise, cramping, flushed skin, light-headedness, dizziness, dry mouth and eyes, nausea and loss of appetite. If dehydration progresses, you can experience difficulty swallowing, clumsiness, shriveled skin, painful urination, numb skin, muscle spasms and delirium.

The simplest way to tell if you're replacing the fluid that your body loses is to check the color and quantity of your urine. You're well hydrated if your urine is very pale yellow, pale yellow or straw colored. You're dehydrated if your urine is dark colored and scanty. If you're taking a multivitamin supplement, your urine may be bright, almost neon, yellow because of a B vitamin called riboflavin. In this case, it's better to judge your need for fluids by the quantity of urine you produce.

You cannot rely on thirst to tell you when you need to drink more. By the time your thirst mechanism has kicked in and you feel parched, your body is already dehydrated. Some people have a blunted thirst mechanism and are at higher risk for becoming dehydrated. Young children, the elderly, people who are sick and people who exercise in warm weather must pay particular attention to their daily fluid intake.

What Counts as Fluid?

Your daily fluids should come from *noncaffeinated, nonalcoholic* beverages, soups and foods. Consuming water, juice, milk, soup and foods containing a lot of water, such as fruit and vegetables, will help you meet your daily food requirements. (Notice that I have not added soft drinks to this list!) Believe it or not, solid foods can actually provide up to 4 cups (1 liter) of fluid each day. And the water generated by your body's metabolic reactions contributes another 1 cup (250 ml). The rest you have to make up by drinking fluids, preferably plain water.

Tap Water

Tap water is drawn from the surface water of lakes, reservoirs and rivers. To eliminate disease-causing bacteria and viruses, most drinking water supplies are disinfected with chlorine. Some cities use ozone to disinfect their water. But because ozone breaks down quickly, small amounts of chlorine must still be added. Our water supplies have been treated with chlorine for more than a century, ensuring our safety from the likes of cholera and typhoid fever.

All levels of government are involved in keeping our drinking water safe, yet there remain concerns over the potential harmful effects of chlorine by-products in tap water. When chlorine is added to water, it reacts with organic matter such as decaying leaves. This chemical reaction forms a group of chemicals known as disinfection by-products, the most common ones being trihalomethanes (e.g., chloroform). Recent scientific data suggest that these by-products might be harmful during pregnancy and increase the risk of bladder and colon cancer.

The provincial governments monitor the level of trihalomethanes in our drinking water in accordance with standards set by Health Canada. The maximum allowable limit for these chemicals in drinking water is associated with a very low cancer risk over the course of a lifetime.

Water Treatment Devices for Home Use

It's not possible to remove all disinfection by-products from your tap water, but you can minimize your exposure to them by using a water treatment device at home. Not only will these devices remove a fair amount of chlorine and its by-products from drinking water, but they will also improve the water's taste and smell. *Point-of-use* treatment devices are installed on taps and treat water used for cooking and drinking. Most of these products use an activated carbon filter, which is effective at removing organic chemicals and improving the taste of water. Other point-of-use devices use one of the following treatment methods:

- *Reverse osmosis* consists of a semi-permeable membrane, a water storage tank and a dispensing faucet. This system removes inorganic chemicals (minerals) and is often combined with an activated carbon filter to remove chlorine and organic compounds.

- *Activated aluminum oxide filters* are relatively new on the market. They remove heavy metals, especially lead.

- *Pitcher-type products* use activated carbon filters, and some may also include an ion-exchange resin to remove inorganic chemicals responsible for the "hardness" of water.

- *Distillation systems* reduce the levels of all chemicals, including minerals, in drinking water. These systems boil water in one compartment and condense the vapor and collect it in another. They are often combined with an activated carbon filter to remove chlorine by-products.

Point-of-entry devices are installed on your home's main water supply and treat all the water entering your house. The most widely used devices are water softeners and greensand filters. Water softeners reduce water hardness by removing minerals, but they don't get rid of organic chemicals like chlorine and chlorine by-products. Greensand filters are used to remove iron, manganese and hydrogen sulfide from water.

If you decide to buy a water treatment device, make sure you follow the manufacturer's instructions. Filters need to be replaced periodically to prevent the build-up of bacteria and organic chemicals. Make sure to store filtered water in the fridge to prevent bacterial contamination.

Bottled Water

More and more Canadians are drinking bottled water instead of filling a glass from their kitchen faucet. Many people think bottled water tastes better than tap water—it doesn't have that chlorine taste. Bottled water is also perceived as being safer and of higher quality than tap water. After the tragedy involving contaminated tap water that occurred in Walkerton, Ontario, in 2000, it's no wonder people reach for bottled water.

Technically, bottled water is simply water that's sold in sealed containers. Bottled water may be labeled as mineral water or spring water. If it's not, then it can be water from any source, including the municipal water supply, that's been treated to make it safe to drink. Treatments can include carbonation, ozonation, ultraviolet irradiation, and filtration to remove harmful bacteria. These bottled waters can be distilled to remove minerals, or they may simply be tap water bottled for sale. Here's a list of the main types of bottled waters available for sale in Canada:

- *Spring water* is bottled water that comes from a protected underground source. The water is collected at the spring or through a borehole tapping the underground formation that supplies the spring. This water contains less than 500 milligrams per liter of dissolved solids (e.g., minerals).

- *Mineral water* is the same as spring water, but it contains more than 500 milligrams per liter of dissolved solids. That means it has more calcium, magnesium and, in some cases, sodium. The ideal mineral water should be rich in magnesium and calcium and low in sodium.

- *Artesian water* is bottled water that is tapped from a well. (Unlike a spring, well water does not flow naturally to the surface of the earth.) This may also be called "artesian well water."

- *Purified water* is bottled water that has been produced by distillation, deionization or reverse osmosis. The water can come from a spring, a well or a public community water supply.

- *Carbonated bottled water* contains natural or added carbonation. This does not include soda water, seltzer water or tonic water—these are considered soft drinks.

Bottled water differs from tap water in two ways. One main difference is the source of water. While tap water comes from the surface of lakes and rivers, most bottled waters originate from a protected underground source. Another difference relates to how these waters are distributed. Municipal water is pumped through miles of piping, whereas bottled water is produced in food plants and packaged in clean, sealed containers. And finally, bottled waters do not contain any chlorine or chlorine by-products.

Besides its improved taste and lack of chlorine, some people drink bottled water for certain health reasons. People with weakened immune systems (the elderly and HIV/AIDS, cancer and transplant patients) are more vulnerable to bacterial infection and should drink bottled water that has been ozonated, carbonated or disinfected in some way.

Some people worry that bottled water can contain bacteria that cause illness. It's true that bacteria levels can increase quickly if bottled water is left at room temperature for six weeks. But since most bottled waters use some type of disinfection process, this is likely not an issue. Like most food products, bottled water contains very low levels of harmless bacteria.

What's most important is that you refrigerate an opened bottle of water in case any harmful bacteria have been introduced upon opening the bottle. Ideally, refrigerate your bottled water once you buy it, and if you can't, store it in a cool place away from heat, sunlight and household chemicals. When buying bottled water, check the bottling date and best-before date to ensure its freshness. Bottled water can be stored for up to two years.

Milk, Soy and Rice Beverages

These beverages are other ways to meet your fluid requirements and get important nutrients at the same time. As well as fluid, low-fat milk offers protein, calcium, vitamin D, B vitamins and zinc. If you are lactose intolerant, lactose-reduced brands are available in the dairy case of your grocery store. Soy and rice beverages are another option. If you use these products, make sure you buy a fortified brand. The label should state "enriched" or "high in calcium."

All these nutritious drinks go a long way to meeting your daily calcium needs. Just 1 cup (250 ml) of milk, fortified soy beverage or fortified rice beverage offers 300 milligrams of calcium, not to mention 100 international units (IU) of vitamin D.

Fruit and Vegetable Juices

Whether you make your own or buy them at the grocery store, fruit and vegetable juices are yet another hydration option. They provide your body with extra fluid, vitamins C and A and folate. Drink one cup of fruit or vegetable juice and you've knocked off a fluid serving and a fruit and vegetable serving at the same time! However, if you're watching your weight, I don't recommend that you fill up on fruit juice. Despite its nutritious qualities, the calories from natural fruit sugar can add up. You're better off hydrating your body with plain water.

When you buy fruit juice, choose unsweetened varieties that don't have added sugars. When it comes to buying juice boxes for your child's lunch, this can be a challenge. Avoid juice boxes labeled "fruit punch" or "fruit drink." These drinks supply sugar, water, artificial fruit flavoring and, sometimes, added vitamin C.

Limit the amount of unsweetened fruit juice your child drinks each day. Juices high in sorbitol and fructose can cause diarrhea in toddlers. Some studies show that toddlers who drink too much juice fail to thrive and have decreased heights for their age. That's because young children have small stomach capacities. Fruit juice fills them up quickly, leaving less room for more nutrient-dense foods. Getting too many calories from fruit juice can also lead to weight problems in older children.

Preschoolers should drink no more than 4 ounces (125 ml) of unsweetened juice per day and older kids no more than 6 to 8 ounces (175 to 250 ml). Encourage your children to drink water when they're thirsty. Offer them milk or a calcium-fortified soy or rice beverage at meals and snacks.

And let's not forget about vegetable juices—these have far less sugar than fruit juice and pack a lot of vitamin C. Tomato-based juices are also a great way to get a boost of lycopene, a natural plant chemical that appears to lower the risk of prostate cancer. In fact, I recommend that all my male clients skip the diet pop or coffee at lunch and drink a glass of tomato juice instead.

The only downside of bottled or canned vegetable juice is its salt content. For instance, a serving of commercial vegetable juice packs close to 700 milligrams of sodium—more than a quarter of the daily recommended intake. If you have high blood pressure or kidney problems, or if you tend to retain fluid, look for sodium-reduced brands.

What about Caffeinated Beverages?

I am sorry to be the bearer of bad news, but I don't count coffee as part of your daily fluid intake. This is because caffeine acts as a diuretic, causing your kidneys to excrete fluid. Caffeine can affect your health in other important ways, too. Here's what you should know.

Caffeine and Bone Health

Caffeine increases not only the amount of fluid you excrete in your urine but also the amount of calcium. It is estimated that every 6-ounce cup of coffee leaches 48 milligrams of calcium from your body. The negative effects of caffeine on bone density are likely most detrimental for women who are not getting enough calcium each day. One study found that 400 milligrams of caffeine (about three small cups of coffee) caused calcium loss in women whose daily diet had less than 600 milligrams of calcium.[17] Another study from Tufts University in Boston found that women getting more than 450 milligrams of caffeine and less than 800 milligrams of calcium had significantly lower bone densities than women who consumed the same amount of caffeine but got more than 800 milligrams of calcium.[18] Coffee drinking has also been associated with a greater risk of bone fracture in post-menopausal women.[19]

Caffeine and Sleep

It's true that caffeine stimulates your central nervous system. While one or two cups of coffee in the morning may give you that gentle lift you were hoping for, the fourth or fifth cup can overstimulate your system and cause insomnia. Studies have shown that as few as one or two cups of coffee in the morning can affect the quality of your sleep that night. Caffeine blocks the action of adenosine, a natural brain chemical that slows the body down. If you're having trouble getting to sleep, or you're waking up during the night, aim for no more than 200 milligrams of caffeine per day (see list below), or preferably none.

Caffeine and Blood Pressure

If you have high blood pressure, you might want to cut coffee out of your diet. Recent studies have found that small doses of caffeine can cause temporary stiffening of the blood vessel walls. Researchers from Greece found that people with mild hypertension who took a pill containing 250 milligrams of caffeine, equivalent to the amount in two to three cups of coffee, experienced a temporary increase in blood pressure and in the stiffness of the aorta, the main artery leaving the heart. In the other study, a small group of people with normal blood pressure who were given a pill containing as much caffeine as one cup of coffee also experienced a temporary increase in the stiffening of arterial walls.[20]

The scientists speculate that this caffeine-induced stiffness of the artery walls might make high blood pressure worse and may also increase the risk of heart attack or stroke in people with high blood pressure. Increased stiffness of the artery walls means that less oxygen is supplied to the heart.

Caffeine, Fertility and Pregnancy

If you're a woman who's trying to get pregnant, limit your caffeine intake to no more than 250 milligrams per day. Consuming more caffeine than this has been linked with decreased female fertility.[21]

The evidence for coffee's ill effect on pregnancy remains unclear. Some studies have linked coffee drinking with an increased risk of early and late miscarriage.[22-25] Despite these findings, other studies have found no harmful effects of moderate coffee drinking on pregnancy outcome. To play it safe, I recommend that women avoid coffee during pregnancy and minimize their intake of caffeine from other sources such as colas, tea and dark chocolate.

How Much Caffeine Is Too Much?

Health Canada recommends a daily upper limit of 450 milligrams of caffeine for healthy people. If you have osteoporosis or high blood pressure, try to consume less caffeine. If you are pregnant or are experiencing a bout of insomnia, eliminate caffeine from your diet. Use the list below to help you keep your caffeine intake to a minimum.

CAFFEINE CONTENT OF BEVERAGES AND MEDICATIONS

Beverage or Food	Caffeine (milligrams)
Coffee, filter drip, 8 fluid oz (235 ml)	110–180 mg
Coffee, filter, Starbucks, 8 fluid oz (235 ml)	200 mg
Coffee, instant, 8 fluid oz (235 ml)	80–120 mg
Coffee, decaffeinated, 8 fluid oz (235 ml)	4 mg
Espresso, 2 fluid oz (60 ml)	90–100 mg
Tea, black, 8 fluid oz (235 ml)	46 mg
Tea, green, 8 fluid oz (235 ml)	33 mg
Cola, 12 fluid oz (350 ml)	35 mg
Dark chocolate, 1 oz (30 g)	20 mg
Milk chocolate, 1 oz (30 g)	6 mg
Chocolate cake, 1 slice	20–30 mg
Medication (2 tablets)	
Anacin	64 mg
Excedrin	130 mg
Midol	64 mg

The Health Benefits of Drinking Tea

Although black and green teas both contain caffeine, they have considerably less than coffee. You would have to drink 12 cups of tea each day to reach Health Canada's upper caffeine limit of 450 milligrams! So I do consider drinking a cup of tea as contributing to your daily fluid requirement.

Black and green teas are also rich in antioxidants, compounds that can protect your health. The antioxidants in tea leaves belong to a special class of compounds called catechins. A study from Tufts University in Boston compared the antioxidant action of tea with that of 22 vegetables (including broccoli, onions, garlic, corn, carrots) and found that 7 ounces (230 ml) of green and black tea brewed for five minutes had the antioxidant power equivalent to the same amount of fruit and vegetable juice.[26]

By mopping up harmful free radical molecules in the body, catechins in tea may protect from heart disease. Dutch researchers recently found that compared with non–tea drinkers, older men and women who enjoyed more than 1 1/2 cups (375 ml) of tea per day were 43 percent less likely to suffer a heart attack.[27] Similar results were observed in an American study: compared with non–tea drinkers, those who enjoyed at least one cup a day had a 44 percent lower risk of heart attack.[28]

There is also a growing body of evidence to suggest that tea protects from certain cancers, including breast cancer. The famous Nurses' Health Study from Harvard University found that drinking four or more cups of tea per day (versus one or fewer) was associated with 30 percent lower risk of breast cancer.[29] Animal studies also show that clear tea, tea with milk and extracts of tea can suppress the growth of cancer cells.

There are three main types of tea: green tea, black tea and oolong. All three come from the same tea plant, but they are processed differently. Green tea leaves are steamed and dried immediately after picking. Black tea (e.g., orange pekoe) leaves are allowed to ferment or oxidize before steaming and drying, causing a darker color. Oolong teas have been partially fermented, giving them a flavor between that of green and black tea.

Herbal teas are *not* made from tea leaves but from grass and, as a result, don't have the antioxidant properties that green and black tea do. The following suggestions will help you incorporate tea into your daily diet:

- If you drink coffee in the afternoon, replace it with a cup of tea.

- Replace all regular and diet soft drinks with tea.

- Enjoy a cup of tea with your midday snack. Try different flavors—Earl Grey, orange spice, apricot and blackcurrant are just a few available.

- The next time you're at your local coffee shop, skip the coffee and order a chai latte instead. This is a spicy hot drink made from tea and Indian spices (but ask for just half the amount of syrup to cut down on the sugar!).

- Visit your local tea shop and buy small quantities of loose green teas to try at home. You'll find a large selection of Japanese and Chinese teas—plain green teas or blends with mango, mint, apricot, vanilla…the list goes on.

Recommendations for Alcohol

No doubt you've heard that a moderate intake of alcohol—one to two drinks per day—is good for your heart. Whether it's from wine, beer or liquor, alcohol raises the level of HDL (good) cholesterol and may reduce blood clotting. There's also evidence that antioxidant compounds in wine, especially red wine, may help prevent LDL cholesterol particles from sticking to your artery walls. Keep in mind, however, that the heart-healthy effects of alcohol are most apparent in people over the age of 50 and in those with more than one risk factor for heart disease.

When it comes to cancer prevention, alcohol is definitely not a friend. Based on a comprehensive review of study findings linking alcoholic beverages to the development of many types of cancer, experts recommend that we do not drink alcohol. Alcohol may make cells in the body more vulnerable to the effects of carcinogens or it may enhance the liver's processing of these substances. Alcohol may also inhibit the ability of cells to repair faulty genes. Finally, alcohol may increase levels of certain hormones that influence the development of cancer.

If you do drink alcohol, keep it to a minimum. Women should consume no more than seven alcoholic beverages per week, or no more than one per day. Men are advised to keep their intake to one or two per day or a weekly maximum of nine alcoholic drinks.

Reducing your alcohol intake will also help you sleep better, boost your energy level and lower elevated triglycerides (blood fat). If you're not in line with the recommendations above, make a plan to cut back. Replace alcoholic beverages with sparkling mineral water, Clamato or tomato juice or soda with a splash of cranberry juice. Eliminate alcoholic beverages on evenings you are not entertaining. Often that " before dinner drink" is a habit that can be easily broken. Instead, save your glass of wine or cocktail for weekends and social occasions.

10 TIPS
FOR BOOSTING YOUR FLUID INTAKE

1. Drink fluids with each meal and snack and throughout the day.

2. Keep a bottle of water on your desk at the office. The water cooler may be close at hand, but how many times do you actually get up to fill your glass?

3. When you travel—by car, plane or train—always carry a bottle of water with you.

4. If you don't like drinking plain water, add a splash of white grape juice, cranberry juice or blackcurrant concentrate. Or try a glass of sparkling mineral with a slice of lemon.

5. If you deprive your body of fluids because you don't like the taste of tap water, buy a water pitcher with an activated carbon filter. Always keep a full pitcher in the fridge. (And don't forget to replace the filter periodically!)

6. Use a water bottle when you exercise. Drink 4 to 8 ounces (125 to 250 ml) of fluid every 15 minutes.

7. If your workout lasts longer than one hour, hydrate with a sports drink such as Gatorade, All Sport or PowerAde.

8. If you drink fruit juice, choose only unsweetened varieties (no sugar added).

9. Keep your coffee intake to a minimum. Ideally, aim for no more than two cups per day. Replace unnecessary coffee (and soft drinks) with herbal tea, black tea or green tea. You get much less caffeine and, in the case of black and green teas, plenty of health-enhancing antioxidants.

10. Limit your intake of alcoholic beverages to no more than seven per week (women) or nine per week (men). When you do drink alcohol, drink a glass of water after each alcoholic beverage you've consumed. This will help you cut back on your alcohol consumption and help prevent dehydration.

ANSWERS TO LESLIE'S IQ QUIZ   FLUIDS

1. True. Turn to page 132 to learn how drinking water can lower your risk for disease.

2. d. The average man requires 12 cups (3 liters) of fluid each day.

3. b. Coffee contains caffeine, which increases the amount of fluid your body excretes.

4. True. Sports drinks contain carbohydrate and electrolytes, which can promote better hydration and enhance physical performance during exercise sessions that last longer than one hour.

5. b. No more than one (women) or two (men) drinks a day. A moderate pattern of drinking does not mean saving up your alcoholic beverages for one or two occasions!

Step 9

Control Your Weight

W eight control is top of mind for many of us these days. Just visit your local bookstore and you'll see what I mean. If you browse through the health section, you'll be hard-pressed not to find some new diet book promising fast weight loss and better health. Whether we want to look better, feel fitter or stay healthy as we age, many Canadians are turning to self-help books, commercial weight-loss programs and nutritionists for help.

It seems that this help could not come at a better time. When it comes to packing on the pounds, Canadians are breaking records. Obesity in Canada is said to be at epidemic levels, and steadily increasing. Since 1981, obesity has soared by 55 percent in men and by 33 percent in women. When researchers examined our bulging waistlines from 1981 to 1996, they found that nearly half of Canadian adults are now overweight, and among the overweight, a quarter are obese. It seems that men have more difficulty staying trim than women do: 57 percent of Canadian men are overweight compared with 35 percent of women.[1]

What's even more alarming is that Canadian kids, aged 7 to 13, are getting fatter and fatter. Over the past 20 years, the number of overweight boys and girls has skyrocketed. One-third of Canadian boys and one-quarter of girls and are now said to be overweight. What's worse is that obesity in boys has risen by 400 percent and in girls by 350 percent.[2,3] If left unmanaged, accumulating weight problems in our kids could spell trouble in their adult years. Overweight and obesity increase the risk for type 2 diabetes (non–insulin dependent), high blood pressure, heart disease, stroke and certain cancers, not to mention psychological problems such as low self-esteem and depression.

Do You Need to Lose Weight?

Body Mass Index (BMI)

After reading these depressing statistics, you may be wondering what the difference is between being overweight and being obese. You may even be wondering if your weight puts you into one of these categories. Researchers, nutritionists and doctors use the body mass index (BMI) to assess your weight. The BMI is a mathematical formula that takes into account your weight and your height and determines whether your weight is putting your health at risk. It's used for adults aged 20 to 65 years. The BMI is not to be used for children, teens, pregnant or breastfeeding women, endurance athletes or very muscular people.

Take a moment to calculate your BMI (you will need a calculator).

CALCULATE YOUR BODY MASS INDEX (BMI)

Determine your weight in kilograms (kg)
  (Divide your weight in pounds by 2.2) _____

Determine your height in centimeters (cm)
  (Multiply your height in inches by 2.54) _____

Determine your height in meters (m)
  (Divide your height in centimeters by 100) _____

Square your height in meters (m)
  (Multiply your height in meters by your height in meters) _____

Now, calculate your BMI
  (Divide your weight (in kg) by your height (in m^2)) _____

But what does your BMI mean? Long-term studies show that the overall risk of developing heart disease, diabetes and high blood pressure is generally related to your BMI as follows:

MAKING SENSE OF YOUR BMI

BMI under 20	You may be more likely to develop certain health problems due to malnutrition, including anemia, osteoporosis and irregular heart rhythms.
BMI 20–24.9	Healthy range. Your risk for health problems is very low.
BMI 25–29.9	Overweight. Having a BMI in this range is a call to action. Your risk for future health problems is increasing.
BMI 30 or higher	Obese. You are at high risk for weight-related health problems.

If your BMI is in the upper end of the healthy zone, say 24 or 25, you might still be carrying extra weight. While a little extra body fat is generally not thought to affect your long-term health, new research begs to differ. According to researchers from the Brigham and Women's Hospital and Harvard Medical School, adults who weigh in at the high end of the healthy range may be at increased risk of type 2 diabetes, gallstones, high blood pressure, heart disease, stroke, colon cancer and high cholesterol.

The investigators observed that men and women in the upper half of the healthy weight category (those whose BMIs were between 22 and 24.9) were significantly more likely than adults with lower BMIs to develop numerous health conditions. They also found, not surprisingly, that having a BMI over 25 was a health hazard. Overweight women with BMIs of 25 to 29.9 were significantly more likely to develop gallstones, high blood pressure, high cholesterol and heart disease. Overweight adults were more than three times as likely to develop type 2 diabetes than their thinner peers, while very obese adults whose BMIs were above 35 were about 20 times more likely than healthy-weight adults to develop diabetes.

People not traditionally considered to be overweight (those with BMIs of 22 to 24.9) were also at greater risk of developing at least one of the chronic diseases compared with their slimmer peers. Based on their findings, the scientists recommend that adults try to maintain a BMI of between 18.5 and 21.9.[4]

Waist–Hip Ratio

Nutritionists don't rely on BMI alone to paint your health picture. In addition to your BMI, your waist–hip ratio can be used to help predict your risk of death and illness. The waist–hip ratio measures where fat is accumulated on your body. It turns out that the circumference of your waist can say a lot about your chances of developing disease. Research has shown that people who develop excess weight in their abdomen, or those with an "apple-shaped" body, have a higher risk of certain health problems than do people who tend to gain weight in their buttocks and thighs, or those who have "pear-shaped" bodies. Statistics clearly show that being overweight, especially if excess weight is carried around the abdomen, significantly increases the risk of heart disease and stroke, type 2 diabetes, osteoarthritis, sleep apnea, gout and gallbladder disease.

In the Iowa Women's Health Study, general obesity did not accurately predict total death rates, but abdominal obesity, as measured by the waist–hip ratio, did. Women with a high waist–hip ratio who had a low BMI were much more likely to die from heart disease. (This does *not* mean that a high BMI is not hazardous.) A high waist–hip ratio was also linked to an increased incidence of bone fracture.[5]

CALCULATE YOUR WAIST–HIP RATIO

1. Using a tape measure, find the circumference of your waist at its narrowest point when your stomach is relaxed.   Waist = _____ inches

2. Next, measure the circumference of your hips at their widest point.   Hips = _____ inches

3. Now, divide your waist measurement by your hip measurement.   Waist ÷ hip = _____

A healthy waist–hip ratio is less than 0.9 for men and less than 0.8 for women. This means you're not carrying excess weight around your abdomen.

Body Fat Measurements

Yet another way to assess your health is to have your percentage of body fat calculated. Many health clubs and commercial weight-loss programs estimate body fat by using calipers on folds of skin or by sending harmless electrical impulses through the body, a technique known as bioelectrical impedance. Your body fat percentage can then be classified according to established ranges for optimal health and optimal physical fitness. Keep in mind, however, that this technique may yield inaccurate results if performed by untrained individuals.

PERCENTAGE BODY FAT STANDARDS FOR HEALTHY ADULTS

	Men	Women
At risk[a]	≤ 5%	≤ 8%
Below average health risk	6–14%	9–22%
Average health risk	15%	23%
Above average health risk	16–24%	24–31%
At risk[b]	≥ 25%	≥ 32%

a. At risk for health problems associated with malnutrition.
b. At risk for health problems associated with obesity.

Heyward, V.H., 1998. *Advanced Fitness Assessments & Exercise Prescription,* 3rd ed. (Champaign, IL: Human Kinetics), 146.

The Pitfalls of Fad Diets

There's no question that a poor diet and a sedentary lifestyle are to blame for the increasing girth of our nation. But the question remains: How should you eat to successfully lose weight? And by successfully, I mean keeping that weight off for good. Should you eat a high-carbohydrate, low-fat diet? Or should you try a high-protein, low-carb plan? Is it better to choose foods based on your blood type? And what about food-combining? I can understand if you're confused. There is no shortage of diet books, each one claiming its own special formula that guarantees a thinner, healthy body.

Many people reach for the latest fad diet to help them shed pounds. After all, most of us are looking for a quick fix—a fast track to weight loss that requires little effort. And each fad diet seems to make sense. That's the lure of fad diets: they all put forth some logical theory as to why their plan works. The fad diets blatantly contradict one another, and yet they all seem to work—up to a point. The truth is, any diet that cuts calories will help you shed pounds. Whether you cut calories by giving up bread and fruit, by not combining meat with starch or by feasting on only cabbage soup, you will lose weight. But here comes the most important question: Can fad diets help you keep those pounds off in a year from now? In five years from now?

Most people can lose weight; in fact, we are pretty darn good at it. But what we are not good at is maintaining a weight loss. Studies have shown that most people in weight-loss programs lose about 10 percent of their initial weight, but then regain most of this weight within three to five years.[6,7] Sound familiar to you? If so, let me make one point very clear. *People don't fail diets, diets fail people.* Here's why fad diets don't work in the long run:

- *Diets are hard to follow.* Diets rely on willpower to keep you on track, something that can be hard to maintain for an extended period, especially if the diet is too strict. As time goes on, people usually feel less inclined to restrict their food intake.

- *Diets make it harder and harder to lose weight.* Crash dieting and rapid weight loss make it harder to keep the weight off. When you put your body through a period of starvation by drastically cutting back on calories, you trigger hormonal changes in your body. Your body becomes more efficient at storing fat by slowing down your metabolism. When you inevitably go off the diet, your metabolism is still sluggish, and you'll end up gaining the weight back even faster.

- *Diets make you feel hungry and deprived.* A diet will not work long term if it leaves you hungry. Research shows that dieting creates overwhelming cravings for the very foods diets tell you to stay away from. When everyone else is enjoying birthday cake, it's hard not to tell yourself that you should have some too. Sooner or later, feelings of hunger and deprivation will break your willpower and you will eat to excess.

- *Diets lead to a sense of failure.* When you do decide to "break" your diet and indulge in that high-fat treat, guilt usually ensues. You tell yourself you've "blown it," so you may as well eat what you like for the rest of the day. After all, you can always start afresh on Monday. Diets create a sense of inadequacy in their followers; people end up viewing harmless lapses as signs of failure.

- *Diets don't address why you eat.* For some people, hunger has nothing to do with eating. Many people turn to food as a means of coping with stress, emotional upset and boredom. Diets don't solve the problem of emotional eating. If anything, they make people feel more depressed and irritable.

- *Diets don't change core habits.* To be successful at losing weight and keeping it off, you have to make permanent changes to your lifestyle. Diets tend to be short-term solutions. Most don't teach skills for shopping for and cooking with low-fat foods, effective exercise or dealing with cravings. And radical plans that cut out entire food groups are near impossible to stick to for life. Can you really see yourself giving up carbohydrates for the rest of your life? Do you think you'll be able to stick to your 1000-calorie plan long term?

- *Many diets are unhealthy over the long term.* Even if you are able to stick to a fad diet for a long period, this may not be a healthy option. High-protein, high-fat diets can raise your blood cholesterol and increase the risk of heart disease. Low-carb diets that promote ketosis (an abnormal body process that occurs because of lack of carbohydrate) cause fatigue, dehydration and constipation. Potential long-term side effects of ketosis include heart disease, bone loss and kidney damage. And many popular diets are very low in calcium and iron. Even the act of repeated dieting has been shown to cause bone loss in women.

Successful Weight Loss

Set a Realistic Goal

Now that you've assessed your weight by calculating your body mass index and waist–hip ratio, you may have decided it's time to lose some weight. But before you embark on your weight-loss plan, you need to have a goal to work toward. You'll recall from Step 1 that your goal needs to be realistic, attainable, measurable and time sensitive (see page 5).

There are many ways you can set a weight-loss goal, and it doesn't have to be tied to the bathroom scale. You might decide to use one of the following ways to measure success:

- *The size of your clothes.* You might decide that you'll be happier and healthier if you reduce one dress size or lose two notches on your belt.

- *Body measurements.* Looking at changes in the measurement of your waist, your hips and your chest is another way to go. If you are starting an exercise program to help you lose weight, I suggest you monitor your measurements monthly. When you build a little bit of muscle, the scale won't drop as quickly as you might like, but your body will show the results. If you work out at a gym, combine your body measurements with your results from a body fat test. Monitor changes to your percentage of body fat every three to six months.

- *Health measurements.* I have many clients who change their diet in order to lower their blood pressure or blood cholesterol level. When they change their diet to accomplish these goals, the weight automatically falls off. Watching these health readings change is a big motivator to keep on making healthy changes to their diets.

- *Fitness level.* You may just want to lose those 10 pounds to be more fit. If so, let measures of your physical fitness be your yardstick of success. Sports clubs perform comprehensive fitness tests on their members, and, for a small fee, nonmembers can usually access this service too. Your first fitness appraisal serves as your starting point. After three months of healthy eating and regular exercise, get retested to see the results. Chances are, you'll see the results in your workouts first. As you get fit, you'll be able to walk faster on the treadmill, lift more weight in the gym or do more push-ups at home.

While these are all great alternatives for goal setting, most of us still check in with the weigh scale. To decide on a realistic weight goal, consider your weight history for the past 10 to 15 years. If you want to weigh 120 pounds, but you haven't weighed that since you graduated from high school, this goal might be difficult to achieve. And depending on your lifestyle today, it may be unrealistic. Ask yourself, What was the lowest weight you were able to maintain for at least one year during your adult life? This might be more achievable.

I also recommend that you strive to achieve a 3- to 5-pound weight range, rather than setting one single number as your goal. Instead of saying, "I want to weigh 135 pounds," it is more realistic to set a goal to maintan a weight of 135 to 139 pounds; you need a little room for holidays and entertaining (after all, lapses are a part of life). This, then, is the weight range you plan to always stay within.

Size Up Your Portions

The next step is to know how much food to eat. Believe it or not, many of us don't know what a serving size is. We've become so used to eating super-sized portions that we've lost touch with what an appropriate serving is. I call this phenomenon "portion distortion." American researchers recently studied 16,000 people, looking at the amount of food they consumed at a single serving. Not surprisingly, the researchers found that oftentimes what Americans eat exceeds what a Food Guide serving size is. French fries are consumed at almost two and half servings at a time (ten French fries equals a Food Guide serving of potatoes). With baked potatoes, most people were eating two or three servings at one sitting. And with pasta, most people were getting about three or four servings at any one meal.[8]

Later in this chapter, I outline a plan for safe, steady weight loss. I tell you how many servings from each food group you should eat each day, and what constitutes a serving size. Once you know how much you should be eating, you can then use the meal plan and recipes presented later in the book.

I strongly recommend that you measure your foods when you begin a weight-loss program. Get to know what 1/2 cup (125 ml) of rice or 1 cup (250 ml) of pasta looks like on your plate. Learn to identify a 3-ounce (90-gram) piece of meat. Don't worry, you won't have to measure out portions of foods forever. But it's not a bad idea to refresh your memory every once in a while. Portion sizes can easily creep back to large sizes.

A few tricks of the trade will help you practice portion-size self-defense:

- *Buy small packages of food.* Bonus-size boxes of cookies, crackers, pretzels and potato chips may be a deal at Costco, but they encourage overeating. If you resist the "more for less" thinking, you'll end up eating less.

- *Serve smaller portions at meal time.* If you sit down to a plate overflowing with food, the chances are good that you'll finish it all. Most of us have a tendency to clear our plates, a habit that's rooted in childhood. If you don't serve yourself at dinner, instruct whoever does to put less food on your plate.

- *Use smaller plates.* A few of my clients find this trick really works. Instead of filling a dinner plate with food, they serve less food on a luncheon-sized plate. And guess what? The plate looks full!

- *Plate your snacks.* Never, ever, snack out of the bag. When you reach your hand into that bag of mini rice cakes or pretzels rather than into a small bowl, you never really get a sense of how much you're eating—it just doesn't register. You end up eating far more than you should. Whether your snack is crackers and low-fat cheese, popcorn or apple slices, first measure out your portion and put it on a plate. And then pay attention to the fact that you're eating!

Get in Touch with Hunger and Satiety

Ideally, you should eat when you feel hungry, when your stomach growls, telling you it needs food. Stomach hunger should not be confused with mouth hunger, the desire for food because it will taste good. Eating in response to how good food looks or smells has to do with your appetite, not your hunger.

Some of my clients have reported never feeling hungry during the day. Yet they eat anyway, either because it was time to eat or because the food was there. If you're out of touch with how hunger feels to you, eat according to schedule for the next two weeks. Eat breakfast, lunch and dinner at approximately the same time each day. You'll find that you will start to feel hungry before your meals.

Pay attention to your hunger signals, and let them dictate how much you eat. When you sit down to a meal, rate your hunger on a scale of one to ten, one being so full you couldn't possibly eat and ten being ravenously hungry. Halfway through your meal, rate your hunger again. Let your score tell you whether it's time to stop eating.

Learning to stop eating when you feel full can also help you eat less. Feeling full does not mean feeling "stuffed." Satiety means that you no longer feel hungry and, in fact, you feel good. Keep in mind that it doesn't take much to feel satisfied. Sometimes all you need is a small snack to keep hunger at bay.

Recognize What Causes You to Overeat

You may eat not because you are hungry, and you may not stop eating when you're satisfied. Some people eat because they feel sad, angry or bored. Others eat because others around them are eating. And still others reach for the wrong foods simply because those foods are in front of them. It is not within the scope of this book to deal with the psychology of eating. However, an important first step is recognizing that these triggers may be part of the reason you struggle with your weight. Here's a look at some common triggers:

If negative emotions trigger overeating, I recommend that you seek counseling to help you work through these issues before you embark on a weight-loss program.

If you succumb to unhealthy foods because they surround you, get rid of them. There's a lot to the saying "out of sight, out of mind." I have many clients who keep a bowl of fresh fruit front and center at home and at the office.

If you mindlessly eat because you're not paying attention, take charge! Become aware of the foods you put in your mouth by eating without distractions. Turn off the television, put down the newspaper and sit down to eat. Watch as the food leaves your plate on its way to your mouth. How many times have you eaten while distracted, only to look down at your empty plate unaware that you had finished your meal? Make sure you savor every mouthful. You'll feel more satisfied after a meal and won't be inclined to search the cupboards for that elusive something you still crave.

Recently, a stay-at-home mom who was having a real battle losing her weight consulted me. She constantly munched throughout the day, partly because she was bored and partly because food was always within reach. I asked her to keep a notepad on the kitchen counter and record each time she reached for a snack. The first day she kept track, she was shocked to learn that she mindlessly munched 12 times! This awareness was all it took for her to cut out the unnecessary eating. She allowed herself only one planned snack between meals and was able to return within four months to her pre-pregnancy weight.

If socializing triggers overeating, make a plan. People tend to eat more in social settings. Eat a snack before you leave home so you don't arrive at the event famished. Curb your alcohol intake, since alcohol, especially on an empty stomach, can cause food cravings. Plan to sit beside someone you can talk to during the meal. The more talking you do, the less you'll eat. And here's a word of advice to women: pay attention to the amount of food you eat compared with your spouse. Often I see female clients who, over time, end up eating the same portion sizes as their partners.

How Much Should You Eat to Lose Weight?

The following meal plans should help you kick-start the weight-loss process. I have divided your food intake into three meals and two snacks. If you're very active, choose the higher number of servings when given a range. If you're sedentary, choose the lower number.

A WEIGHT-LOSS PLAN FOR WOMEN (1200–1400 CALORIES)

Breakfast:

Protein servings: 1 (optional)

Starchy food servings: 1

Fruit servings: 1

Milk servings: 1

Water: 2 cups (500 ml)

Lunch:

Protein servings: 2 or 3

Starchy food servings: 2

Vegetable servings: 1 or 2

Fat servings: 2

Water: 2 cups (500 ml)

Dinner:

Protein servings: 3 to 5

Starchy food servings: 0 to 2**

Vegetable servings: 2 to 3

Fat servings: 1 to 2

Water: 2 cups (500 ml)

Morning Snack:*

Fruit servings: 1 OR

Milk servings: 1

Water: 1–2 cups (250–500 ml)

Afternoon Snack:*

Fruit servings: 1 AND

Milk servings: 1

Water: 2 cups (500 ml)

* Choose the larger snack if your meals are longer than five hours apart. For example, if you eat breakfast at 6 a.m. and don't sit down to lunch until 1 p.m., have the bigger snack.

** If you skip the starch, choose the higher protein serving.

A WEIGHT-LOSS PLAN FOR MEN (1600–1800 CALORIES)

Breakfast:

Protein servings: 1 (optional)

Starchy food servings: 2

Fruit servings: 1 or 2

Milk servings: 1

Water: 2 cups (500 ml)

Morning Snack:*

Fruit servings: 1 OR

Milk servings: 1

Water: 1–2 cups (250–500 ml)

Lunch:

Protein servings: 4

Starchy food servings: 2 or 3

Vegetable servings: 1 or 2

Fat servings: 2

Water: 2 cups (500 ml)

Afternoon Snack:*

Fruit servings: 1 AND

Milk servings: 1

Water: 2 cups (500 ml)

Dinner:

Protein servings: 4 to 6

Starchy food servings: 0 to 3**

Vegetable servings: 2 to 4

Fat servings: 2

Water: 2 cups (500 ml)

* Choose the larger snack if your meals are longer than five hours apart. For example, if you eat breakfast at 6 a.m. and don't sit down to lunch until 1 p.m., have the bigger snack.

** If you skip the starch, choose the higher protein serving.

Recommended Supplements:

- Multivitamin/mineral once daily
- Calcium citrate, 300 milligrams with vitamin D, once or twice daily. (To determine if you need a calcium supplement, see page 106, Chapter 6.)

A Guide to Serving Sizes

Wondering what one serving is? Here's a selected list to help you determine your daily portions:*

SERVING SIZES OF FOODS

Food Group	One Serving Equals...
Protein Foods	
Fish, lean meat, poultry, cooked	1 oz (30 g)
Egg, whole	1
Egg whites	2
Legumes (beans, chickpeas, lentils)	1/3 cup (75 ml)
Soy nuts, roasted	2 tbsp (25 ml)
Tempeh	1/4 cup (50 ml)
Tofu, firm	1/3 cup (75 ml)
Texturized vegetable protein	1/3 cup (75 ml)
Veggie dog, small	1
Veggie burger	1/2

Food Group	One Serving Equals...
Starchy Foods (choose whole grain!)	
Whole-grain bread	1 slice
Bagel	1/4
Roll, large	1/2
Pita pocket	1/2
Tortilla, 6"	1
Crackers, soda	6
Cereal, dry flake	3/4 cup (175 ml)
Cereal, 100% bran	1/2 cup (125 ml)
Cereal, low-fat granola	1/3 cup (75 ml)
Cereal, hot, cooked	1/2 cup (125 ml)

SERVING SIZES OF FOODS (continued)

Food Group	One Serving Equals...
Starchy Foods (continued)	
Corn	1/2 cup (125 ml)
Corn on the cob	1/2
Grains, cooked	1/2 cup (125 ml)
Pasta, cooked	1/2 cup (125 ml)
Popcorn, plain	3 cups (750 ml)
Potato	1/2 cup (125 ml)
Rice, cooked	1/3 cup (75 ml)
Fruits and Vegetables	
Vegetables, raw or cooked	1/2 cup (125 ml)
Vegetables, leafy green	1 cup (250 ml)
Fruit, whole	1
Fruit, small (plums, apricots)	4
Fruit, cut up	1 cup (250 ml)
Berries	1 cup (250 ml)
Juice, unsweetened	1/2 to 3/4 cup (125 to 175 ml)

Food Group	One Serving Equals...
Milk and Alternatives	
Milk, 1% MF (milk fat) or skim	1 cup (250 ml)
Yogurt, 1% MF or less	3/4 cup (175 ml)
Cheese, 20% MF or less	1 1/2 oz (45 g)
Rice beverage, fortified	1 cup (250 ml)
Soy beverage, fortified	1 cup (250 ml)
Fats and Oils	
Butter, margarine, mayonnaise	1 tsp (5 ml)
Nuts, seeds	1 tbsp (15 ml)
Peanut and nut butters	1 1/2 tsp (7 ml)
Salad dressing	2 tsp (10 ml)
Vegetable oil	1 tsp (5 ml)

*All serving sizes are based on measures *after* cooking.

Choosing a Weight–Loss Program

Perhaps you've decided you can't carry out a weight-loss plan on your own. There's absolutely nothing wrong with that. The majority of clients who come to see me about weight loss know what they should be doing—or not doing—but they enlist my support because they need a kick in the butt to get going. Many people benefit from the structure and support that formal weight-loss programs offer.

Shop around to find a program that matches your needs and personality. Ask yourself these questions:

1. Would I benefit from the support of a group or would I be better off with one-on-one attention? (A program like Weight Watchers is famous for its group approach. If you want personalized attention and a custom-made meal plan, you're better off seeking the help of a registered dietitian in private practice. To find a dietitian in your community, log on to www.dietitians.ca.)

2. Do I need a highly structured diet or just some general strategies?

3. Do I need to be accountable (e.g., do I need to be weighed regularly or have food records monitored)?

4. Do I need a program that offers both nutrition and exercise advice?

5. Do I need a program that incorporates behavioral therapy or stress management techniques?

Other questions to ask include:

- Does the program teach lifelong healthy eating skills?

- Does the program exclude any food group?

- Does the program rely on specially purchased foods?

- Does the program promote a safe loss of 1 to 2 pounds (0.5 to 1 kilogram) per week?

- Does the program emphasize weight maintenance?

- How much does the program cost?

Answering these questions will help you determine what you need most in order to be successful. Your responses will narrow your search for a program that best suits your needs. However, keep in mind that the perfect weight-loss program does not exist. Most programs do a good job at providing some of the components necessary for weight loss but lack expertise in other areas. Inevitably, you'll have to do some work on your own.

Smart Strategies to Help You *Keep* the Weight Off

Over the past 14 years, I have helped scores of people successfully lose weight. I have done so by teaching people *what to eat* and *how to eat*—skills we are never taught in school. My philosophy is very straightforward: *everything you do to lose weight must be everything you do to keep it off.* So there is no sense in cutting out your favorite food or exercising fanatically seven days per week. It just won't stick.

Clients often ask me what they will do differently once they reach their weight goal. My answer often surprises them: nothing. The only thing (besides pregnancy) that will dictate how much food healthy people can eat is their level of physical activity. If a client's exercise level increases, I will revise that client's food plan by increasing the food intake to help him or her maintain body weight. If exercise goes out the window for a time due to a busy work schedule or injury, the food plan is revised in the opposite direction. Adjusting food intake to match activity level is not an automatic reaction for most people. But it's an important skill you need to learn in order to successfully manage your weight over the long haul.

But there's more to weight-loss success. By studying the habits of successful dieters, researchers have now learned key strategies that help keep the weight off. The National Weight Control Registry is a database of over 2000 people from all over the United States who have successfully maintained a 30-pound weight loss for at least one year.[9,10] The average registrant has lost about 60 pounds and has kept it off for about five years. What's more, about half these people lost weight on their own; that is, without the help of any type of formal program. What makes these people so successful? Here's a look (while these strategies may not sound sexy, they really work!):

1. Eat a high-carbohydrate, low-fat diet Most people in the registry lost weight and kept it off by following the very eating principles I've discussed throughout this book. The average registrant consumes 1400 calories per day, with 24 percent of those calories coming from fat. Successful weight-loss maintainers say they don't use fat as a seasoning, avoid frying foods and substitute low-fat for high-fat foods. Whole grains, legumes, fruit, vegetables and low-fat dairy products make up the bulk of their diets.

2. Keep high-fat foods out of the house This sounds so simple, yet that's what 85 percent of weight-loss registrants say they do to help them stick with their low-fat diet. Almost all say that, to stay on track, they stock their kitchen with plenty of healthy foods, and about one-third say they eat in restaurants less often.

3. Eat five times per day Instead of devouring three big meals, successful dieters eat more often. Spreading out their food keeps their stomach always partly full and prevents overeating at any one time. Plan to eat three meals plus two snacks, or divide your calories evenly into five smaller meals eaten every three to four hours. (See Chapter 7 for more on this technique.)

4. Don't deny yourself People in the National Weight Control Registry say they don't give up their favorite foods. They continue to enjoy them, but perhaps just not as often as they did when they were overweight.

5. Keep a food diary One-half of all successful weight-loss participants say they record their daily food intake and workouts. Doing so provides focus and motivation. You are forced to see, in black and white, the foods you are eating and the foods you are not eating. It will make you think twice about eating that second helping at dinner or that handful of potato chips while watching television.

I encourage you to record your food intake for the next seven days. Each day, take a moment to assess it. What do you notice? No fruit? No vegetables? No breakfast? Too many sweets? Make a plan for change. Each week, set one new goal for changing your diet and write down exactly what you plan to change. Think back to the discussion of goal-setting in

Step 1, and be specific in your goals. It's not enough to say that you will eat less fat. How will you do this? By replacing the cream in your coffee with milk, by skipping the butter on your vegetables or by replacing those afternoon cookies with a low-fat yogurt and fruit?

6. Weigh yourself often Almost 80 percent of the registrants weigh themselves on a regular basis, even after six years of maintaining their loss. Monitoring your progress provides motivation and impetus to keep on going. It also allows you to nip small weight gains in the bud. Knowing that you've gotten off track and probably put on a few pounds is one thing, but getting on the scale and staring at the result of your indulgences is quite another. You'll be much more likely to do something about it before those 5 pounds turn into 10!

7. Learn about nutrition Seventy-five percent of successful dieters say they buy books and magazines related to nutrition and exercise, and they continue to do so years after they have lost the weight. When you create an environment that fosters healthy eating, you're more likely to stay on track and make these changes permanent.

8. Get planned exercise We'll talk more about this strategy in Step 10. But suffice it to say that nine out of ten registrants report getting one hour of scheduled exercise each day. Many participants get their calorie burn from brisk walking. Exercise makes you feel good about yourself, making you want to eat healthy. And there's an added bonus—you can enjoy more food if you work out regularly!

9. Sneak in activity Another common denominator among weight-loss registrants was that they add little bits of activity into their daily routine. Small things such as taking the stairs instead of the escalator, parking at the end of the lot and getting off the bus a few stops early add up.

10. Expect failure, but keep on trying People who are successful at losing weight don't expect to be perfect. They consider lapses as momentary setbacks, not the ruin of all their hard work. Whether you've had a busy social schedule or you've just returned from a food-laden vacation, you're bound to put on a few pounds. As I mentioned above, the key to long-term weight maintenance is dealing with small weight gains when they occur. You'll be amazed at how easy it is to return to your usual healthy routine by telling yourself that you're human and it's okay to have slipped a little. Go back now and read my "relapse prevention" tips on page 10, Step 1.

10 TIPS
FOR MANAGING YOUR WEIGHT

1. Using the instructions on page 149, calculate your body mass index and waist–hip ratio. What do these numbers say about your weight? Do you need to lose?

2. Put all fad-diet books away. This time you're going to do it right. Let's make this your last weight-loss attempt.

3. Keep a food diary for one week. Study it every day. Pay attention to what you are eating, what you are not eating enough of and how often you are eating. You might also want to record why you are eating. Did you eat because you were hungry? Upset? Bored?

4. Reread Step 1, Get Ready to Change Your Diet Permanently. Then take a few minutes to write down a realistic weight-loss goal. Remember, your goal does not have to relate to the weigh scale. Write down how you will measure your progress and when you plan to attain this goal.

5. Reread Step 3, Choose the Right Carbohydrates. Make sure most of your meals contain whole-grain starches. Choose low glycemic carbohydrates for snacks.

6. Plan to eat four or five times per day (while you're at it, reread Step 7, Eat More Often). If you choose to follow the plan I have provided in this chapter, your schedule is already mapped out for you.

7. Monitor your progress regularly—by keeping food records, taking your measurements or weighing yourself. To maintain your weight loss, weigh yourself weekly to nip small weight gains in the bud.

8. Get to know portion sizes. For one week, measure out the food you eat. Compare your portion with the amounts listed in the serving-size table on page 157. When you notice that your portion sizes are starting to grow, bring back the measuring cup.

9. Assess your level of hunger before and halfway through each meal. Learn to stop eating when you're satisfied, not stuffed.

10. Now, start to think about getting some exercise. Read Step 10, Be Active Every Day, to help you do this.

ANSWERS TO LESLIE'S IQ QUIZ   WEIGHT LOSS AND MAINTENANCE

1. True. Read page 151 to learn how crash diets can slow down your metabolism.

2. c. A whopping 50 percent of Canadians are now overweight.

3. True. Apple-shaped people who carry more fat around their abdomen have a much higher risk of health problems compared with their pear-shaped peers.

4. d. 1/2 cup cooked pasta is considered one grain serving. All the others are considered two servings.

5. True. The National Weight Control Registry found that among people who maintained a 60-pound (27-kg) weight loss for one year or longer, most did so by following a high-carb, low-fat diet.

Step 10

Be Active Every Day

LESLIE'S PHYSICAL ACTIVITY IQ QUIZ   EXERCISE

1. True or false? Being sedentary is as dangerous to your health as cigarette smoking.

2. How many Canadians are not active enough to achieve health benefits?
    a. none
    b. one-third
    c. two-thirds
    d. all

3. True or false? Weight training will give women bulky muscles.

4. How much physical activity do experts say it takes to stay healthy?
    a. 10 minutes, once a day
    b. 15 minutes of vigorous activity, two times per week
    c. 30 minutes, three times per week
    d. 60 minutes of light activity accumulated during the day

5. True or false? If you want to lose body fat, it's best to do cardiovascular exercise at a slow pace.

I couldn't possibly write a book about healthy eating without including a chapter on exercise—the two go hand in hand. Adding physical activity to your life can go a long way to keeping you lean and healthy. The good news is that you don't have to spend hours sweating in the gym to reap the health benefits of exercise. In fact, you don't even have to join a gym! If the health club scene intimidates you, you can whip your body into shape at home, at work, at school and on the road. Believe it or not, regular exercise can be fun, invigorating and very rewarding.

If you're among the 63 percent of Canadians who don't get enough exercise, it's time to get your body moving. Exercise can make you look better, feel better and move better as you age. This isn't exactly news. As far back as 400 B.C., the Greek physician Hippocrates professed the benefits of healthy eating and exercise. But we've come a long way since then. Today, we know that being active does a whole lot more than energize your body. A growing body of evidence shows that exercise can prevent, and may even help treat, a wide range of health problems.

Reasons to Exercise

Control Your Weight

For many of us, a trip to the gym or a power walk at lunch is a way of controlling our weight. Whether we want to drop weight or just keep it off, pounding the pavement (or treadmill) helps burn calories and body fat. To lose weight you must expend more calories than you consume. And there's no better way to an energy deficit than burning calories through regular exercise. Exercise uses up calories while you do it and increases your resting metabolic rate, the speed at which your body burns calories at rest. This means your body is burning more calories following exercise than it was before you started to work out.

Exercise helps you lose body fat while maintaining the amount of muscle you have. If you lose muscle (as you do on many crash diets), your metabolism will slow down. When the diet is over and you return to your old eating habits, your slower metabolism makes it very easy to regain the weight. You stand a much better chance of preserving your muscle and your metabolism if you add exercise to the mix (and drop the crash diet!).

The bottom line is clear: exercise helps people lose weight, and is a key strategy in maintaining a weight loss. (I'll tell you what kind of exercise works best later on in this chapter.)

Improve Your Mood

Most of us know how good it feels when we're finished a workout. Not only do you feel more energetic, but there's also a huge sense of accomplishment. By boosting your self-esteem and self-confidence, exercise can make a big impact on your mood. The psychological benefits of exercise have been documented in many studies. People who exercise regularly are less likely to experience depression, anger, distrust and stress.

Physical activity is becoming regarded as a feasible treatment for patients with clinical depression and anxiety disorders. Researchers have found that regular exercise, such as walking on a treadmill for 30 minutes a day, can produce substantial mood enhancement in a short period.[1,2] Some studies even find that the therapeutic effects of exercise on mood disorders are as beneficial as meditation and relaxation.

Boost Immunity

If you're looking for a way to prevent the common cold, try regular exercise. A handful of studies show that fit people get sick less often.[3,4] One study even found that overweight women who walked for 45 minutes five days a week for 12 weeks suffered half as many cold and flu symptoms as people who didn't exercise.[5]

When you exercise, your increased circulation transports beneficial immune compounds throughout your body, boosting protection from cold and flu viruses. Exercise can increase the number, activity and circulation of immune cells during exercise and for 90 minutes afterward. Physical activity may also keep the bugs at bay through its stress-relieving effects. Ongoing stress is known to impair the body's immune function, and many studies show that exercise reduces stress and improves mood.

New research suggests that there's no need to let a runny nose or scratchy throat prevent you from working out. In fact, moderate activity may even be beneficial when you have a head cold. But if you have a fever, muscle aches or cough, take a break and rest until you feel better.

Reduce Your Risk of Diabetes

Physical activity can help people with type 2 diabetes manage their condition, by itself and when combined with diet and medication. Exercise influences several aspects of diabetes. It enhances the action of insulin and makes your cells more sensitive to its effects. Mild to moderate exercise also lowers blood sugar levels, and this effect continues for a period of time after you stop exercising.

Perhaps you don't have type 2 diabetes. Maybe you're at risk because you're overweight or the disease runs in your family. Did you know that exercise can prevent type 2 diabetes from developing in the first place? One of the most encouraging studies was a six-year trial of diabetes prevention from China. In the study, 577 people with glucose intolerance (a pre-diabetes condition) followed one of four programs: exercise only, diet only, diet and exercise, or nothing (the control group). The people in the exercise group were told to increase their activity level each day by an amount comparable to a 20-minute brisk walk. After six years of treatment, the incidence of type 2 diabetes was 68 percent in the control group, but much lower in the other groups: 44 percent in the diet-only group, 41 percent in the exercise-only group and 46 percent in the diet-plus-exercise group.[6]

Harvard researchers have also learned that exercise is a powerful way to lower the odds of getting diabetes. Women who engaged in regular vigorous exercise, including fast walking, were 42 percent less likely to have type 2 diabetes.[7] Among men, exercising once a week was linked with a 36 percent lower risk of the disease. And the risk decreased further as exercise frequency increased.[8]

Ward off Heart Disease

There's plenty of good evidence to show that regular exercise prevents the development of coronary heart disease. And you don't have to take up jogging to keep your heart in shape; walking is just as beneficial. The Nurses' Health Study from Harvard University found that women who walked briskly for at least three hours per week had a much lower risk of heart disease and stroke compared with women who walked the least.[9,10] If you already have heart disease, being physically active can lower your risk of suffering a second heart attack. Being sedentary is considered to be an independent risk factor for heart disease. That means that inactivity, just like cigarette smoking, increases your risk of suffering a heart attack or stroke.

Exercise training helps your heart function better. As you get fit, your heart requires less oxygen to perform the same amount of work. And it becomes more effective at pumping oxygen-rich blood to your muscles. But you have to exercise *regularly* to maintain these effects. Regular exercise can protect from heart disease in other ways, too. It can lower elevated blood triglycerides (blood fats), raise your HDL (good) cholesterol and lower blood pressure. Finally, exercise can keep your heart healthy by controlling obesity and diabetes.

Prevent Cancer

A number of studies find that regular exercise lowers the risk of cancer, especially colon cancer.[11-13] In fact, it's been estimated that 13 percent of colon cancer cases can be blamed on a sedentary lifestyle. One study from the University of Utah revealed that men and women whose lifestyle was characterized by high levels of physical activity were 58 percent less likely to get colon cancer.

Being more active may also help prevent breast cancer, although its protective effects may be more modest. The Nurses' Health Study discovered that women who participated in moderate or vigorous exercise for seven or more hours per week (e.g., an hour each day) were less likely to develop breast cancer than their inactive peers.[14]

Exercise may protect from cancer in a number of ways. For starters, it boosts your immune system, helping your body defend itself from disease. Exercise also speeds the passage of waste through your intestinal tract. This means there's less time for cancer-causing substances to make contact with the walls of the colon. Regular activity can also lower the level of certain hormones that may be linked with cancer. And let's not forget that exercise can prevent overweight, a risk factor for certain cancers.

Slow Down Bone Loss

We know that children who spend the greatest amount of time being physically active have stronger bones than those who are sedentary. But the effects of exercise on bone strength don't stop once you reach adulthood. Participating in weight-bearing activities such as brisk walking or stair climbing stimulates bones to increase in strength and density during the pre- and postmenopausal years too.[15] One recent study found that postmenopausal women who worked out three times a week for nine months actually increased their bone mass by 5.2 percent.[16]

Strength training exercises such as lifting weights can also delay bone loss in women. Researchers from Ohio State University learned that, compared with nonexercising women, women who worked out with weights for one hour three times a week gained 1.6 percent bone mass in their spine. The nonexercisers actually lost 3.6 percent of their bone![17]

If you have osteoporosis, a safe exercise program can help you slow bone loss, improve posture and balance and build muscle strength and tone. All these benefits can reduce your risk for falling and fracturing a bone.

Breaking Down Barriers to Exercise

Perhaps by now you're thinking, "I really should get moving … it's time to do something active." And you know what? *You can.* The toughest part is just getting started. How many times in the past have you committed to getting fit only to get bogged down with reasons why you can't exercise? "I don't have time … the weather's bad … business travel gets in the way … I don't like exercise … I'm too tired at the end of the day …" At one time or another, we've all come up with plenty of reasons why not to exercise.

Before those same old excuses prevent you from tying up your laces, let's take a moment to overcome some common obstacles. If you understand what your barriers are (or will be), you'll be in a better position to work through them and stick with your exercise program.

"I Don't Have Time"

No time to exercise? It's true that making time for exercise can be challenging. Work and family demands often leave little time or energy for getting to the gym or going for a walk. One strategy is to schedule exercise in your calendar like any other appointment. If it's written down for a planned time, your workout becomes more important. You'll regard it as a meeting that you must attend.

While lack of time is a legitimate obstacle for many busy people, it's often used to explain away other barriers, like not believing in your ability or feeling self-conscious in workout clothes. If you think that time really is the issue, take a few minutes to chart your down time each day. How many hours do you spend watching television or surfing the Internet? You might be surprised to learn how much time you spend being sedentary each day. Logging your daily activities could open your eyes to possible time slots for exercise.

If you really don't have time for a formal workout, increase your daily physical activity in any way you can—take the stairs at work instead of the elevator or park at the far end of the parking lot. And remember that small bouts of exercise interspersed throughout the day can quickly add up to 60 minutes' worth of exercise. If you only have time to sneak in a 15-minute walk on your lunch break and another one after dinner, that's fine. At least you're getting out there. If exercising intermittently throughout the day makes it easier for you to stick with it, then all the better.

I am often told by clients who stray from their exercise routines that there was "no time to make it to the gym." They just weren't able to make time for their usual 60-minute program. I am quick to remind these clients that a 20-minute workout is better than no workout at all. You'll release stress, burn calories and feel good that you did it, even if it was a downsized workout. And most importantly, your mindset will still be one of working out regularly. If you stop exercising until your calendar becomes less hectic, it will be more difficult to get back at it.

"I Need to Lose Weight First"

Concerns about appearance keep some people from exercising, especially those who think of themselves as sedentary. They feel self-conscious about their bodies and feel embarrassed in exercise clothes. "If I just lose a little weight first," they say, "I'll feel more comfortable going to the gym."

The irony is that the shape of your body will change faster if you exercise. If the thought of exercising with other people intimidates you, start exercising in the privacy of your home. Use exercise videos, a stationary bike or a treadmill. Or check out the exercise classes at your local community center. More and more facilities offer classes that cater to large-size people. There are also water aerobic classes that are easier on your knees and back.

"Exercising Is Boring"

Many people drop out of a fitness program because of boredom. Exercise can easily become monotonous because the activities are often continuous and repetitive. When you're bored, your mind wanders and you become less focused on what you're doing. You end up putting less effort into your workout and won't get the results you want. And if exercise feels more like drudgery than fun, chances are you won't be doing it for long.

Variety is a key ingredient in any exercise program. Combat boredom by trying different types of exercise classes or moving from a StairMaster to an Elliptical Trainer. If you fight with your brain to stay on the treadmill for 40 minutes, break up your routine. Run for 20 minutes, then try another machine for the remaining 20 minutes. Perhaps you need to take a break from the gym and join a sports team. New exercises not only engage your mind, but also work different muscles and challenge your body.

"I Don't Like Exercising"

Let's face it, some people just can't stand the thought of participating in any type of formal exercise. Fortunately there is an option for those of you who fall into this category. I call it the "lifestyle approach" to exercise. *Your goal is to accumulate 30 minutes of moderate physical activity during the course of the day.* Instead of going for a run or taking an aerobics class, you build activity into your daily routine. Short bouts of exercise accumulate and make a difference to your health and your waistline. Here are some ways to activate your day:

- Walk whenever you can, get off the bus early, park at the back of the lot, walk partway to work, take the dog for an extra walk and so on.

- Instead of driving to a friend's house, ride your bicycle.

- Take the stairs instead of the escalator at the shopping mall.

- Avoid using walking sidewalks at airports (unless you're late for a flight!).

- Use the stairs instead of the elevator, even if it's for only partway.

- Walk at lunch hour with coworkers or friends.

- Walk to visit a coworker instead of sending an e-mail.

- Play actively with your kids.

- Get up off the couch and stretch for a few minutes each hour.

- Ride a stationary bicycle while watching TV.

Get Motivated and Stay Motivated

If you want to get motivated and stay motivated, here are a few strategies to consider.

Set Realistic Goals

If you think back to Step 1, Get Ready to Change Your Diet Permanently, you'll recall I talked a lot about goal setting. Establishing goals, whether they're diet or exercise related, keeps you motivated and provides a way of tracking your progress. Your exercise goals should be realistic but challenging. They should be based on what you are capable of achieving given your fitness level and your schedule.

If you're new to exercise, begin by working out for a reasonable amount of time, say 10 minutes at a time. Increase that time gradually each week. I became a runner 15 years ago. But I didn't start by running a marathon. To be honest, I couldn't even run a full city block to my local corner store. Instead I set a goal to walk a few minutes, run a minute, then walk again, and so on. It was pretty exciting to see how quickly I improved. Within two months I was running for 45 minutes straight!

If it's been awhile since you've hit the gym, don't try to start back at the same level you left off. Pick a moderate level and give yourself time to work back up to your higher level. The same principle applies if you're starting an exercise program to shed weight. Break down your long-term goal of losing 20 pounds into smaller goals that keep you motivated. It's much more satisfying to see 5 pounds come off each month, rather than focusing only on what you'll look like months down the road.

Reward Yourself

It's important to celebrate small achievements, whether it's losing the first 5 pounds or mastering a new intensity level on the StairMaster. As you stick with your program, make progress and see the results, congratulate yourself by giving yourself a small reward. I like to reward myself with a pedicure or manicure. Some people buy a new CD, lipstick or an item of clothing. Do whatever works for you…just don't wait too long. To stay motivated, it's important to reward yourself for achieving all the small steps that lead you to your final destination.

Enlist the Support of Others

It's often easier to exercise if you have someone to exercise with. Personally, I'm not sure I would do weight training on my own. Working with a personal trainer motivates me to do it. For starters, I have someone waiting for me, so I can't just not go. But a trainer also makes me work harder, and I enjoy the company along the way.

You don't have to hire a personal trainer to gain a workout partner. If you're having trouble motivating yourself to get out the door, ask a friend or family member to join you. Or try a group exercise class. Working out with people who share a common goal can be a big motivator. And if that doesn't keep you coming back, the lively music ought to!

When to Check in with Your Doctor First

Most healthy people can safely start an exercise program. However, if you're a male over 45 or a female over 55 and have not been regularly active, or have any health concerns, consult your doctor first. Regardless of your age, consult your doctor if you have two or more of the following risk factors:

- High blood pressure

- High blood cholesterol

- Diabetes

- Smoking

- You have a family history of early-onset heart disease (father before the age of 55 or mother before the age of 65)

Other reasons to visit your doctor before starting an exercise program include:

- You feel pain in your chest during physical activity.

- In the past you have felt pain in your chest when you're not active.

- You sometimes lose your balance or become dizzy.

- You have a bone or joint condition that could be made worse by exercise.

Putting Together Your Exercise Program

After reading about the many ways that exercise can keep you healthy, it's hard to justify sitting on the couch watching television night after night. So it's time to get started! The experts recommend that we *accumulate 60 minutes of physical activity every day* to stay healthy or improve our health. The time you need to spend being active depends on the amount of effort the activity takes. As you progress to activities of moderate intensity, you can cut down to 30 minutes, four days a week. In other words, the higher the exercise intensity, the shorter the duration of exercise. But keep in mind that 45 minutes of moderate to vigorous activity may further reduce the risk of breast and colon cancer.

Here's a list showing the level of exercise intensity of various activities. Those requiring moderate and vigorous effort are considered cardiovascular ("cardio") or aerobic workouts (see below).

INTENSITY LEVEL OF VARIOUS ACTIVITIES

Light Effort	Moderate Effort	Vigorous Effort
60 minutes	30–60 minutes	20–30 minutes
Easy gardening	Biking	Aerobics
Light walking	Brisk walking	Fast dancing
Stretching	Dancing	Basketball
Volleyball	Raking leaves	Hockey
	Swimming	Jogging
	Water aerobics	Spinning
		Fast swimming

Your body needs three types of exercise to keep healthy: cardiovascular, flexibility and strength.

Cardiovascular Exercises

Aerobic or cardiovascular activities help keep you slim and get your heart, lungs and circulatory system in shape. To improve your health and level of fitness, cardio exercise should involve large muscle groups (such as your legs) and should be maintained continuously. When you continuously exercise the big muscles in your legs, they require more oxygen than usual. This challenges your cardiovascular system to deliver more oxygen to your working muscles. Not only do your legs get a workout, but your heart and lungs get fit too!

CARDIOVASCULAR ACTIVITIES (FOUR TO SEVEN DAYS PER WEEK)

Group 1 Activities	Group 2 Activities	Group 3 Activities
Cycling (indoor)	Aerobic classes	Basketball
Jogging	Step aerobics	Handball
Walking	Hiking	Hockey
Stair-climbing	In-line skating	Racquet sports
Rowing	Skipping rope	Soccer
Cross-country skiing	Swimming	Volleyball
Distance cycling	Water aerobics	Circuit training

Group 1 activities provide constant intensity that is not dependent on skill; group 2 activities may provide constant or variable intensity, depending on skill; group 3 activities provide variable intensity that is highly dependent on skill.

If you're new to cardiovascular exercise, begin with activities that can be maintained continuously and don't require special skill (for example, group 1 activities). Depending on the amount of effort you're expending, exercise for 20 to 60 minutes continuously.

Calculate Your Target Heart Rate Zone

You are exercising hard enough if you're working out at between 65 and 90 percent of your maximum heart rate (the maximum number of times your heart can beat in one minute). This is called your target heart rate zone. Beginners and older adults should aim to work out at 40 to 50 percent of their maximum heart rate. Here's how to estimate your target heart rate zone:

1. Calculate your estimated maximum heart rate (220 minus your age).

2. Multiply your maximum heart rate by 0.65 for the lower end of your heart rate zone.

3. Multiply your maximum heart rate by 0.90 for the upper end of your heart rate zone.

Here's my target heart rate zone:

$220 - 37 = 183$ (This is my estimated maximum heart rate.)

$183 \times 0.65 = 119$

$183 \times 0.90 = 165$

As you can see, my target heart rate zone is 119 to 165 beats per minute. If my heart rate drops below 119, I need to pick up the pace. Conversely, if it exceeds 165, I need to slow down a little. You might be wondering how to determine your heart rate during exercise. If you want to spend approximately $200, you can buy a heart rate monitor, consisting of a chest band that transmits your heart rate to a wristwatch.

It's cheaper to count the number of times your heart beats in 15 seconds. Just hold two fingers (your pointer and middle finger) to the inside of your wrist or on your neck. Once you find your pulse, look at the second hand of your watch and count the number of beats in 15 seconds. (If you can't find your pulse, ask a fitness professional at the gym for help.) Now all you have to do is multiply that number by four to get "beats per minute." During my workout on the stationary bike, my heart usually beats 35 times in 15 seconds. That means it is beating 140 times per minute, which is within my target heart rate zone.

Use the Talk Test

There's a much easier way still to tell if you're slacking off or working too hard. If you can comfortably carry on a conversation while you exercise, you're not overdoing it. But if you don't become winded at all while talking, you need to increase the intensity.

Flexibility Exercises

Being flexible means that your joints can move fluidly through a full range of motion. Gentle reaching, bending and stretching your muscles all keep your joints flexible and your muscles relaxed. The more flexible you are, the less likely it is that you'll get injured during exercise. If you get into the habit of doing flexibility exercises now, you'll be glad you did when you're older. That's because flexibility enhances the quality of life and independence for older adults.

FLEXIBILITY ACTIVITIES (FOUR TO SEVEN DAYS PER WEEK)

Mopping	Pilates	Bowling
Sweeping	Stretching	Curling
Vacuuming	T'ai Chi	Dancing
Gardening	Yoga	Golfing
Yard work		

© Her Majesty The Queen in Right of Canada. All rights reserved. Source: *Handbook for Canada's Physical Activity Guide to Healthy Active Living,* Health Canada, 1998. Reproduced with the permission of the Minister of Public Works and Government Services, 2002.

Follow these guidelines for safe stretching:

- Warm up with light activity for five minutes before stretching. This increases your body temperature and your range of motion. Or do your stretching after a cardio or weight workout.

- Stretch all your major muscle groups (back, chest, shoulders, arms, legs).

- Stretch slowly and smoothly without bouncing or jerking. Use gentle continuous movement or stretch-and-hold (for 10 to 30 seconds), whichever is right for the exercise.

- Focus on the target muscle you're stretching. Relax the muscle and minimize the movement of other body parts.

- Stretch to the limit of the movement but not to the point of pain. Aim for a stretched, relaxed feeling.

- Don't hold your breath. Keep breathing slowly and rhythmically while holding the stretch.

- If you're not sure what to do, get help from a fitness expert at your health club or gym. Or pick up a book on stretching at your local bookstore.

Strength Exercises

Muscular strength, tone and endurance are important to your overall health and physical fitness. Strength training (also called resistance training) improves your posture, prevents injuries, gives definition to your muscles, reshapes problem areas, increases your metabolism and helps prevent osteoporosis. Research suggests that virtually all the health benefits of resistance training can be obtained in two 15 to 20 minute sessions per week.[18] Of course, if your goal is to gain weight by building muscle mass, you'll have to work out longer and more often.

STRENGTH ACTIVITIES (TWO TO FOUR DAYS PER WEEK)

Heavy yard work	Abdominal crunches	Cybex machines	Pilates
Raking and carrying leaves	Chin-ups	Free weights (dumbbells, barbells)	Yoga
Stair-climbing	Lunges	Nautilus machines	
	Push-ups		
	Squats		

People with low initial strength who work with weights will show greater improvements and at a faster rate than people who start out with higher strength levels. As you get stronger, it will become easier and easier to lift the same amount of weight or perform the same number of push-ups. Throughout your program, you must periodically (and gradually) increase the amount of work your muscles perform so that further improvements can be made. This means you need to increase the amount of weight you lift or the number of push-ups and sit-ups you do.

Follow these guidelines for safe strength training:

- Warm up with five minutes of light aerobic activity and stretching to get your circulation going and your joints moving.

- Ask a personal trainer to show you proper technique in order to protect your back and joints.

- Breathe regularly when doing an exercise.

- Rest for at least one day between strength training sessions.

Reps and Sets

Repetitions (reps) refers to the number of times you do an exercise such as a leg lunge. A set is a group of repetitions. Depending on your fitness goals, you would usually do one to three sets per exercise. For instance, if my goal is to tone my arms, I might do three sets of 12 bicep curls. Here's a handy guide:

GOAL	REPS	SETS	FREQUENCY
Toning	12–15	3	3 times per week
Endurance	15–20	3	3 times per week
Strength (beginner)	6–8	3	3 times per week
Strength (novice)	4–8	5–6	5 times per week

You'll improve your muscular fitness by performing only one set of a given exercise, but research suggests that multiple sets will optimize gains in muscle strength and endurance. The amount of weight you lift will depend on your muscle strength and the number of reps you need to perform to achieve your goals. For example, if you want to tone your muscles, pick a weight that becomes difficult after 10 to 12 repetitions. The last 3 to 5 reps of the set should definitely challenge you. Your muscles should feel fatigued, but not painful.

If you are new to the world of strength training, I strongly recommend that you consult a certified personal trainer for your first few sessions. A personal trainer will instruct you on proper technique, specific exercises and the appropriate amount of weight to use.

Consult a Certified Personal Trainer

You might want to hire someone to show you the ropes and get you started. An expert can help motivate you and guide you through a weight program. Or you might prefer weekly sessions to keep you focused.

If you belong to a health club, there's bound to be a few personal trainers on staff. If you work out at home and would like the help of a personal trainer, call the Canadian Personal Trainers Network at (416) 979-1654. You can also e-mail the network at info@cptn.com. Tell them your goals, where you live and whether you prefer a male or female trainer. They'll set you up with a referral.

What's the Best Time of Day to Exercise?

How well you exercise may relate to the time of day and the type of workout you do. Studies have found that people perform better at strength training exercises when the exercises are done in the afternoon or early evening. This is probably because during the day, our body temperature increases and our joints become looser. This is also why it's thought that athletes are less prone to injury later in the day.

Despite this, there are benefits to working out in the morning. Men may be better off weight training in the morning, when their testosterone levels are naturally higher. Sex aside, studies show that people who work out in the morning are more likely to be working out one year later. If you work out first thing in the morning, it's more likely to develop into a routine. Your workout gets done because there's nothing to compete with it—no last-minute meetings, no telephone ringing and no household chores that have to get done. People say a morning workout starts their day off on a positive note. They feel better and tend to make healthy food choices throughout the day.

But not everybody is a morning person. What's most important is that you pick a time when your energy level is still high, when you feel motivated and when you won't be distracted to do something else. If the only time you have to exercise is after dinner when the kids are asleep, so be it. That's likely going to be the time that sticks.

15 TIPS
FOR GETTING MORE ACTIVE

1. Make a list of the reasons why you want to start exercising (for example, how will exercising make you feel?) Then think about what might cause you to stop being active. Make a list of the obstacles you might encounter along the way. Beside each barrier to exercise, write down a possible solution.

2. Make a list of the activities you would like to incorporate into your daily life. These must be activities you will enjoy doing and that you can do given your current fitness level.

3. Find out what exercise you can do in your community. Get information from your local YMCA, YWCA and community center. Or call the local parks and recreation department. You might ask for a map of walking trails and cycling paths in your area. Find out if a nearby mall has a walking route posted or a regular walking program.

4. Pull out your calendar. Schedule at least 10 minutes of lifestyle activity into each day. Then pick a few days each week when you will do a planned workout for 20 to 30 minutes. As the weeks go by, gradually increase your frequency and intensity of planned exercise.

5. Create a new morning routine. Start your day with ten minutes of stretching or a short walk around the block (or on your treadmill).

6. Take stretch breaks during meetings or during long stints on the computer. Roll your shoulders and stretch your neck.

7. Take the stairs whenever you can. Pretend the elevator or escalator is out of service.

8. Wear a pedometer every day and watch your daily steps increase in number.

9. Park your car ten minutes away from the store you are going to. Or if you take public transit, get off a few stops early and walk the rest of the way.

10. Make a commitment to try a new activity each season—cross country skiing, snow shoeing, skating, hiking, tennis, paddling, roller blading or biking. Take lessons if you need to.

11. Arrange to meet a friend for a walk each evening. Or get outside and play with your kids when the weather permits.

12. Pedal a stationary bicycle while you're watching TV.

13. Ride your bike to work in the summer.

14. Try a new group exercise class. Check out spinning, yoga or Pilates.

15. If you belong to a gym, hire a certified personal trainer to develop a well-rounded exercise program for you. Work with your trainer for the first few sessions to learn proper technique. As your fitness improves, check back with your trainer every few months to revamp your program.

ANSWERS TO LESLIE'S IQ QUIZ   INCLUDE REGULAR EXERCISE

1. True.

2. c. A whopping 63% of Canadians don't exercise enough to reap its health benefits.

3. False. Because women have lower testosterone levels than men do, weight training tones and strengthens muscles without increasing their size that much. The amount of weight you lift and the number of reps you perform also determine the end result.

4. d. To get health benefits from exercise, all you have to do is accumulate 60 minutes of light activity each day.

5. False. When it comes to losing weight, what matters is the *total number* of calories you burn. A 140 pound woman will burn approximately 300 calories whether she walks briskly for 70 minutes or runs for 25 minutes.

Leslie's
14–Day Meal Plan
for Healthy Eating

Now that you know what the ten steps to healthy eating are, it's time to put them into action! One of the best strategies to help you eat healthy is cooking for yourself rather than relying on restaurants, take-out places and processed ready-to-eat meals. Preparing delicious and nutritious meals for your family and yourself is empowering. And it's easy.

All the recipes included in my 14-Day Meal Plan come from The Canadian Living Test Kitchen. This means they have been Tested Till Perfect. It was a real pleasure working with food and nutrition editor Elizabeth Baird and chef Daphna Rabinovitch, the food editors responsible for bringing you so many great-tasting recipes each month in *Canadian Living* magazine.

efore we came up with the recipes, I discussed my philosophy about healthy eating. Here's the framework from which the meal plan was built.

- The meal plan follows the principles of a plant-based diet. This means more emphasis is placed on whole grains, vegetables and beans than on animal foods. You'll find meals based on beans, lentils and tofu, but you'll also see chicken and meat, just less often.

- The meal plan offers fish three times each week.

- The meal plan emphasizes whole-grain choices as often as possible.

- Most recipes are lower in fat (30 percent of calories or less). Sometimes this isn't possible, but that's okay. Remember, it's what you eat over the course of a day that counts, not one single food or meal.

The professionals at Canadian Living came up with more than 65 recipes—including extra recipes not specified in the meal plan to help you eat more vegetables and whole grains—that taste great (a top priority), use ingredients that are easy to find and can be quickly prepared (usually in less than 30 minutes). And all the recipes specified in the 14-Day Meal Plan include a nutritional analysis that tells you the calories and grams of protein, carbohydrate, fat and fiber per serving. (Most of the extra recipes have a nutritional analysis, too.) You'll also see how one serving of each recipe stacks up in terms of providing the recommended dietary intake (% RDI) for key vitamins and minerals.

Think of the recipes that follow as your starter kit to eating well. By giving you a two-week plan for breakfasts, lunches and dinners, I've eliminated the work involved in the first strategy of getting organized—planning your meals ahead. All you have to do is follow the remaining strategies I discussed in Step 1, page 11. These tips will help you get organized and make your healthy eating plan a reality.

Strategy #2: Schedule Time for Once-a-Week Grocery Shopping

Read through the recipes in the next section and develop your shopping list. I suggest doing this on the weekend or whenever it is that you have a little more time. And remember—don't shop on an empty stomach.

Strategy #3: Buy It Pre-Prepped

To save time cooking, buy chickpeas, beans and lentils canned, ready to use. Buy your veggies chopped, ready to throw into a salad or steamer basket. You'll need partly skim mozzarella for the Vegetarian Lasagna on page 209—why not buy it already grated?

Strategy #4: Plan for Leftovers

You can easily prepare each recipe just before each meal. But if you lead a hectic lifestyle like most of us do, I suggest you do some batch cooking on the weekend and take advantage of your freezer. Preparing food in advance will be a lifesaver during your busy week. Here are a few time-saving suggestions for using my 14-Day Meal Plan:

- Monday breakfasts include high-fiber, low-fat quick breads. Make these on Sunday. Freeze what you don't plan to use for another breakfast or an after-school snack for the kids.

- Monday lunches include a hearty lentil soup and vegetarian chili. You will need to prepare these on Sunday, too. Freeze what you won't eat on Monday in single-serving containers. This way you'll have a quick meal ready to defrost for any day of the week. The meal plan includes an antioxidant-packed carrot soup for lunch on Thursday, Week 2. Make this in advance, too.

- There are two other breakfasts that can be made ahead whenever you have a little extra time. On Friday, Week 1, I've planned a delicious low-fat granola—the recipe is straight from the Wickaninnish Inn on Vancouver Island. This granola can be stored in the refrigerator for up to two weeks! You'll also find apple oat muffins for breakfast on Wednesday, Week 2.

You'll need to add your own side dishes to some of the meals. When it's not included, add a fruit and milk serving to breakfast. Add vegetables to lunch and dinners—you'll find ten tasty vegetable recipes starting on page 191. When soup or salad is on the menu for lunch, enjoy a whole-wheat roll, half a pita pocket or a slice of whole-grain pumpernickel bread.

Strategy #5: Surround Yourself with Healthy Tools

You won't need anything special to cook the healthy recipes that follow. Just some nonstick baking pans (or nonstick cooking spray), pots and pans, a blender for breakfast smoothies, the standard utensils and a few sharp knives.

Don't feel you have to use the meal plan exactly as it's presented here. You might not want to adhere to a two-week schedule. Perhaps you'd rather pick and choose recipes to add to your own repertoire of healthy meals. If that's the case, you'll find plenty to choose from. In addition to the 14 breakfasts, lunches and dinners, I've provided 24 quick recipes for vegetables, whole grains, sandwiches and marinades (see page 184).

And now it's time to move on to the meal plan and recipes. I hope you enjoy all the recipes and make them a regular part of your diet. Have fun eating well.

The 14-Day Meal Plan

WEEK 1

BREAKFAST	LUNCH	DINNER

MONDAY

Date Bran Muffins (p. 202) with Melon Berry Fruit Salad (p. 198)	Smoky Turkey Sausage, Tomato & Chickpea Soup (p. 186)	Garlic Gratin Fish (p. 215) with Roasted Broccoli and Red Pepper (p. 196)

TUESDAY

Orange Date Oat Bran Porridge (p. 199)	Cheesy Pita Pockets (p. 187)	Chicken Fajitas (p. 218)

WEDNESDAY

Grab-a-Snack Mix (p. 200)	Southwestern Three Bean Salad (p. 211)	Tofu & Vegetable Skewers with Peanut Sauce (p. 211)

THURSDAY

Strawberry Banana Smoothie (p. 213)	Mango Chicken Wrap (p. 188)	Roasted Cajun Halibut (p. 217) with Cherry Tomato and Mushroom Sauté (p. 191)

FRIDAY

Wickaninnish Inn Granola (p. 213)	Quick Potato Lentil Soup (p. 185)	Healthy Pizza with your choice of toppings (p. 207)

SATURDAY

Buttermilk Berry Pancakes (p. 203) with Standby Stewed Fruit (p. 198)	Salmon Melt (p. 189)	Vegetarian Lasagna (p. 209)

SUNDAY

Western Omelet Pockets (p. 214)	Mediterranean Tuna Pasta (p. 216)	Balsamic Honey Pork Tenderloin (p. 220) with Orzo Salad (p. 195)

WEEK 2

BREAKFAST	LUNCH	DINNER

MONDAY

Orange Apricot Loaf (p. 202)	Vegetarian Chili with Squash (p. 212)	Asian Fish Steaks (p. 215) with Mango, Cucumber, and Red Pepper Salad (p. 195)

TUESDAY

Maple Walnut Multigrain Porridge (p. 200)	Tuna Wrap (p. 190)	Chicken in Spicy Spinach Sauce (p. 219)

WEDNESDAY

Apple Oat Muffins (p. 201)	Bean Spread and Veggie Sandwich (p. 187)	Cumin Carrot Tofu Patties (p. 210)

THURSDAY

Tropical Fruit Shake (p. 213)	Creamy Carrot Soup (p. 185)	Roasted Fillets with Orange Caramelized Onions (p. 217)

FRIDAY

Apple Cinnamon Oatmeal Porridge (p. 199)	Vegetable Tofu Salad (p. 212)	Citrus Mustard Chicken (p. 219)

SATURDAY

French-Toasted Banana Sandwich (p. 204)	Tuna and Pepper Panini Melt (p. 189)	Sicilian Beans with Pasta (p. 210)

SUNDAY

Super Nutritious Frittata (p. 214)	Chicken Club Pita (p. 188)	Garlic Horseradish Sirloin Roast (p. 220) with Roasted Roots Salad (p. 197)

The Recipes

SOUPS

Creamy Carrot Soup 185
Quick Potato Lentil Soup 185
Smoky Turkey Sausage,
   Tomato and Chickpea Soup
   186

SANDWICHES AND WRAPS

Bean Spread and Veggie
   Sandwich 187
Cheesy Pita Pockets 187
Chicken Club Pita 188
Mango Chicken Wrap 188
Salmon Melt 189
Tuna and Pepper Panini Melt
   189
Tuna Wrap 190
Five Fast Sandwich Ideas 190

VEGETABLES AND SALADS

Asparagus Leek Braise 191
Cherry Tomato and Mushroom
   Sauté 191
Cold Sesame Swiss Chard
   Leaves 192
Curried Carrots 192
Green Beans Gremolata 193
Honey Lemon Beets 193
Kale with Apples and Onion
   194
Lemon Broccoli Salad 194
Mango, Cucumber and Red
   Pepper Salad 195
Orzo Salad 195
Rapini with Lemon Anchovy
   Vinaigrette 196
Roasted Broccoli and Red
   Pepper 196
Roasted Roots Salad 197
Snow Peas and Peppers 197
Four Fast Green Pea Dishes
   197

FRUIT

Melon Berry Fruit Salad 198
Standby Stewed Fruit 198

GRAIN FOODS

Cereals

Apple Cinnamon Oatmeal
   Porridge 199
Orange Date Oat Bran
   Porridge 199
Maple Walnut Multigrain
   Porridge 200
Grab-a-Snack Mix 200
Wickaninnish Inn Granola 201

Quick Breads and Pancakes

Apple Oat Muffins 201
Date Bran Muffins 202
Orange Apricot Loaf 202
Buttermilk Berry Pancake Mix
   203
Buttermilk Berry Pancakes 203
French-Toasted Banana
   Sandwich 204

Side Dishes

Barley 204
Couscous 205
Kasha 205
Wheat Berries 206
Eight Great Ideas for Grains
   206

Pizza and Pasta

Healthy Pizza Base 207
Artichoke Pizza 207
Hot and Spicy Pizza 208
Veggie Spinach Pizza 208
Vegetarian Lasagna 209

LEGUMES AND SOY

Cumin Carrot Tofu Patties 210
Sicilian Beans with Pasta 210
Southwestern Three-Bean
   Salad 211
Tofu and Vegetable Skewers
   with Peanut Sauce 211
Vegetarian Chili with Squash
   212
Vegetable Tofu Salad 212

DAIRY AND EGGS

Strawberry Banana Smoothie
   213
Tropical Fruit Shake 213
Super Nutritious Frittata 214
Western Omelet Pockets 214

FISH

Asian Fish Steaks 215
Garlic Gratin Fish 215
Mediterranean Tuna Pasta 216
Roasted Cajun Halibut 217
Roasted Fillets with Orange
   Caramelized Onions 217

POULTRY

Marinated Chicken Breasts
   218
Chicken Fajitas 218
Chicken in Spicy Spinach
   Sauce 219
Citrus Mustard Chicken 219

MEAT

Balsamic Honey Pork
   Tenderloin 220
Garlic Horseradish Sirloin
   Roast 220

Five Fast Marinades for Fish, Poultry and Meat

Adobo Marinade 221
Chimichurri Marinade 221
Moroccan Marinade 221
Red Wine Marinade 221
Teriyaki Marinade 221

SOUPS

Creamy Carrot Soup

You'll pack a week's worth of vitamin A into one meal when you make this soup. But you probably won't even stop to think about its nutritional wallop because you'll be so taken with its taste. Round out the meal with a green salad and some crusty dinner rolls.

1 tbsp	butter	15 mL
2	onions, chopped	2
1 1/4lb	carrots (about 10), coarsely chopped	625 g
1	sweet potato, peeled and coarsely chopped	1
4 cups	vegetable stock	1 L
1 1/2 tsp	ground cumin	7 mL
1/2 tsp	each salt and pepper	2 mL
1/2 cup	milk	125 mL
1 cup	croutons	250 mL

In saucepan, heat butter over medium heat; cook onions, stirring often, for about 5 minutes or until softened. Add carrots, sweet potato, stock, cumin, salt and pepper; bring to boil. Reduce heat to medium; cover and simmer for 20 minutes.

Purée in food processor or blender until smooth. Blend in milk. Return to pan and reheat. Serve sprinkled with croutons.

Makes 4 servings.

Per serving: about 236 cal, 6 g pro, 5 g total fat (2 g saturated fat), 43 g carb, 6 g fiber, 10 mg chol, 1109 mg sodium. % RDI: 11% calcium, 16% iron, 431% vit A, 27% vit C, 16% folate.

Quick Potato Lentil Soup

This is a quick and easy soup that can easily be made the night before in 30 minutes. Or, it can be made on the weekend and frozen in easy-to-microwave 1 cup (250 mL) containers, ready to tuck into a lunchbag any day of the week.

1 tbsp	vegetable oil	15 mL
1	onion, chopped	1
2	potatoes, peeled and chopped	2
1	stalk celery, chopped	1
1 cup	red lentils	250 mL
1	clove garlic, minced	1
1 tsp	dried thyme	5 mL
1/2 tsp	each salt and pepper	2 mL
1/4 tsp	ground cumin	1 mL
Pinch	cayenne pepper	Pinch
4 cups	vegetable stock	1 L

In large saucepan, heat oil over medium heat; cook onion, potatoes, celery, lentils, garlic, thyme, salt, pepper, cumin and cayenne pepper, stirring often, until onion is softened, about 5 minutes.

Add stock; bring to boil. Reduce heat to low; simmer until potatoes and lentils are tender, about 20 minutes.

Makes 4 servings.

Per serving: about 280 cal, 15 g pro, 5 g total fat (trace saturated fat), 47 g carb, 8 g fiber, 0 mg chol, 931 mg sodium. % RDI: 5% calcium, 39% iron, 1% vit A, 15% vit C, 120% folate.

Smoky Turkey Sausage, Tomato and Chickpea Soup

Here's a hearty and spicy way to dispel that chilled-to-the-bone feeling during the colder months. The soup keeps for up to 2 days, ready to reheat after a curling match or morning of cross-country skiing. Fresh chorizo or mild Italian sausage can replace the turkey sausage; omit paprika.

3/4 lb	lean fresh turkey sausage	375 g
1 tsp	vegetable oil	5 mL
1	onion, chopped	1
4	cloves garlic, minced	4
1	large carrot, chopped	1
1	stalk celery, chopped	1
2	jalapeño peppers, sliced thinly	2
1 tsp	ground cumin	5 mL
1/2 tsp	each ground coriander and paprika	2 mL
1/4 tsp	each chili powder and pepper	1 mL
1	can (19 oz/540 mL) tomatoes	1
1	can (19 oz/540 mL) chickpeas	1
3 cups	chicken stock	750 mL
1/4 cup	chopped fresh coriander or parsley	50 mL
1	lime	1

Remove casings from sausage; cut into slices or break into chunks. In large pot, heat oil over medium heat; cook sausage, without stirring, for 5 minutes. Add onion, garlic, carrot and celery; cook, stirring often, for about 10 minutes or until vegetables are softened and sausage is cooked through. Drain off any excess fat.

Stir in jalapeño peppers, cumin, ground coriander, paprika, chili powder and pepper; cook, stirring, for 1 minute. Pour in tomatoes, breaking up into small pieces with back of spoon; bring to boil. Reduce heat and simmer, covered, for 10 minutes.

Meanwhile, drain and rinse chickpeas; stir into pot along with stock and 2 tbsp (25 mL) of the fresh coriander. Cover and simmer for 20 minutes.

Soup can be cooled, covered and refrigerated for up to 2 days. Reheat gently, adding up to 1/3 cup/75 mL more stock if too thick.

Slice lime into 4 wedges. Garnish each serving with lime wedge. Sprinkle with remaining coriander.

Makes 8 servings.

Per serving: about 167 cal, 13 g pro, 5 g total fat (1 g saturated fat), 20 g carb, 3 g fiber, 26 mg chol, 910 mg sodium. % RDI: 5% calcium, 15% iron, 36% vit A, 28% vit C, 15% folate.

Tip: If you don't have jalapeño peppers, substitute 1/4 tsp (1 mL) cayenne pepper or hot pepper flakes.

SANDWICHES AND WRAPS

Bean Spread and Veggie Sandwich

This bean spread not only is wonderful in a sandwich but will win raves as a dip at your next party. For dipping, serve with raw vegetables or baked Cajun-spiced pita bread sliced into triangles.

For a vegetarian lunch, spread 2 tbsp (25 mL) bean spread over two slices of 12-grain bread. Top with tomato and cucumber slices, arugula leaves and grilled zucchini or eggplant slices. For added convenience and to ensure that your sandwich is as fresh and crunchy as can be, package all the vegetables in separate containers and assemble at lunchtime.

Bean Spread

1	can (19 oz/540 mL) white kidney beans, drained and rinsed	1
2 tbsp	lemon juice	25 mL
2 tbsp	olive oil	25 mL
1/2 tsp	salt	2 mL
1/4 tsp	pepper	1 mL

In food processor, purée together all ingredients. Store in refrigerator for up to 3 days.

Makes 1 2/3 cups (400 mL).

Per Serving: about 328 cal, 13 g pro, 8 g total fat (1 g sat. fat), 53 g carb, 7 g fibre, 0 mg chol, 668 mg sodium. % RDI: 2% calcium, 6% iron, 7% vit A, 33% vit C, 17% folate.

Cheesy Pita Pockets

This lunch, a combination of carbohydrates (from the whole-grain pita) and protein (from the cheese), will help you store energy to use later in the day, thereby dispelling that late-afternoon urge to doze.

1/3 cup	light cream cheese, softened	75 mL
1/4 cup	shredded light old cheddar cheese	50 mL
1	carrot, shredded	1
1/4 tsp	pepper	1 mL
2	whole-wheat pita breads	2
Quarter	large cucumber, sliced	Quarter
1/2 cup	shredded spinach or lettuce	125 mL

In small bowl, mash together cream and cheddar cheese, shredded carrot and pepper until blended.

Cut top quarter off each pita and tuck inside bottom of pita. Spread half of the cheese mixture inside each; fill with cucumber and sprouts.

Pita pockets can be wrapped in plastic wrap and refrigerated or stored in cooler pack for up to 24 hours.

Makes 2 servings.

Per serving: about 316 cal, 15 g pro, 10 g total fat (6 g saturated fat), 42 g carb, 6 g fiber, 34 mg chol, 607 mg sodium. % RDI: 20% calcium, 12% iron, 119% vit A, 12% vit C, 19% folate.

Chicken Club Pita

Smoky chicken and ham piled onto pitas with juicy tomatoes make the best sandwich of the season.

1 lb	boneless skinless chicken breasts	500 g
4	slices prosciutto ham (75 g) or slices of bacon	4
2 tbsp	Dijon mustard	25 mL
2 tbsp	liquid honey	25 mL
2 tsp	cider vinegar	10 mL
1 tsp	vegetable oil	5 mL
1/4 tsp	pepper	1 mL
4	pita breads	4
1/4 cup	light mayonnaise	50 mL
1	tomato, chopped	1
1 cup	shredded lettuce	250 mL

Cut chicken into 1 1/2-inch (4-cm) chunks. Cut prosciutto into 1 1/2-inch (4-cm) wide strips. Thread onto skewers, weaving ham around and alternating with chicken.

In small bowl, whisk together mustard, honey, vinegar, oil and pepper. Place skewers on greased grill over medium-high heat; close lid and cook, brushing with mustard mixture and turning occasionally, for 15 minutes or until chicken is no longer pink inside. Meanwhile, wrap pitas in foil; heat on grill for 5 minutes.

Spread pitas with mayonnaise. Removing skewers, divide chicken and ham over pitas. Top with tomato and lettuce; fold in half.

Makes 4 servings.

Per serving: about 477 cal, 47 g pro, 11 g total fat (2 g saturated fat), 45 g carb, 1 g fiber, 106 mg chol, 731 mg sodium. % RDI: 7% calcium, 22% iron, 4% vit A, 12% vit C, 27% folate.

Mango Chicken Wrap

Sweet, delicious mango complements leftover sliced chicken beautifully. And it doesn't get any easier than store-bought coleslaw, which adds an inviting note of crunchiness. When buying mangoes—which are rich in vitamins A and C—look for smooth, unblemished skin, tinged with red, that yields slightly to pressure.

Spread light mayonnaise, mustard or chutney over large whole-wheat flour tortillas. Sprinkle with about 1/2 cup (125 mL) packaged undressed precut coleslaw. Line with slices of precooked, sliced chicken or turkey breast; cover with a single layer of sliced fresh mango. Roll up.

Per Serving: about 397 cal, 21 g pro, 12 g total fat (2 g sat. fat), 53 g carb, 5 g fibre, 48 mg chol, 412 mg sodium. % RDI: 5% calcium, 17% iron, 57% vit A, 73% vit C, 12% folate.

Salmon Melt

To save time, assemble your melt the day before, wrap well with plastic wrap and store in the refrigerator overnight; then simply unwrap and place it in a toaster oven while you and the kids slice fresh fruit for dessert. Consider mashing the bones in with the rest of the salmon for an extra kick of calcium.

Drain 1 can salmon; mash salmon and bones with about 2 tbsp (25 mL) yogurt or light sour cream, chopped green onions or chives, some dried dillweed, a spoonful of Dijon mustard and salt and pepper. Heap onto 4 whole-wheat English muffin halves.

Place on baking sheet and top each with 1/4 cup (50 mL) shredded light Cheddar or Monterey Jack cheese. Bake in oven or toaster oven until cheese is melted and English muffin is toasted.

Per Serving: about 219 cal, 20 g pro, 9 g total fat (4 g sat. fat), 15 g carb, 2 g fibre, 31 mg chol, 496 mg sodium. % RDI: 41% calcium, 11% iron, 1% vit A, 2% vit C, 17% folate.

Tuna and Pepper Panini Melt

Serve with crisp green salad tossed with vinaigrette.

2	cans (each 6 oz/170 g) water packed tuna, drained	2
Half	sweet red pepper, diced	Half
1	stalk celery, diced	1
2	green onions, chopped	2
2 tbsp	light mayonnaise	25 mL
2 tbsp	plain yogurt or light sour cream	25 mL
1 tbsp	drained capers	15 mL
1/2 tsp	each ground cumin and pepper	2 mL
1/4 tsp	each salt and cayenne pepper	1 mL
4	soft panini (Italian) buns	4
1/2 cup	shredded light cheddar or Swiss cheese	125 mL

In bowl, mix together tuna, red pepper, celery, green onions, mayonnaise, plain yogurt, capers, cumin, pepper, salt and cayenne pepper.

Cut buns in half horizontally; spread tuna mixture evenly over bottom half of each. Sprinkle each evenly with cheese. Replace bun tops.

In nonstick skillet or grill pan or on grill, cook sandwiches over medium heat, pressing often to flatten and turning once, for about 5 minutes or until crusty and cheese is melted.

Makes 4 servings.

Per serving: about 352 cal, 26 g pro, 11 g total fat (4 g saturated fat), 35 g carb, 2 g fiber, 36 mg chol, 862 mg sodium. % RDI: 16% calcium, 22% iron, 12% vit A, 43% vit C, 25% folate.

Tip: Using soft buns such as Italian rolls, or panini, instead of a crusty variety ensures that the sandwiches will flatten easily when pressed.

Tuna Wrap

There's a reason why wraps are the new sandwich of choice for lunch and even dinner. First, flour tortillas are low in fat and lighter than bagels or kaiser rolls. They're also ideal for packing with delicious, good-for-you ingredients, which means you'll never get that bored, lunchbag-letdown feeling.

For a Greek twist, spread your tortilla with prepared tzatziki sauce and sprinkle lightly with sliced black olives. Or mix tuna with a low-fat niçoise dressing for a taste of Provence.

Spread Dijon mustard, light mayonnaise or mango chutney over small whole-wheat flour tortillas. Line each with curly lettuce or baby spinach leaves and 1/4 cup (50 mL) shredded carrots. Drain can of water-packed tuna; combine with 2 tbsp (25 mL) low-fat mayonnaise and 1 stalk finely chopped celery. Spread 1/3 cup (75 mL) tuna over carrots; roll up.

Per Serving: about 292 cal, 21 g pro, 12 g total fat (1 g sat. fat), 24 g carb, 2 g fibre, 20 mg chol, 669 mg sodium. % RDI: 4% calcium, 18% iron, 81% vit A, 10% vit C, 10% folate.

FIVE FAST SANDWICH IDEAS

Sandwiches need not be boring; the key is to keep interesting spreads and add-ins in your refrigerator at all times.

•   Try pairing leftover sliced grilled chicken with roasted red pepper strips and leaves of arugula. Or even up the ante a bit by spreading the rolls with prepared pesto or olive tapenade.

•   Make a sun-dried tomato hummus, spread on a whole-wheat kaiser and heap your sandwich high with leftover grilled veggies.

•   Keep on hand in the freezer whole-wheat flour tortillas, whole-wheat, muesli or flaxseed pitas and cheese buns.

•   If you've had roast or grilled pork the night before, make a quick tzatziki sauce by combining yogurt with grated cucumber and dill. Presto, you've got a brown bag souvlaki!

•   And don't forget about fish meals—grill up some salmon fillets, keep whole or flake and combine with homemade tartar sauce (chop some pickles and green onion into light mayonnaise along with some green pepper relish), tomato slices and shredded lettuce.

BEYOND BREAD

Go whole grain, whole wheat or whole rye for the fiber, then spread or top your slice with a protein pleaser of choice: lean meat, low-fat cheese, chicken breast, tuna, salmon or, for vegetarians, hummus or bean spread.

VEGETABLES AND SALADS

Asparagus Leek Braise

Whether you prefer plump or pencil-thin spears, always choose asparagus with tightly closed tips that are some-what purplish green in color. Asparagus are always best cooked the same day you buy them but can be stored in the refrigerator, either tightly wrapped in damp paper towels or standing vertically in a wet measuring cup in a small amount of water, for up to 3 days.

1	leek (white and green part), thickly sliced	1
1 lb	asparagus, trimmed and cut into 2-inch (5-cm) lengths	500 g
1 tbsp	butter	15 mL
2/3 cup	vegetable stock	150 mL
2 tsp	chopped fresh dill (optional)	10 mL

In skillet, heat butter over medium heat; cook leek for 2 minutes, stirring often. Add vegetable stock; cover and cook for 8 minutes or until tender.

Add asparagus; cook, covered, over medium heat for about 6 minutes or until tender. Serve sprinkled with chopped fresh dill, if desired.

Makes 4 servings.

Per serving: about 56 cal, 2 g pro, 3 g total fat (2 g satu-rated fat), 6 g carb, 2 g fiber, 7 mg chol, 145 mg sodium. % RDI: 2% calcium, 6% iron, 7% vit A, 17% vit C, 56% folate.

Cherry Tomato and Mushroom Sauté

Tomatoes and mushrooms complement each other deliciously, particularly cherry tomatoes, which are more flavorful than regular tomatoes when the latter are not in season.

1 tbsp	vegetable oil	15 mL
1	onion, chopped	1
1	clove garlic, minced	1
3 cups	quartered mushrooms (about 8 oz/250 g)	750 mL
1/4 tsp	each salt and pepper	1 mL
1 tbsp	all-purpose flour	15 mL
1/2 cup	chicken or vegetable stock	125 mL
2 cups	cherry tomatoes, halved	500 mL

In skillet, heat oil over medium heat; cook onion, garlic, mushrooms, salt and pepper, stirring occasionally, for about 5 minutes or until softened.

Sprinkle with flour; cook, stirring, for 1 minute. Stir in stock and bring to boil; reduce heat and simmer for 2 minutes. Add tomatoes; cook for about 3 minutes or until some juice is released.

Makes 4 servings.

Per serving: about 75 cal, 3 g pro, 4 g total fat (trace sat-urated fat), 9 g carb, 2 g fiber, 0 mg chol, 247 mg sodi-um. % RDI: 1% calcium, 9% iron, 7% vit A, 20% vit C, 7% folate.

Cold Sesame Swiss Chard Leaves

Put a little Asian flavor on your table with this cold side dish, inspired by Japanese and Korean spinach salads.

2	bunches Swiss chard (2 1/2 lb/1.25 kg total)	2
4 tsp	soy sauce	20 mL
1 tbsp	toasted sesame seeds	15 mL
2 tsp	sesame oil	10 mL
1 tsp	granulated sugar	5 mL

Remove stems from Swiss chard and reserve for another use. In large pot of boiling salted water, cook leaves for 1 minute. Drain in colander and rinse under cold water; press to extract as much liquid as possible. Transfer to bowl.

In small bowl, mix together soy sauce, sesame seeds, sesame oil and sugar; pour over leaves and toss to coat.

Makes 4 servings.

Per serving: about 88 cal, 5 g pro, 4 g total fat (1 g saturated fat), 12 g carb, 5 g fiber, 0 mg chol, 769 mg sodium. % RDI: 13% calcium, 41% iron, 75% vit A, 72% vit C, 11% folate.

Curried Carrots

Curry lovers, beware! Your ranks will swell with new members once people taste this recipe. The inherent sweetness of the cooked carrots, coupled with the raisins and apple juice, beautifully tempers and subdues the curry paste, resulting in a sweet and delicately flavorful side dish. Serve with roast pork, pork chops or roast chicken.

8	carrots (about 1 1/2 lb/750 g), peeled and sliced diagonally	8
3/4 cup	apple juice	175 mL
1/4 tsp	each salt and pepper	1 mL
1/2 cup	chopped golden raisins	125 mL
1 tsp	curry paste	5 mL
1	clove garlic, minced	1
2 tbsp	vegetable oil	25 mL
2	green onions, finely chopped	2

In large saucepan, bring carrots, apple juice, salt and pepper, raisins, curry paste and garlic to boil; cover and cook over medium heat for 5 to 7 minutes or until almost tender.

Uncover and increase heat to high; cook, stirring often, for 3 to 4 minutes or until liquid is evaporated yet carrots are still moist. Remove from heat. Stir in oil and chopped green onions.

Makes 4 servings.

Per serving: about 217 cal, 3 g pro, 8 g total fat (1 g saturated fat), 38 g carb, 6 g fiber, 0 mg chol, 246 mg sodium. % RDI: 6% calcium, 11% iron, 364% vit A, 32% vit C, 11% folate.

Green Beans Gremolata

The classic northern Italian gremolata mixture of parsley, citrus rind and garlic livens up cooked green beans—a midsummer favorite.

1 lb	green beans, trimmed	500 g
2 tbsp	olive oil	25 mL
1 tbsp	wine vinegar	15 mL
1/4 tsp	each salt and pepper	1 mL
1 tbsp	chopped fresh parsley	15 mL
2 tsp	grated lemon rind	10 mL
1	clove garlic, minced	1

In large pot of boiling salted water, cook beans until tender-crisp, about 5 minutes; drain well.

In large bowl, whisk together olive oil, vinegar, salt and pepper; add beans and toss to coat. Combine parsley, lemon rind and garlic; sprinkle over beans.

Makes 4 servings.

Per serving: about 97 cal, 2 g pro, 7 g total fat (1 g saturated fat), 8 g carb, 3 g fiber, 0 mg chol, 380 mg sodium. % RDI: 5% calcium, 10% iron, 7% vit A, 20% vit C, 15% folate.

Honey Lemon Beets

Vibrant both in color and flavor, this dish turns the humble beet into delicious upscale fare.

8	small beets (about 2 lb/1 kg)	8
1 tbsp	butter	15 mL
1	onion, sliced	1
2 tbsp	liquid honey	25 mL
2 tbsp	lemon juice	25 mL
1/2 tsp	ground nutmeg	2 mL
1/4 tsp	each salt and pepper	1 mL

In large pot of boiling salted water, cover and cook beets for about 40 minutes or until tender. Drain and let cool slightly; slip off skins. Cut in half; cut into wedges.

Meanwhile, in large nonstick skillet, melt butter over medium heat; cook onion, stirring occasionally, for 8 minutes or until tender. Stir in honey, lemon juice, nutmeg, salt and pepper.

Add beets; cook, stirring to coat, for 5 minutes or until glazed.

Makes 4 to 6 servings.

Per each of 6 servings: about 98 cal, 2 g pro, 2 g total fat (1 g saturated fat), 19 g carb, 3 g fiber, 5 mg chol, 205 mg sodium. % RDI: 2% calcium, 7% iron, 2% vit A, 10% vit C, 43% folate.

Kale with Apples and Onion

Kale goes well with apples; here, curry paste makes it more fragrant.

1	bunch kale (8 oz/250 g)	1
1	apple	1
1 tbsp	vegetable oil	15 mL
1	onion, sliced	1
1 tsp	curry paste	5 mL
1/2 cup	vegetable or chicken stock	125 mL
Pinch	each salt and pepper	Pinch

Trim off stems and ribs from kale. Chop leaves coarsely and set aside. Peel and cut apple into 1/4-inch (5-mm) thick slices.

In large shallow Dutch oven, heat oil over medium-high heat; cook onion until golden, about 3 minutes. Add apple and curry paste; cook until apple is almost tender, about 2 minutes.

Add reserved chopped leaves, stock, salt and pepper; cover and cook, stirring occasionally, until kale is tender and most of the liquid is evaporated, about 5 minutes.

Makes 4 servings.

Per serving: about 80 cal, 1 g pro, 4 g total fat (trace saturated fat), 11 g carb, 2 g fiber, 0 mg chol, 87 mg sodium. % RDI: 6% calcium, 1% iron, 14% vit A, 13% vit C, 3% folate.

Lemon Broccoli Salad

Lemon adds sparkle and almonds add crunch to a tender-crisp broccoli salad.

2 tbsp	slivered almonds	25 mL
4 cups	chopped broccoli	1 L
2 tbsp	vegetable oil	25 mL
4 tsp	lemon juice	20 mL
1 tsp	Dijon mustard	5 mL
1/2 tsp	granulated sugar	2 mL
1/4 tsp	each salt and pepper	1 mL
1/4 cup	chopped red onion	50 mL

In small skillet, toast almonds over medium heat, shaking pan occasionally, for about 5 minutes or just until golden.

Meanwhile, in large pot of boiling water, cook broccoli for 3 minutes or until tender-crisp. Drain and chill under cold running water. Drain and pat dry.

In salad bowl, whisk together oil, lemon juice, mustard, sugar, salt and pepper. Add broccoli, onion and almonds; toss to coat.

Makes 4 servings.

Per serving: about 116 cal, 4 g pro, 9 g total fat (1 g saturated fat), 7 g carb, 3 g fiber, 0 mg chol, 184 mg sodium. % RDI: 5% calcium, 7% iron, 12% vit A, 113% vit C, 22% folate.

Mango, Cucumber and Red Pepper Salad

Fresh, crisp and spicy, this salad is the perfect accompaniment to Asian stir-fries and noodle dishes.

1	mango	1
1	sweet red pepper	1
Half	English cucumber (about 6 inches/15 cm)	Half
2 tbsp	lime juice	25 mL
1 tbsp	fish sauce	15 mL
1 1/2 tsp	granulated sugar	7 mL
1 tsp	minced hot pepper	5 mL
1/4 cup	each chopped unsalted peanuts and fresh coriander	50 mL

Peel mango. Slice mango, sweet red pepper and English cucumber into thin strips.

In bowl, whisk together lime juice, fish sauce, sugar and hot pepper. Add mango, red pepper and cucumber; toss to coat. (Make ahead: Cover and refrigerate for up to 6 hours.) Sprinkle with peanuts and coriander.

Makes 4 servings.

Per serving: about 110 cal, 4 g pro, 5 g total fat (1 g saturated fat), 16 g carb, 3 g fiber, 0 mg chol, 353 mg sodium. % RDI: 2% calcium, 4% iron, 39% vit A, 127% vit C, 13% folate.

Tip: For the best peanut flavor, use raw peanuts; roast, stirring constantly, in dry skillet over medium heat for 5 minutes.

Orzo Salad

An ideal substitute for rice, orzo is a tiny, rice-shaped pasta perfect for soups and salads. Remember, salting the water before boiling any type of pasta is an important step. It makes the water boil faster and, more importantly, it will make the pasta taste better and complement the rest of the flavors in the dish.

1 cup	orzo	250 mL
1/4 cup	olive oil	50 mL
3 tbsp	lemon juice	50 mL
1	clove garlic, minced	1
3 tbsp	chopped fresh parsley	50 mL
1 tsp	dried oregano	5 mL
1/4 tsp	each salt and pepper	1 mL
1	field cucumber (or half English cucumber), seeded and diced	1
2	tomatoes, seeded and diced	2
Quarter	red onion, chopped	Quarter
	lettuce leaves (optional)	

In saucepan of boiling salted water, cook orzo for about 6 minutes or until tender but firm. Drain and cool under cold water; drain and place in bowl.

Meanwhile, in small bowl, whisk together olive oil, lemon juice, minced garlic, 2 tbsp (25 mL) of the parsley, oregano, salt and pepper; stir into orzo. Add cucumber, tomatoes and red onion; stir to combine.

Line serving platter with lettuce (if using). Mound salad in center; garnish with remaining parsley.

Makes 6 servings.

Per serving: about 207 cal, 5 g pro, 10 g total fat (1 g saturated fat), 26 g carb, 2 g fiber, 0 mg chol, 177 mg sodium. % RDI: 2% calcium, 6% iron, 4% vit A, 23% vit C, 10% folate.

Tip: The tomatoes are seeded to prevent the salad from becoming too watery. To seed a tomato, slice in half horizontally. Hold cut side down over a bowl and gently squeeze out seeds.

Rapini with Lemon Anchovy Vinaigrette

This quick dish makes an attractive side vegetable served either hot or at room temperature. Or serve it as a salad course with bread or as an addition to an antipasto platter.

1	bunch rapini (1 lb/500 g)	1
1	clove garlic	1
1/4 tsp	salt	1 mL
1	anchovy fillet (or 1 tsp/ 15 mL anchovy paste)	1
3 tbsp	extra-virgin olive oil	50 mL
1 tbsp	lemon juice	15 mL
1/4 tsp	pepper	1 mL

Trim 1/4 inch (5 mm) off bottom of rapini stems and discard. In large pot of boiling salted water, blanch rapini until tender-crisp, about 2 minutes. Drain well; place on tea towel.

On cutting board, chop garlic; sprinkle with salt. Using side of chef's knife or fork, rub together to form paste. Chop anchovy and mash into garlic paste.

In bowl, whisk together oil, lemon juice, pepper and paste; add rapini and toss to coat.

Makes 4 servings.

Per serving: about 130 cal, 4 g pro, 11 g total fat (1 g saturated fat), 5 g carb, 2 g fiber, 1 mg chol, 434 mg sodium. % RDI: 23% calcium, 13% iron, 31% vit A, 57% vit C, 4% folate.

Roasted Broccoli and Red Pepper

Packed with color and flavor, these vegetables are roasted together and ready fast—cook them while the fish is roasting.

6 cups	broccoli florets (about 1 large bunch)	1.5 L
1	sweet red pepper, cut in chunks	1
2	cloves garlic, minced	2
1/2 tsp	salt	2 mL
1/4 tsp	pepper	1 mL
Pinch	cayenne pepper	Pinch
1 tbsp	olive oil	15 mL

In large bowl, toss together broccoli, red pepper, garlic, salt, pepper and cayenne pepper; spray with oil. Spread on foil-lined baking sheet.

Roast in 450°F (230°C) oven until broccoli is tender-crisp, 10 to 15 minutes.

Makes 4 servings.

Per serving: about 60 cal, 3 g pro, 4 g total fat (1 g saturated fat), 6 g carb, 2 g fiber, 0 mg chol, 306 mg sodium. % RDI: 4% calcium, 6% iron, 21% vit A, 170% vit C, 18% folate.

Tip: Save the broccoli stalks for snacks; peel and cut into finger-size lengths for dipping into dip or dressing.

Roasted Roots Salad

Roasting root vegetables caramelizes them, releasing their natural sweetness to balance the roasted garlic dressing.

1	head garlic	1
4	beets (about 1 lb/500 g), peeled	4
4	carrots (about 1 lb/500 g), peeled	4
2	sweet potatoes (about 1 lb/500 g), peeled	2
1	celery root (about 1 lb/500 g), peeled	1
3 tbsp	olive oil	50 mL
1/2 tsp	each salt and pepper	2 mL

Roasted Garlic Dressing

1/4 cup	chopped fresh mint (or 1 tsp/5 mL dried)	50 mL
2 tbsp	each olive oil and balsamic vinegar	25 mL
1/4 tsp	salt	1 mL

Trim tip off garlic head. Cut beets, carrots, sweet potatoes and celery root into 1-inch (2.5-cm) cubes; place in large bowl along with garlic. Add oil, salt and pepper; toss to coat. Spread on large greased or foil-lined rimmed baking sheet; roast in 425°F (220°C) oven, stirring once, for 45 to 55 minutes or until tender and potatoes are golden.

To make the dressing, squeeze garlic pulp into a large bowl. Add mint, oil, vinegar and salt; mash together. (Make ahead: Cover and refrigerate for up to 4 hours.) Add vegetables; toss to coat. Serve hot or warm.

Makes 6 servings.

Per serving: about 247 cal, 4 g pro, 12 g total fat (2 g saturated fat), 35 g carb, 6 g fiber, 0 mg chol, 441 mg sodium. % RDI: 8% calcium, 13% iron, 273% vit. A, 37% vit. C, 33% folate.

Substitution: You can improvise with the kinds of root vegetables used as long as you respect the amounts and method of preparation. For example, a half rutabaga can replace carrots, and 4 potatoes the celery root.

Snow Peas and Peppers

A captivating and nutritious side dish to any meal, this recipe takes only minutes to make. Up the flavor ante by substituting balsamic vinegar or sherry vinegar for the wine vinegar.

1 tbsp	butter or vegetable oil	15 mL
2	cloves garlic, minced	2
1/4 tsp	each salt and pepper	1 mL
1	sweet red pepper, sliced	1
3 cups	snow peas, trimmed	750 mL
1 tbsp	wine vinegar	15 mL

In deep skillet, heat butter over medium heat; cook garlic and salt and pepper until fragrant, about 30 seconds. Add sweet red pepper and snow peas. Cook, stirring occasionally, until tender-crisp, 5 minutes. Stir in vinegar.

Makes 4 servings.

Per serving: about 59 cal, 2 g pro, 3 g total fat (2 g saturated fat), 6 g carb, 2 g fiber, 8 mg chol, 176 mg sodium. % RDI: 3% calcium, 9% iron, 14% vit A, 125% vit C, 9% folate.

FOUR FAST GREEN PEA IDEAS

Frozen peas are a go-with-anything vegetable that requires no preparation—the answer to many a rush-hour dilemma. Here's how to add variety to this everyday favorite.

In microwaveable dish, cover and cook 2 cups (500 mL) frozen peas at high for about 3 minutes or until hot. Stir in 1 tsp (5 mL) butter, a pinch of salt and pepper and one of the following combinations.

Mint Red Pepper Peas: Half sweet red pepper, diced; 1/4 tsp (1 mL) dried mint.

Honey Almond Peas: 1/3 cup (75 mL) toasted sliced almonds; 1 tsp (5 mL) liquid honey.

Ginger Pepper Peas: 1 tsp (5 mL) sesame oil; 1/4 tsp (1 mL) each ground ginger and hot pepper sauce.

Lemon Dill Peas: 1 tsp (5 mL) grated lemon rind; 1/4 tsp (1 mL) dried dillweed.

FRUIT

Melon Berry Fruit Salad

A refreshing and colorful way to kick-start your day, this fruit salad uses fruit nectar, which is slightly thicker than fruit juice. Try peach, pear or guava for a hint of exotic flavor.

3 cups	cubed cantaloupe (about 1/2 cantaloupe)	750 mL
3 cups	cubed honeydew melon (about 1/3 honeydew)	750 mL
2 cups	sliced strawberries	500 mL
1/4 cup	bottled fruit nectar	50 mL

Combine cantaloupe and honeydew pieces in bowl with strawberries. Pour nectar over; toss gently to combine.

Can be covered with plastic wrap and refrigerated for up to 3 days.

Makes 8 cups (2 L).

Other Suggestions:

Citrus fruit is perfect for breakfast any time of the year—be it a fresh orange cut into sections, or a pretty pink or red half grapefruit, just waiting to be sectioned and slurped.

Combine cubed cantaloupe with a dash of freshly squeezed lemon juice and have on standby in your refrigerator during the week.

Try the extra sweet (golden) pineapple—many stores stock them already peeled and cored, making short shrift of your work. Cube and combine with blueberries and a bit of frozen orange juice concentrate thinned out with some water.

Per serving: about 59 cal, 1 g pro, trace total fat (trace saturated fat), 15 g carb, 2 g fiber, 0 mg chol, 13 mg sodium. % RDI: 1% calcium, 2% iron, 20% vit A, 108% vit C, 16% folate.

Standby Stewed Fruit

Keep a jar in the refrigerator to spoon over yogurt or cereal, or freshen up with grapes, bananas or orange or grapefruit sections.

4 cups	water	1 L
1 cup	dried apples	250 mL
1 cup	pitted prunes	250 mL
1/3 cup	dried apricots	75 mL
Pinch	cinnamon	Pinch
2 tsp	grated orange rind	10 mL
2 tbsp	orange juice	25 mL
	granulated sugar or liquid honey (optional)	

In saucepan, combine water, apples, prunes, apricots, cinnamon, orange rind and juice; bring to boil. Reduce heat, cover and simmer for 10 to 15 minutes or until tender but not mushy. Let cool. Add sugar (if using) to taste.

Compote can be covered and refrigerated for up to 1 week; stir occasionally.

Makes 8 servings.

Per serving: about 84 cal, 1 g pro, trace total fat (0 g saturated fat), 22 g carb, 4 g fiber, 0 mg chol, 11 mg sodium. % RDI: 1% calcium, 6% iron, 5% vit A, 7% vit C, 0% folate.

GRAIN FOODS

CEREALS

Apple Cinnamon Oatmeal Porridge

To add variety to your mornings, try substituting dried apples or pears for the fresh apple called for in this recipe and replacing the raisins with dried cherries or cranberries.

3 cups	unsweetened apple juice or water	750 mL
1/2 tsp	salt	2 mL
1 1/3 cups	quick-cooking rolled oats	325 mL
Half	apple, peeled and diced	Half
1/3 cup	raisins (optional)	75 mL
1/2 tsp	cinnamon	2 mL

Stove top: In saucepan, bring unsweetened apple juice or water and salt to boil. Whisk in rolled oats, apple, raisins (if using) and cinnamon. Reduce heat and simmer, whisking constantly, for 4 to 5 minutes or until desired thickness.

Microwave: In 12-cup (3-L) microwaveable casserole dish, microwave unsweetened apple juice or water with salt at High for 3 minutes or until boiling. Whisk in oats; apple, raisins (if using) and cinnamon. Microwave, covered, at High, stirring often, for 4 minutes or until desired thickness.

Makes 4 servings.

Per serving: about 149 cal, 4 g pro, 2 g total fat (trace saturated fat), 30 g carb, 4 g fiber, 0 mg chol, 290 mg sodium. % RDI: 2% calcium, 11% iron, 0% vit A, 37% vit C, 3% folate.

Orange Date Oat Bran Porridge

Here's a lip-smacking porridge that sticks to your ribs. This recipe includes a hint of orange and the goodness of dried fruit. Oat bran is particularly high in soluble fiber, a leading contender in the fight against cholesterol.

4 cups	water	1 L
1/2 tsp	salt	2 mL
1 1/3 cups	oat bran	325 mL
1 cup	chopped dates	250 mL
1 tsp	grated orange rind	5 mL
Pinch	ground cloves	Pinch

Stove top: In saucepan, bring water and salt to boil. Whisk in oat bran, dates, orange rind and ground cloves. Reduce heat and simmer, whisking constantly, for 3 to 4 minutes or until desired thickness.

Microwave: In 12-cup (3-L) microwaveable casserole dish, microwave water with salt for 3 minutes or until boiling. Whisk in oat bran, dates, orange rind and ground cloves. Microwave, covered, at High, stirring often, for 3 minutes or until desired thickness.

Makes 4 servings.

Per serving: about 200 cal, 6 g pro, 2 g total fat (trace saturated fat), 54 g carb, 9 g fiber, 0 mg chol, 296 mg sodium. % RDI: 3% calcium, 16% iron, 0% vit A, 2% vit C, 6% folate.

Maple Walnut Multigrain Porridge

When buying shelled walnuts, look for ones that are plump, meaty and crisp. Avoid those that appear shriveled or dried out. And always store them tightly wrapped in a plastic bag.

3 cups	low-fat milk	750 mL
1/2 tsp	salt	2 mL
1 cup	multigrain cereal such as Red River or Sunny Boy	250 mL
1/2 cup	chopped walnuts	125 mL
2 tbsp	maple syrup	25 mL
1 tsp	vanilla	5 mL

Stove top: In saucepan, bring milk and salt to boil. Whisk in multigrain cereal, walnuts, maple syrup and vanilla. Reduce heat and simmer, whisking constantly, for 6 to 7 minutes or until desired thickness.

Microwave: In 12-cup (3-L) microwaveable casserole dish, microwave milk with salt at High for 3 minutes or until boiling. Whisk in multigrain cereal, chopped walnuts, maple syrup and vanilla. Microwave, covered, at High, stirring often, for 6 minutes or until desired thickness.

Makes 4 servings.

Per serving (based on 2% milk): about 349 cal, 14 g pro, 14 g total fat (3 g saturated fat), 45 g carb, 5 g fiber, 14 mg chol, 392 mg sodium. % RDI: 22% calcium, 9% iron, 9% vit A, 2% vit C, 17% folate.

Grab-a-Snack Mix

In a rush with no time to eat in the morning? This snack mix is the perfect breakfast you and your kids can munch on while on your way to work or school. Bring along with a small carton of milk or unsweetened fruit juice. It's even great to snack on during the day or while watching a movie in the evening.

1 cup	whole-wheat cereal squares	250 mL
1/2 cup	raisins	125 mL
1/3 cup	banana chips, broken	75 mL
1/4 cup	dried apricots, quartered	50 mL
2 tbsp	chopped toasted almonds	25 mL

In glass bowl, mix together cereal squares, raisins, banana chips, dried apricots and almonds.

Mix can be covered with plastic wrap or transferred to resealable plastic bag for up to 2 weeks; do not store in airtight container.

Makes 2 cups (500 mL).

Per 2/3 cup (150 mL) serving: about 255 cal, 4 g pro, 6 g total fat (3 g saturated fat), 50 g carb, 5 g fiber, 0 mg chol, 149 mg sodium. % RDI: 4% calcium, 26% iron, 8% vit A, 3% vit C, 7% folate.

SUPER CEREAL

Add fiber and vitamins A and C to your bowl by topping it with a couple of spoonfuls of one, or a juicy combination, of the following: blueberries, raspberries; sliced bananas, peaches, strawberries or nectarines; dried cranberries.

For an extra 4 g of fiber, sprinkle your favorite cereal with 2 tbsp (25 mL) Kellogg's All-Bran Buds with Psyllium.

Wickaninnish Inn Granola

This healthy and versatile granola, laden with nuts, seeds and all manner of dried fruits, was developed at the Wickaninnish Inn on Vancouver Island by chef Jim Garraway. You won't give ordinary granola a second glance!

2 cups	large-flake rolled oats	500 mL
1/2 cup	shredded coconut	125 mL
1/2 cup	wheat germ	125 mL
1/4 cup	natural bran	50 mL
1/4 cup	slivered almonds	50 mL
1/4 cup	pecan halves	50 mL
1/4 cup	sunflower seeds	50 mL
2 tbsp	sesame seeds	25 mL
1/4 cup	liquid honey	50 mL
2 tbsp	vegetable oil	25 mL
1 1/2 tsp	grated orange rind	7 mL
1 tsp	vanilla	5 mL
Pinch	salt	Pinch
1 cup	raisins	250 mL
3/4 cup	dates, pitted and quartered	175 mL
1/2 cup	dried apricots, quartered	125 mL
1/2 cup	dried figs, quartered	125 mL
1/4 cup	banana chips	50 mL
3 tbsp	currants	50 mL

In large bowl, toss together rolled oats, coconut, wheat germ, bran, almonds, pecans, and sunflower and sesame seeds.

Whisk together honey, oil, orange rind, vanilla and salt; add to dry ingredients, stirring, until moistened. Spread on ungreased large rimmed baking sheet.

Bake in 250°F (120°C) oven, stirring occasionally, for 1 hour and 20 minutes or until golden. Let cool. Stir in raisins, dates, apricots, figs, banana chips and currants.

Makes 8 cups (2 L).

Per 1 cup (250 mL): about 457 cal, 10 g pro, 16 g total fat (4 g saturated fat), 76 g carb, 9 g fiber, 0 mg chol, 23 mg sodium. % RDI: 6% calcium, 26% iron, 6% vit A, 3% vit C, 19% folate.

Tip: To store, refrigerate in airtight container for up to 2 weeks. Enjoy 1/2 cup (125 mL) as a cold cereal with low-fat milk, or sprinkle a few tablespoons (25–50 mL) over a bowl of yogurt and fresh fruit.

QUICK BREADS AND PANCAKES

Apple Oat Muffins

Start your day with a hearty muffin that combines whole wheat and oats with apples and warm spices.

1 3/4 cups	quick-cooking rolled oats	425 mL
1 3/4 cups	plain 1% or 2% yogurt	425 mL
2	eggs	2
1 cup	shredded peeled apple	250 mL
1/4 cup	vegetable oil	50 mL
1 tsp	vanilla	5 mL
2 cups	whole-wheat flour	500 mL
3/4 cup	packed brown sugar	175 mL
4 tsp	baking powder	20 mL
2 tsp	cinnamon	10 mL
1 tsp	baking soda	5 mL
1/2 tsp	each nutmeg and salt	2 mL
3/4 cup	raisins or dried cranberries	175 mL

In bowl, combine oats and yogurt; let stand for 10 minutes. Whisk in eggs, apple, oil and vanilla. In large bowl, combine flour, sugar, baking powder, cinnamon, baking soda, nutmeg and salt. Pour yogurt mixture over dry ingredients. Sprinkle with raisins; stir just until moistened. Spoon into greased or paper-lined muffin cups.

Bake in center of 375°F (190°C) oven for 35 minutes or until golden brown and tops are firm to touch. Let cool in pan on rack for 5 minutes; transfer to rack and let cool completely.

Can be stored in airtight container for up to 1 day or frozen for up to 2 weeks.

Makes 12 large muffins.

Per muffin: about 278 cal, 8 g pro, 7 g total fat (1 g saturated fat), 49 g carb, 5 g fiber, 37 mg chol, 322 mg sodium. % RDI: 13% calcium, 16% iron, 2% vit A, 2% vit C, 7% folate.

Date Bran Muffins

These high-fiber, flavorful muffins are a great way to start your day, and they're also easy to make.

3/4 cup	each natural wheat bran and All-Bran cereal	175 mL
11/3 cups	buttermilk	325 mL
2 cups	all-purpose flour	500 mL
3/4 cup	whole-wheat flour	175 mL
1/2 cup	packed dark brown sugar	125 mL
2 tbsp	flaxseeds, ground	25 mL
4 tsp	baking powder	20 mL
2 tsp	baking soda	10 mL
1/2 tsp	cinnamon	2 mL
1/4 tsp	salt	1 mL
1 cup	chopped dates	250 mL
3/4 cup	fancy molasses	175 mL
1/3 cup	vegetable oil	75 mL
1	egg, beaten	1
1 1/2 tsp	vanilla	7 mL

In bowl, stir bran and cereal into buttermilk; let stand for 10 minutes. Meanwhile, in large bowl, whisk together flours, sugar, flaxseeds, baking powder, baking soda, cinnamon and salt; stir in dates.

Into bran mixture, whisk molasses, oil, egg and vanilla; pour over flour mixture and stir together just until combined.

Grease tops of muffin pans; line cups with paper or grease. Pour in batter, filling three-quarters full; bake in center of 375°F (190°C) oven for about 25 minutes or until golden and tops are firm to the touch. Let cool in pans on rack for 2 minutes. Remove from pans; let cool on rack.

Makes 12 muffins.

Per muffin: about 330 cal, 6 g pro, 8 g total fat (1 g saturated fat), 64 g carb, 6 g fiber, 19 mg chol, 413 mg sodium. % RDI: 13% calcium, 27% iron, 1% vit A, 0% vit C, 18% folate.

Orange Apricot Loaf

This muffin-like loaf is ideal for brunch or to serve with tea. If using a dark pan, check after one hour, as loaves bake slightly faster in dark pans.

1 3/4 cups	whole-wheat flour	425 mL
1 cup	all-purpose flour	250 mL
2/3 cup	packed brown sugar	150 mL
2 tsp	baking powder	10 mL
1/2 tsp	baking soda	2 mL
1/2 tsp	salt	2 mL
1	medium seedless orange (unpeeled)	1
2	eggs	2
3/4 cup	milk (approx)	175 mL
1/4 cup	vegetable oil	50 mL
2 tsp	vanilla	10 mL
3/4 cup	chopped dried apricots	175 mL
2 tsp	icing sugar	10 mL

In large bowl, combine whole-wheat and all-purpose flours, sugar, baking powder, baking soda and salt; set aside.

In food processor or blender, mince orange into small pieces. Using on/off motion, blend in eggs, milk, oil and vanilla; pour into measure and add more milk to make 2 cups (500 mL). Pour over dry ingredients; sprinkle with apricots. Stir just until moistened.

Spread in greased 8-× 4-inch (1.5-L) loaf pan. Bake in center of 350°F (180°C) oven for 1 to 1 1/4 hours or until tester inserted in center comes out clean. Let cool in pan on rack for 10 minutes; turn out onto rack and let cool completely. Dust with icing sugar.

Slices can be individually wrapped in plastic wrap and frozen in airtight container for up to 1 month; or wrap and freeze whole.

Makes 1 loaf, or 12 slices.

Per slice: about 234 cal, 6 g pro, 6 g total fat (1 g saturated fat), 42 g carb, 4 g fiber, 37 mg chol, 211 mg sodium. % RDI: 7% calcium, 14% iron, 8% vit A, 15% vit C, 6% folate.

Buttermilk Berry Pancake Mix

Vary the fruit in this mix, which stores well. Or omit it altogether and add pieces of your favorite fresh fruit when mixing up the batter. Look for buttermilk powder in bulk-food stores. You can substitute skim milk powder but omit the baking soda.

4 cups	all-purpose flour	1 L
2 cups	whole-wheat flour	500 mL
1 1/3 cups	buttermilk powder	325 mL
1/4 cup	granulated sugar	50 mL
2 tbsp	baking powder	25 mL
2 tsp	baking soda	10 mL
1 tsp	ground nutmeg	5 mL
1 tsp	salt	5 mL
3 cups	dried blueberries or other dried berries, raisins or currants	750 mL

In bowl, stir together all-purpose and whole-wheat flours, buttermilk powder, sugar, baking powder, baking soda, ground nutmeg and salt until combined. Stir in berries. (Make ahead: Store in airtight containers in dry place for up to 3 weeks; stir before using.)
Makes about 9 1/3 cups (2.3 L).

Buttermilk Berry Pancakes

When you have a mix in the cupboard just waiting to blend, pancakes are fast breakfast fare.

1	egg	1
1 1/4 cups	water	300 mL
3 tbsp	vegetable oil or butter, melted (approx)	50 mL
2 1/3 cups	Buttermilk Berry Pancake Mix (recipe, this page)	575 mL

In bowl, beat together egg, water and 2 tbsp (25 mL) of the oil. Stir in pancake mix until blended.

Heat skillet over medium-high heat; brush with some of the remaining oil. Pour 1/4 cup (50 mL) batter per pancake into skillet, brushing with more oil as necessary; cook for about 2 minutes or until golden and bubbles break on top but do not fill in. Turn and cook for about 1 minute or until bottoms are golden brown.
Makes about 12 4-inch (10-cm) pancakes.

Per pancake: about 132 cal, 4 g pro, 4 g total fat (1 g saturated fat), 21 g carb, 2 g fiber, chol (not analyzed), 152 mg sodium. % RDI: 6% calcium, 7% iron, 1% vit A, 0% vit C, 3% folate.

French-Toasted Banana Sandwich

If you like, you can dust this with a little cinnamon sugar.

1 tbsp	peanut butter (optional)	15 mL
4	slices whole-grain bread	4
2	bananas	2
2	eggs	2
1/3 cup	milk	75 mL
1/2 tsp	vanilla	2 mL
Pinch	each cinnamon and salt	Pinch
2 tsp	butter	10 mL

Spread peanut butter (if using) over bread. Slice each banana lengthwise into 4; sandwich between bread. In pie plate, whisk together eggs, milk, vanilla, cinnamon and salt; add sandwiches, turning to soak up all mixture. In nonstick skillet, heat butter over medium-high heat; cook sandwiches for about 5 minutes or until browned on both sides.
Makes 2 servings.

Per serving: about 369 cal, 14 g pro, 13 g total fat (5 g saturated fat), 55 g carb, 6 g fiber, 199 mg chol, 413 mg sodium. % RDI: 11% calcium, 20% iron, 14% vit A, 12% vit C, 25% folate.

SIDE DISHES

Barley

An important consideration when buying grains is freshness. Try to purchase grains in amounts that you can use within a month, especially if they are whole grains. Barley, because it is more processed than brown rice, for example, will keep for at least 6 months in an airtight container in a cool pantry.

2 cups	water or vegetable or chicken stock	500 mL
1/4 tsp	salt	1 mL
1 cup	pot or pearl barley	250 mL

In saucepan, bring water and salt to boil over high heat; stir in barley. Reduce heat to low; cover and simmer for 40 minutes or until tender and liquid is evaporated.
Makes 4 servings.

Tip: Pot barley is a little bit more nutritious than pearl barley because it has been less heavily processed.

Couscous

Technically a pasta, couscous is the hurried cook's dream. It cooks in just 5 minutes, can be made with stock or water, and can be used as a side dish, as a salad mixed with chopped vegetables or dried fruit, or even in stews.

1 1/2 cups	water or vegetable or chicken stock	375 mL
Pinch	salt	Pinch
1 cup	couscous	250 mL

In saucepan, bring water and salt to boil; stir in couscous. Remove from heat; cover and let stand for 5 minutes. Fluff with fork.
Makes 4 servings.

Kasha

Mixing kasha or roasted buckwheat groats with an egg before steaming keeps the grains firm and separate. Try substituting stock for water; it boosts flavor without adding fat.

1 cup	kasha	250 mL
1	egg	1
1/2 tsp	salt	2 mL
Pinch	pepper	Pinch
1 1/2 cups	boiling water	375 mL
1 tbsp	butter	15 mL

In saucepan, combine kasha, egg, salt and pepper; cook over medium-low heat, stirring, for 3 minutes or until dry and kernels separate. Stir in water and butter; cover and cook, without stirring, for 10 to 12 minutes or until water is absorbed. Fluff with fork.
Makes 2 servings.

Wheat Berries

Wheat berries are whole-wheat kernels with the bran and germ intact. They hold all the same nutrients wheat has to offer and are wonderfully chewy.

4 cups	water	1 L
1/2 tsp	salt	2 mL
1 1/2 cups	soft wheat berries	375 mL

In large saucepan, bring water and salt to boil over high heat; add wheat berries. Reduce heat to low; cover and simmer for 45 to 60 minutes or until tender but firm. Drain. Serve hot or cold with chopped fresh herbs and enough vinaigrette to moisten.

Makes 4 to 6 servings.

EIGHT GREAT IDEAS FOR GRAINS

• Use quinoa or barley in a salad. Cook 1 cup (250 mL) quinoa or barley. Once cool, combine with 6 dried apricots, diced, 1/3 cup (75 mL) minced green onion, 1/4 cup (50 mL) currants and 1/4 cup (50 mL) each finely chopped sweet red and green pepper. Toss lightly with your favorite dressing.

• Try tossing together dried cherries, some toasted cashews and some chopped fresh mint into your favorite grain.

• Use barley or bulgur in a pilaf. In saucepan, sauté chopped fresh mushrooms in a little bit of butter along with salt, pepper and some chopped fresh rosemary. Combine with some chopped rehydrated dried porcini mushrooms. Stir in liquid and grain of choice. Lower heat and simmer until cooked.

• Cook 1 cup (250 mL) couscous. Stir in strips of sun-dried tomatoes or chunks of roasted sweet red pepper, some chopped fresh basil and some toasted pine nuts. Serve warm.

• For another Mediterranean-inspired dish, cook barley, bulgur or couscous with some saffron threads and combine with chopped grilled zucchini and eggplant and halved cherry tomatoes; top with crumbled feta or goat cheese.

• In skillet, melt a little bit of butter. Add walnut halves (or corn), chopped green onion and some dried thyme; sauté until golden. Combine with cooked kasha.

• When you have a bit of time, try substituting pot barley for arborio rice in your favorite risotto.

• Combine cooked bulgur or barley with some grated orange rind and juice, a hint of chopped fresh marjoram and some julienned roasted beets (or just some julienned beets from a can). This is also fantastic if you add some strips of roasted fennel.

PIZZA AND PASTA

Healthy Pizza Base

You can refrigerate this dough overnight and make the pizza the next day.

1 cup	whole-wheat flour	250 mL
1 1/2 cups	all-purpose flour (approx)	375 mL
1	pkg quick-rising (instant) dry yeast (or 1 tbsp/15 mL)	1
1 tsp	salt	5 mL
1/2 tsp	granulated sugar	2 mL
2 tsp	olive oil	10 mL

In food processor, combine whole-wheat flour, 1 cup (250 mL) all-purpose flour, yeast, salt and sugar. With motor running, gradually pour in oil and 3/4 cup (175 mL) very hot water (125°F/50°C) and beat, adding up to 1/4 cup (50 mL) more water if necessary, just until dough begins to form ball. Process for 1 minute. Turn out onto lightly floured surface. Knead for 5 minutes or until smooth and elastic, adding more flour if necessary; cover and let rest for 10 minutes or refrigerate for up to 2 days. On lightly floured surface, roll out dough into 12-inch (30-cm) circle.

Makes one 12-inch (30-cm) pizza round, enough for 4 servings.

Per serving: about 300 cal, 10 g pro, 3 g total fat (trace saturated fat), 59 g carb, 6 g fiber, 0 mg chol, 578 mg sodium. % RDI: 2% calcium, 24% iron, 0% vit A, 0% vit C, 49% folate.

Artichoke Pizza

Pizza can be lively and robust in flavor even when ingredients may be out of season. Take this artichoke pizza with its strong Mediterranean affinity: all you need is a well-stocked pantry and refrigerator—and a little imagination—for a highly creative and satisfying pizza.

1 lb	pizza dough	500 g
1/3 cup	softened cream cheese	75 mL
2 tbsp	pesto	25 mL
1/3 cup	oil-packed sun-dried tomatoes, drained and chopped	75 mL
1	jar (6 oz/170 mL) marinated artichoke hearts, drained and halved	1
4	bocconcini cheese balls, sliced (or 1 1/4 cups/300 mL shredded mozzarella cheese)	4

On lightly floured surface, roll 1 lb (500 g) pizza dough into 12-inch (30-cm) circle. Transfer to cornmeal-dusted pizza pan or baking sheet.

In bowl, mix together cream cheese with pesto until well combined; spread over dough right to edge.

Arrange sun-dried tomatoes and artichoke hearts over top.

Arrange bocconcini slices over. Bake in bottom third of 500°F (260°C) oven until crust is golden and cheese is bubbly, about 10 minutes.

Makes 4 servings.

Per serving: about 558 cal, 22 g pro, 24 g total fat (12 g saturated fat), 66 g carb, 8 g fiber, 60 mg chol, 985 mg sodium. % RDI: 28% calcium, 30% iron, 22% vit A, 22% vit C, 59% folate.

Tip: To reduce the fat content, use part skim mozzarella; look for mozzarella that contains less than 20% milk fat.

Hot and Spicy Pizza

This pizza proves what pizza lovers already know: keep it simple and you'll create a winning combination. One of the keys to making really memorable pizza is to avoid sprinkling too much cheese on top.

1 lb	pizza dough	500 mL
1/2 cup	pizza or pasta sauce	125 mL
1/3 cup	pitted and sliced green olives	75 mL
8	slices hot or sweet salami (3 oz/90 g)	8
1/4 cup	sliced hot or mild banana peppers	50 mL
2 cups	shredded provolone or mozzarella cheese	500 mL

On lightly floured surface, roll 1 lb (500 g) pizza dough into 12-inch (30-cm) circle. Transfer to corn-meal-dusted pizza pan or baking sheet.

Spread pizza sauce over dough right to edge.

Arrange olives, salami and peppers over top.

Sprinkle with provolone or mozzarella cheese. Bake in bottom third of 500°F (260°C) oven until crust is golden and cheese is bubbly, about 10 minutes.

Makes 4 servings.

Per serving: about 592 cal, 28 g pro, 25 g total fat (12 g saturated fat), 65 g carb, 7 g fiber, 53 mg chol, 1806 mg sodium. % RDI: 42% calcium, 33% iron, 29% vit A, 33% vit C, 52% folate.

Tip: Instead of dough, use ready-made baked pizza crust (available in supermarkets), but bake it in the center of the oven.

Veggie Spinach Pizza

An appealing vegetarian option, this Greek-inspired pizza is topped with little clumps of warmed cheese that blanket the vegetables and simply melt in your mouth. To make the olives go even further, slice them thinly before sprinkling them on top.

1 lb	pizza dough	500 mL
2 tbsp	extra-virgin olive oil	25 mL
1 1/2 cups	cooked and squeezed-dry spinach	375 mL
2	tomatoes, sliced	2
1/3 cup	thinly sliced red onion	75 mL
1/3 cup	pitted black olives	75 mL
1/2 cup	goat cheese or crumbled feta cheese	125 mL

On lightly floured surface, roll 1 lb (500 g) pizza dough into 12-inch (30-cm) circle. Transfer to corn-meal-dusted pizza pan or baking sheet.

Spread olive oil over dough right to edge.

Arrange spinach, tomatoes, onion and olives over top.

Sprinkle with goat or feta cheese. Bake in bottom third of 500°F (260°C) oven until crust is golden and cheese is bubbly, about 10 minutes.

Makes 4 servings.

Per serving: about 443 cal, 15 g pro, 15 g total fat (4 g saturated fat), 66 g carb, 9 g fiber, 7 mg chol, 784 mg sodium. % RDI: 14% calcium, 49% iron, 69% vit A, 27% vit C, 96% folate.

Vegetarian Lasagna

You get to add your own special touch to the mushroom tomato sauce, and the rest of the lasagna is simply an assembly-and-baking job. Presliced mushrooms, fresh lasagna noodles and prepared spaghetti sauce accelerate preparation.

1 tbsp	vegetable oil	15 mL
1	onion, chopped	1
5 cups	sliced mushrooms (about 1 lb/500 g)	1.25 L
1	jar (750 mL) spaghetti sauce	1
1	pkg (300 g) frozen spinach, thawed	1
2 cups	1% cottage cheese	500 mL
1	egg	1
1/4 tsp	each salt and pepper	1 mL
3/4 lb	fresh lasagna noodles	375 g
2 cups	shredded part skim mozzarella	500 mL
1/4 cup	freshly grated Parmesan cheese	50 mL

In skillet, heat oil over medium-high heat; cook onion and mushrooms for about 7 minutes or until liquid has evaporated. Stir in spaghetti sauce; set aside.

Squeeze excess moisture from spinach; place in bowl and combine with cottage cheese, egg, salt and pepper; set aside.

Spread 1/2 cup (125 mL) of the sauce in greased 13-× 9-inch (3-L) baking dish. Top with 1 layer of lasagna noodles, trimming to fit if necessary; spread with one-quarter of the sauce. Spread with one-third of the cheese mixture; sprinkle with 1/2 cup (125 mL) of the mozzarella. Beginning with noodles, repeat layers twice.

Arrange layer of noodles over top. Spread with remaining sauce; sprinkle with remaining mozzarella and Parmesan. Bake in 350°F (180°C) oven for 30 to 40 minutes or until bubbly. Let stand for 10 minutes before serving.

Makes 8 servings.

Per serving: about 400 cal, 26 g pro, 12 g total fat (5 g saturated fat), 47 g carb, 5 g fiber, 44 mg chol, 974 mg sodium. % RDI: 33% calcium, 21% iron, 30% vit A, 22% vit C, 51% folate.

LEGUMES AND SOY

Cumin Carrot Tofu Patties

We all know about salmon and tuna patties, but why not try something new and use tofu? Tofu, because of its bland nature, has an extraordinary ability to absorb other flavors, as seen in this recipe inspired by Middle Eastern cuisine. Be sure to use extra-firm tofu, since the other types will have too soft a consistency for the patties to hold together.

1 tbsp	olive oil	15 mL
1	onion, chopped	1
1/2 cup	grated carrot	125 mL
2	cloves garlic, minced	2
1/4 tsp	ground cumin	1 mL
Pinch	cayenne pepper	Pinch
1	pkg (350 g) extra-firm tofu	1
1/4 cup	tahini (sesame paste)	50 mL
1/2 cup	chopped fresh parsley	125 mL
1/4 cup	dry bread crumbs	50 mL
2 tbsp	lemon juice	25 mL
1/4 tsp	each salt and pepper	1 mL
1 cup	pasta sauce	250 mL
1 tsp	grated lemon rind	5 mL
Pinch	cinnamon	Pinch

In nonstick skillet, heat 1 tsp (5 mL) of the oil over medium heat; cook onion, carrot, garlic, pinch of the cumin and cayenne pepper, stirring occasionally, for 5 minutes or until onion is softened. Set aside.

In food processor, blend tofu with tahini. Add onion mixture, half of the parsley, the bread crumbs, lemon juice, salt and pepper; pulse to combine. Form into 8 1/2-inch (1-cm) thick patties.

Heat remaining oil in clean nonstick skillet over medium heat; cook patties, in batches, for 4 minutes per side or until golden.

Meanwhile, in saucepan, combine pasta sauce, lemon rind, cinnamon and remaining cumin and parsley; bring to simmer over medium-high heat, stirring often, about 3 minutes. Serve over patties.

Makes 4 servings.

Per serving: about 284 cal, 14 g pro, 18 g total fat (3 g saturated fat), 20 g carb, 4 g fiber, 0 mg chol, 480 mg sodium. % RDI: 18% calcium, 29% iron, 37% vit A, 23% vit C, 26% folate.

Sicilian Beans with Pasta

Serve with mixed greed salad with Italian vinaigrette.

1 tbsp	olive oil	15 mL
1	onion, chopped	1
2	cloves garlic, minced	2
1	stalk celery, chopped	1
2	bay leaves	2
Pinch	cloves or cinnamon	Pinch
1/4 tsp	each salt and pepper	1 mL
1	can (28 oz/796 mL) tomatoes	1
1 1/2 cups	vegetable stock	375 mL
1	can (19 oz/540 mL) kidney beans, drained and rinsed	1
4 cups	small shell pasta or recchiette (12 oz/375 g)	1 L
1/2 tsp	grated lemon rind	2 mL
1/4 cup	grated Romano cheese	50 mL
	chopped fresh oregano, marjoram, parsley or basil	

In saucepan, heat oil over medium-high heat; cook onion, garlic, celery, bay leaves, cloves or cinnamon, salt and pepper, stirring occasionally, for 3 to 5 minutes or until onion is softened. Add tomatoes and stock, breaking up tomatoes with spoon. Add beans; bring to boil. Reduce heat and simmer for 20 minutes or until thick enough to mound on spoon. Discard bay leaves.

Meanwhile, in large pot of boiling salted water, cook pasta for 8 minutes or until tender but firm; drain and return to pot. Add sauce and lemon rind; toss to coat. Serve sprinkled with cheese and oregano.

Makes 4 servings.

Per serving: about 545 cal, 23 g pro, 8 g total fat (2 g saturated fat), 96 g carb, 14 g fiber, 7 mg chol, 1333 mg sodium. % RDI: 16% calcium, 32% iron, 13% vit A, 37% vit C, 82% folate.

Southwestern Three-Bean Salad

A little change in the beans and a bigger change in the dressing make for a great change in an old picnic and buffet standby. Vary the amount of jalapeño pepper to taste.

1	can (19 oz/540 mL) red kidney beans, drained and rinsed	1
1	can (19 oz/540 mL) chickpeas, drained and rinsed	1
1	can (19 oz/540 mL) black beans, drained and rinsed	1
2	tomatoes, seeded and chopped	2
1	sweet green pepper, chopped	1
Half	red onion, chopped	Half
1/4 cup	chopped fresh coriander or parsley	50 mL

Dressing

1/3 cup	vegetable oil	75 mL
1/4 cup	lime juice	50 mL
1	jalapeño pepper, seeded and minced	1
3/4 tsp	salt	4 mL
1/4 tsp	each ground cumin, chili powder, granulated sugar and pepper	1 mL

Place kidney beans in serving bowl. Add chickpeas, black beans, tomatoes, green pepper, red onion and coriander.

To make the dressing, whisk together all ingredients in a small bowl.

Pour dressing over salad and toss to mix well.
Makes 6 servings.

Per serving: about 377 cal, 16 g pro, 14 g total fat (1 g saturated fat), 49 g carb, 13 g fiber, 0 mg chol, 783 mg sodium. % RDI: 5% calcium, 23% iron, 6% vit A, 57% vit C, 78% folate.

Tofu and Vegetable Skewers with Peanut Sauce

Versatility is built right into these skewers; if you've forgotten to pick up tofu, use chunks of chicken or pork. And don't cheat yourself by limiting the peanut sauce to just this recipe; try drizzling it on top of a grilled chicken sandwich or over a noodle salad complete with sliced red pepper, snow peas and miniature corn.

Serve these tofu and veggie skewers with steamed rice.

1	pkg (350 g) extra-firm tofu	1
1 1/2 cups	small mushrooms	375 mL
2 cups	snow peas, trimmed	500 mL
2 cups	cherry tomatoes	500 mL
2 tbsp	extra-virgin olive oil	25 mL
1/4 tsp	salt and pepper	1 mL

Peanut Sauce

1/2 cup	peanut butter	125 mL
1/4 cup	soy sauce	50 mL
2 tbsp	ketchup	25 mL
2 tbsp	lemon juice	25 mL
2	cloves garlic, minced	2
2	green onions, chopped	2

To make the peanut sauce, whisk together peanut butter, 1/2 cup (125 mL) warm water, soy sauce, ketchup, lemon juice and garlic in a bowl. Set aside 1/2 cup (125 mL).

Drain and pat tofu dry. Cut tofu in half horizontally. Cut each piece in half lengthwise and then cut crosswise into 1/2-inch (1-cm) pieces. Add to bowl, let stand 10 minutes. (Make ahead: Cover and refrigerate for up to 8 hours.)

Meanwhile, in separate bowl, toss mushrooms, snow peas and cherry tomatoes with oil, salt and pepper. Thread vegetables alternately onto eight skewers.

Thread tofu onto four skewers.

Place vegetable and tofu skewers on greased grill, over medium-high heat. Close lid and cook, turning once, until tofu is browned and vegetables are tender-crisp, about 10 minutes. Drizzle with reserved peanut sauce and sprinkle with chopped green onions.
Makes 4 servings.

Per serving: about 336 cal, 18 g pro, 25 g total fat (4 g saturated fat), 17 g carb, 4 g fiber, 0 mg chol, 1121 mg sodium. % RDI: 15% calcium, 26% iron, 8% vit A, 50% vit C, 29% folate.

Vegetarian Chili with Squash

When the temperature outdoors dips and our thoughts turn to comfort foods, nothing fits the bill better than this warm and hearty chili. Thickened with good-for-you lentils and brightened with colorful and sweet butternut squash, it's ideally served with baked pita bread or bagel chips.

1 tbsp	vegetable oil	15 mL
2 tbsp	chili powder	25 mL
1 tbsp	dried oregano	15 mL
1 tsp	each ground cumin and coriander	5 mL
1 tsp	each salt and pepper	5 mL
1	large sweet red or green pepper, chopped	1
1	large red onion, chopped	1
3	stalks celery, sliced	3
3	large cloves garlic, minced	3
1/2 cup	green lentils	125 mL
1/2 cup	red lentils	125 mL
1	can (19 oz/540 mL) tomatoes	1
3 cups	cubed peeled butternut squash	750 mL

In Dutch oven or large heavy saucepan, heat oil over medium heat. Add chili powder, oregano, cumin, coriander, salt and pepper; cook, stirring, for 1 minute. Add red pepper, red onion, celery and garlic; cook, stirring occasionally, for about 6 minutes or until softened.

Meanwhile, sort green and red lentils, discarding any discolored ones; rinse and drain. Add lentils to pan; cook, stirring, for 3 minutes. Add 4 cups (1 L) water; bring to boil. Reduce heat to low; cover and simmer for 15 minutes or until vegetables are tender and green lentils begin to soften. Add tomatoes, breaking up with back of spoon. Add squash; simmer, uncovered and stirring often, for 30 minutes or until tender and liquid is thickened.

Makes 6 servings.

Per serving; about 230 cal, 12 g pro, 4 g total fat (trace saturated fat), 42 g carb, 9 g fiber, 0 mg chol, 581 mg sodium. % RDI: 11% calcium, 39% iron, 79% vit A, 122% vit C, 93% folate.

Vegetable Tofu Salad

If you're in the habit of toting your lunch to work, let your tofu marinate in the dressing until lunchtime. Keep your vegetables in a separate container and then toss everything together once the lunch bell chimes.

1	pkg (350 g) extra-firm tofu	1
2 cups	cherry tomatoes	500 mL
1	sweet green pepper	1
2	carrots	2
2 cups	small mushrooms	500 mL

Dressing

1/3 cup	red wine vinegar	75 mL
1/4 cup	chopped fresh basil (or 2 tsp/10 mL dried)	50 mL
1/4 cup	olive oil	50 mL
1	clove garlic, minced	1
1/4 tsp	dry mustard	1 mL
1/4 tsp	each salt and pepper	1 mL

To make the dressing, whisk together vinegar, basil, oil, garlic, mustard, salt and pepper until combined in a large bowl.

Drain and pat tofu dry; cut into 1/2-inch (1-cm) cubes. Add to dressing; let stand for 10 minutes.

Meanwhile, cut tomatoes in half. Cut green pepper in half lengthwise; seed and core. Cut in half crosswise; cut lengthwise into strips. Slice carrots. Add vegetables to bowl along with mushrooms; toss to coat.

Makes 4 servings.

Per serving: about 250 cal, 11 g pro, 19 g total fat (3 g saturated fat), 14 g carb, 3 g fiber, 0 mg chol, 174 mg sodium. % RDI: 14% calcium, 20% iron, 119% vit A, 73% vit C, 24% folate.

Tip: This salad is also delicious with cooked sliced chicken or turkey breast, sliced hard-cooked eggs or cubed low-fat cheese.

DAIRY AND EGGS

Strawberry Banana Smoothie

Who needs an ice-cream shake when banana adds body to a breakfast drink? This one is fragrant with vitamin C–rich strawberries and is based on an all-important calcium source—milk.

2 cups	sliced strawberries or raspberries (fresh or thawed)	500 mL
1 cup	milk (1%, skim or calcium-enriched soymilk)	250 mL
1	banana	1
1 tbsp	lemon juice	15 mL
1 tbsp	liquid honey	15 mL
Pinch	cinnamon	Pinch

In blender, combine strawberries, milk, banana, lemon juice, honey and cinnamon; purée until thick and frothy.
Makes 2 servings.

Per serving: about 182 cal, 6 g pro, 2 g total fat (1 g saturated fat), 39 g carb, 4 g fiber, 5 mg chol, 65 mg sodium. % RDI: 16% calcium, 6% iron, 8% vit A, 155% vit C, 20% folate.

Tropical Fruit Shake

Tofu is an increasingly popular soybean-based source of protein.

1 cup	chilled pineapple juice	250 mL
1/2 cup	soft tofu or soy milk	125 mL
1	ripe banana	1

In blender or food processor, purée pineapple juice, tofu and banana until smooth. Serve immediately.
Makes 2 servings.

Per serving: about 153 cal, 4 g pro, 2 g total fat (1 g saturated fat), 32 g carb, 2 g fiber, 0 mg chol, 6 mg sodium. % RDI: 4% calcium, 8% iron, 1% vit A, 77% vit C, 18% folate.

Tip: To boost the calcium content, buy a calcium-enriched soy beverage.

Super Nutritious Frittata

Weekends call out for more luxurious breakfasts, and this Italian version of an omelet, in which the ingredients are mixed in with the eggs rather than folded inside, is wonderful first thing upon waking or a few hours later, for brunch. The broccoli can be replaced with broccoli rabe or even rapini.

2 cups	chopped broccoli	500 mL
6	eggs	6
1/2 tsp	salt	2 mL
1/4 tsp	pepper	1 mL
2 tsp	vegetable oil	10 mL
1/4 cup	chopped green onion	50 mL
2	cloves garlic, minced	2
1 tsp	dried tarragon	5 mL
1/4 cup	shredded Fontina cheese or light cheddar cheese	50 mL

Place broccoli in steamer over saucepan of boiling water; cook, covered, for 4 minutes or until broccoli is tender-crisp.

In bowl, whisk eggs, salt and pepper; set aside. In 9-inch (23-cm) ovenproof skillet, heat oil over medium heat; cook onion, garlic and tarragon, stirring, for 2 minutes or until softened.

Arrange broccoli mixture over skillet; pour egg mixture over top. Reduce heat to medium-low; cover and cook for about 12 minutes or until bottom is golden and edge is set but center still jiggles slightly. Sprinkle cheese over top; broil for 2 to 3 minutes or until light golden and cheese is bubbly.

Makes 4 servings.

Per serving: about 168 cal, 12 g pro, 12 g total fat (4 g saturated fat), 3 g carb, 1 g fiber, 287 mg chol, 442 mg sodium. % RDI: 9% calcium, 9% iron, 18% vit A, 32% vit C, 24% folate.

Tip: If skillet is not ovenproof, wrap handle in double thickness of foil.

Western Omelet Pockets

Fast enough to make and enjoy as breakfast on the run, this is a great meal for lunchtime, too. Use whole-wheat pita bread and accompany with orange segments or unsweetened juice.

1 tsp	butter	5 mL
4	mushrooms, sliced	4
Half	sweet green pepper, chopped	Half
1/4 cup	chopped cooked ham	50 mL
1	green onion, chopped	1
Half	tomato, chopped	Half
4	eggs	4
1/4 tsp	dried basil	1 mL
Pinch	each salt and pepper	Pinch
2	6-inch (15-cm) whole-wheat pita breads	2
4	lettuce leaves (optional)	4

In nonstick skillet, melt butter over medium-high heat; cook mushrooms, green pepper, ham and onion, stirring often, for about 3 minutes or until vegetables are slightly tender. Add tomato; cook just until heated through.

Whisk together eggs, basil, salt and pepper; pour over vegetable mixture. Cook for 3 minutes or until almost set, gently lifting edges with spatula to allow uncooked eggs to flow underneath. Remove from heat; let stand for 3 minutes or until eggs are completely set.

Cut pitas in half to form pockets. Line each with lettuce leaf (if using). Cut omelet into 4 wedges; place in pockets.

Makes 4 servings.

Per serving: about 189 cal, 12 g pro, 7 g total fat (2 g saturated fat), 19 g carb, 3 g fiber, 193 mg chol, 358 mg sodium. % RDI: 5% calcium, 11% iron, 12% vit A, 23% vit C, 19% folate.

Variation:
Quick Western Sandwich: Omit mushrooms. Cut omelet into quarters; place each between 2 slices of toast.

Tip: For an easy change, roll up the omelet and lettuce in a large tortilla instead of slipping them into pita pockets.

FISH

Asian Fish Steaks

Halibut and salmon steaks are available frozen in packs of two, sealed airtight for freshness. Or ask at the fresh fish counter for whatever is in season.

2 tbsp	hoisin sauce	25 mL
1 tbsp	cider vinegar	15 mL
1 tsp	minced gingerroot	5 mL
1	bunch bok choy, chopped	1
4	halibut or salmon steaks, each 1-inch (2.5-cm) thick (1 1/2 lb/750 g total)	4
2 tbsp	fresh bread crumbs	25 mL
1 tbsp	toasted sesame seeds	15 mL
1	small clove garlic, minced	1
1 tbsp	olive oil	15 mL

In small bowl or glass measure, stir together hoisin, vinegar and ginger.

In large ovenproof skillet, toss bok choy with half the hoisin mixture. Sprinkle with 2 tbsp (25 mL) water. Place fish steaks over top; brush with remaining hoisin mixture. Bring to boil over medium-high heat; cover, reduce heat to medium and cook for 10 minutes or until bok choy is tender and fish is opaque and flakes easily with fork.

Meanwhile, in small bowl, combine bread crumbs, sesame seeds and garlic; stir in olive oil. Sprinkle evenly over fish and broil for about 30 seconds or until golden brown and crispy.

Makes 4 servings.

Per serving: about 285 cal, 40 g pro, 10 g total fat (1 g saturated fat), 9 g carb, 4 g fiber, 54 mg chol, 347 mg sodium. % RDI: 27% calcium, 29% iron, 67% vit A, 100% vit C, 52% folate.

Garlic Gratin Fish

Fish is the ultimate quick-supper solution for time-crunched cooks. Use fillets of fish, such as cod, haddock or halibut, that are about 1-inch (2.5 cm) thick.

1 cup	fresh bread crumbs	250 mL
2 tbsp	butter, melted	25 mL
2 tsp	chopped fresh oregano (or 1/2 tsp/2 mL dried)	10 mL
1 tsp	grated lemon rind	5 mL
2	cloves garlic, minced	2
1/4 tsp	each salt and pepper	1 mL
1 lb	fish fillets (cod, haddock, halibut or sole)	500 g
1 tbsp	Dijon mustard	15 mL
	lemon wedges	

In small bowl, toss together bread crumbs, butter, oregano, lemon rind and garlic. Sprinkle salt and pepper all over fillets; place on greased foil-lined baking sheet. Brush with mustard; evenly spoon bread crumb–gratin mixture over top.

Bake in 450°F (230°C) oven until topping is golden and crisp and fish flakes easily when tested, 10 to 15 minutes. Serve with lemon wedges to squeeze over top.

Makes 4 servings.

Per serving: about 179 cal, 21 g pro, 7 g total fat (4 g saturated fat), 6 g carb, trace fiber, 64 mg chol, 371 mg sodium. % RDI: 4% calcium, 6% iron, 7% vit A, 3% vit C, 8% folate.

Tip: Keep fresh bread crumbs handy to sprinkle on casseroles or to coat chicken or fish. In food processor, pulse bread until crumbly; freeze in resealable plastic bag for up to 2 months.

Tip: Keep boxes of frozen fish fillets on hand in the freezer. They thaw quickly and mean that you can have fish any time of the week.

Mediterranean Tuna Pasta

Don't let the ingredient list fool you: this dish actually goes together quickly and effortlessly. The key, of course, is to have everything ready and set to go. And aside from chopping an onion, some garlic and olives, all that means is removing some basics from your pantry. And remember to bring the pot of water to a boil before you reach for your chef's knife.

2 tbsp	olive oil	25 mL
1	small onion, chopped	1
4	cloves garlic, minced	4
1/2 tsp	dried Italian herb seasoning	2 mL
1/4 tsp	hot pepper flakes	1 mL
1	pkg (300 g) frozen chopped spinach, thawed	1
1	can (28 oz/796 mL) stewed tomatoes	1
1/4 cup	oil-cured olives, pitted and chopped	50 mL
2 tbsp	drained rinsed capers	25 mL
1 tsp	salt	5 mL
2	cans (each 170 g) tuna, packed in water, drained	2
4 cups	penne rigate (12 oz/375 g)	1 L
	grated Parmesan cheese (optional)	

In large skillet, heat oil over medium heat; cook onion, garlic, Italian herb seasoning and hot pepper flakes, stirring occasionally, until softened, about 5 minutes.

Squeeze spinach dry; add to pan along with tomatoes, breaking up tomatoes with spoon. Add olives, capers and salt; bring to boil. Reduce heat and simmer until thickened, about 10 minutes. Break tuna into chunks; add to sauce.

Meanwhile, in large pot of boiling salted water, cook pasta until tender but firm, 8 to 10 minutes; drain and return to pot. Add sauce and toss to coat. Serve sprinkled with cheese (if using).

Makes 4 servings.

Per serving: about 565 cal, 32 g pro, 12 g total fat (2 g saturated fat), 84 g carb, 8 g fiber, 20 mg chol, 1960 mg sodium. % RDI: 17% calcium, 39% iron, 52% vit A, 58% vit C, 84% folate.

Roasted Cajun Halibut

A New Orleans–style spice rub jazzes up halibut steaks without adding fat. For cooler tastes, cut the amount of chili powder in half.

1 tbsp	lime or lemon juice	15 mL
1 1/2 tsp	chili powder	7 mL
1 tsp	each paprika, pepper, dried oregano and dried thyme	5 mL
1/4 tsp	each garlic powder and salt	1 mL
4	halibut or salmon steaks (1 1/2 lb/750 g total)	4

In small bowl or glass measure, whisk together lime juice, 2 tsp (10 mL) water, chili powder, paprika, pepper, oregano, thyme, garlic powder and salt; rub gently onto both sides of fish steaks. Place on foil-lined baking sheet; roast in 450°F (220°C) oven for about 10 minutes or until fish flakes easily with fork.

Makes 4 servings.

Per serving: about 215 cal, 34 g pro, 7 g total fat (2 g saturated fat), 2 g carb, trace fiber, 66 mg chol, 306 mg sodium, % RDI: 2% calcium, 16% iron, 12% vit A, 5% vit C, 1% folate.

Tip: This rub also works well with fillets as long as they are at least 3/4 inch (2 cm) thick. Choose monkfish, catfish, whitefish or snapper.

Roasted Fillets with Orange Caramelized Onions

The pink flesh of salmon looks lovely with the orange-and-green-flecked caramelized onions. If you wish, choose other types of tender fish, such as halibut, snapper, pickerel or tilapia.

1 tbsp	vegetable oil	15 mL
2	onions, thinly sliced	2
4	cloves garlic, minced	4
3 tbsp	chopped fresh dill	50 mL
1	orange	1
1/4 tsp	each salt and pepper	1 mL
4	fish fillets, i.e., salmon, snapper, pickerel or tilapia (about 1 lb/500 g)	4

In large ovenproof skillet, heat vegetable oil over medium heat; cook onions, stirring occasionally, until golden, about 15 minutes. Add garlic and 1 tbsp (15 mL) of the dill.

Meanwhile, grate 2 tsp (10 mL) rind from orange; set aside. Cut orange crosswise in half. Squeeze one of the halves to make 2 tbsp (25 mL) juice; add juice to onions. Cut remaining half into 4 wedges; set aside.

In small bowl, combine reserved orange rind, 1 tbsp (15 mL) of the remaining dill and salt and pepper; rub onto fillets. Place fillets on onions.

Bake in 425°F (220°C) oven until fish is opaque and flakes easily when tested, about 12 minutes. Sprinkle with remaining dill. Serve with reserved orange wedges.

Makes 4 servings.

Per serving: about 242 cal, 24 g pro, 13 g total fat (3 g saturated fat), 8 g carb, 1 g fiber, 67 mg chol, 69 mg sodium. % RDI: 3% calcium, 4% iron, 1% vit A, 28% vit C, 18% folate.

POULTRY

Marinated Chicken Breasts

Chicken breasts frozen right in the marinade eliminates the usual time lag required for this type of seasoning.

2 lb	boneless skinless chicken breasts	1 kg
1/4 cup	balsamic or wine vinegar	50 mL
1/4 cup	vegetable oil	50 mL
1 tbsp	Dijon mustard	15 mL
1 tsp	dried thyme	5 mL
1/4 tsp	pepper	1 mL

Slice chicken crosswise into 1/2-inch (1-cm) thick strips; divide between 2 freezer bags. Whisk together vinegar, oil, mustard, thyme and pepper; pour half into each bag. Seal and turn to coat chicken.

Chicken can be frozen for up to 2 weeks; thaw in refrigerator.

Makes 10 servings.

Per serving: about 158 cal, 21 g pro, 7 g total fat (1 g saturated fat), 2 g carb, trace fiber, 53 mg chol, 71 mg sodium. % RDI: 1% calcium, 4% iron, 0% vit A, 2% vit C, 1% folate.

Tip: For quick thawing, flatten bag of marinated chicken breasts before freezing. Or microwave one bag at Thaw/Defrost for 8 to 10 minutes.

Chicken Fajitas

Gather around the dinner table for a fun weeknight supper. Set out succulent chicken, toppings and tortillas in individual dishes and let everyone customize dinner.

1 lb	marinated chicken breasts (recipe, this page)	500 g
1 tbsp	chicken stock	15 mL
1	onion, sliced	1
1	clove garlic, minced	1
1/2	each sweet red and green pepper, sliced	1/2
1 tsp	chili powder	5 mL
1 tbsp	balsamic or wine vinegar	15 mL
6	large whole-wheat flour tortillas	6
3 cups	shredded lettuce	750 mL
2/3 cup	shredded light cheddar cheese	150 mL
1/3 cup	light sour cream	75 mL

In large skillet, over medium-high heat, cook marinated chicken breasts with marinade, stirring often, for 5 minutes or until no longer pink inside. Transfer to plate. Add stock to pan; cook onion, garlic, sweet red and green peppers and chili powder for 3 minutes. Return chicken to pan. Stir in vinegar; cook for 1 minute.

Meanwhile, wrap tortillas in foil; heat in 350°F (180°C) oven for 5 minutes or until warm. Divide lettuce among tortillas; top with chicken mixture, cheese and sour cream. Roll up.

Makes 4 to 6 servings.

Per serving: about 390 cal, 28 g pro, 13 g total fat (3 g saturated fat), 39 g carb, 3 g fiber, 54 mg chol, 452 mg sodium. % RDI: 15% calcium, 19% iron, 8% vit A, 43% vit C, 14% folate.

Chicken in Spicy Spinach Sauce

Serve with basmati rice or flatbread and a side plate of sliced cucumber, and onion if desired, with a wedge of lemon or lime to refresh the palate and subdue the mild heat of the sauce.

Bring the flavors of North India to your table with this chicken-and-vegetable dish. Garam masala is a ground spice mixture often used in Indian cuisine to add another layer of flavor. It is available in many supermarkets and all Indian grocery stores.

1 tbsp	vegetable oil	15 mL
1	small onion, finely chopped	1
2	cloves garlic, minced	2
2 tsp	minced gingerroot	10 mL
2 tbsp	minced seeded jalapeño pepper	25 mL
2 tbsp	chopped fresh coriander	25 mL
2 tbsp	mild curry paste	25 mL
1	pkg (300 g) frozen chopped spinach, thawed and squeezed dry	1
1	tomato, chopped	1
1 cup	chicken stock	250 mL
1/4 tsp	salt	1 mL
1 lb	boneless skinless chicken breasts, cut in 1-inch (2.5-cm) cubes	500 g
1 tsp	garam masala	5 mL

In deep skillet, heat oil over medium heat; cook onion, garlic and ginger, stirring occasionally, for 3 minutes. Add jalapeño pepper, coriander and curry paste; cook, stirring, for 1 minute.

Add spinach, tomato, stock and salt; cook over medium-high heat for 2 minutes. Add chicken; cook for 7 minutes or until no longer pink inside. Stir in garam masala.

Makes 4 servings.

Per serving: about 236 cal, 30 g pro, 9 g total fat (1 g saturated fat), 8 g carb, 3 g fiber, 66 mg chol, 449 mg sodium. % RDI: 9% calcium, 14% iron, 48% vit A, 40% vit C, 29% folate.

Substitution: For a milder flavor, replace the jalapeño pepper with 1/3 cup (75 mL) finely chopped sweet green pepper.

Citrus Mustard Chicken

Use this marinade on chicken legs or halves, too. Simply grill legs until juices run clear when pierced. Chicken halves are done when a meat thermometer inserted in thickest part of thigh registers 185°F (85°C).

1/4 cup	lemon juice	50 mL
1/4 cup	Dijon mustard	50 mL
1 tbsp	olive oil	15 mL
4	chicken breasts	4
1/4 cup	marmalade	50 mL

In shallow dish, mix together lemon juice, mustard and oil; add chicken, turning to coat. Cover and marinate in refrigerator for at least 2 hours or up to 8 hours, turning occasionally. Let stand at room temperature for 30 minutes.

Place chicken, skin side down, on greased grill over medium heat; cover and cook, turning once, for 20 minutes. Brush with marmalade; cook for 5 to 10 minutes or until no longer pink inside.

Makes 4 servings.

Per serving: about 303 cal, 31 g pro, 14 g total fat (3 g saturated fat), 15 g carb, 1 g fiber, 97 mg chol, 239 mg sodium. % RDI: 3% calcium, 6% iron, 3% vit A, 5% vit C, 6% folate.

Per serving without skin: about 250 cal, 28 g pro, 9 g total fat (2 g saturated fat), 15 g carb, 1 g fiber, 87 mg chol, 231 mg sodium. % RDI: 3% calcium, 5% iron, 2% vit A, 5% vit C, 4% folate.

Tip: Can be served with baked potatoes and topped with crumbled goat cheese mixed with fresh oregano and chopped sun-dried tomatoes, or light herbed cream cheese mixed with blanched broccoli florets.

MEAT

Balsamic Honey Pork Tenderloin

Succulent pork tenderloin is perfect for the grill. It needs little time for cooking and is a great medium for marinades and spices. This sweet yet sour marinade glazes the meat and turns into a delicious crust.

2 tbsp	liquid honey	25 mL
2 tbsp	grainy mustard	25 mL
2 tbsp	balsamic vinegar	25 mL
1 tbsp	olive oil	15 mL
1	clove garlic, minced	1
1/4 tsp	each salt and pepper	1 mL
2	pork tenderloins	2

In large bowl, combine honey, mustard, vinegar, oil, garlic, salt and pepper; add pork, turning to coat. (Make ahead: Cover and refrigerate for up to 24 hours.)

Reserving marinade, place pork on greased grill over medium-high heat; brush with marinade. Close lid and cook, turning occasionally, for about 18 minutes or until just a hint of pink remains inside.

Transfer to cutting board; tent with foil and let stand for 5 minutes. Cut into 1/2-inch (1-cm) thick slices.

Makes 6 servings.

Per serving: about 182 cal, 27 g pro, 5 g total fat (1 g saturated fat), 5 g carb, 0 g fiber, 61 mg chol, 167 mg sodium. % RDI: 1% calcium, 10% iron, 0% vit A, 0% vit C, 2% folate.

Garlic Horseradish Sirloin Roast

Red meat is one of the best sources of iron. Iron-rich foods are needed to help prevent iron-deficiency anemia, which is one of the most common nutrient deficiencies among Canadian women. Cooking the roast on a bed of sliced onions infuses the gravy with their sweet flavor.

3 lb	top sirloin premium oven roast	1.5 kg
4	cloves garlic, slivered	4
1/4 cup	light mayonnaise	50 mL
2 tbsp	prepared horseradish	25 mL
1/2 tsp	each dried sage, salt and pepper	2 mL
4	onions, thickly sliced	4
1 cup	beef stock	250 mL
1/2 tsp	Worcestershire sauce	2 mL
1 tbsp	cornstarch	15 mL

With sharp tip of knife, cut about 40 slits all over roast. Stuff each with garlic sliver. In small bowl, whisk together mayonnaise, horseradish, sage, salt and pepper; brush all over roast.

Place onions in center of roasting pan; place roast on onions. Roast in 325°F (160°C) oven until thermometer registers 160°F (70°C) for medium, about 2 hours. Transfer to cutting board and tent with foil; let stand for 10 minutes before carving.

Skim fat from pan juices. Pour in beef stock and Worcestershire sauce; bring to boil, stirring and scraping up brown bits. Whisk cornstarch with 1 tbsp (15 mL) water; whisk into pan and cook, whisking, until thickened and glossy, about 2 minutes. Strain and serve with beef.

Makes 8 to 12 servings.

Per each of 12 servings: about 164 cal, 21 g pro, 7 g total fat (3 g saturated fat), 2 g carb, 0 g fiber, 53 mg chol, 239 mg sodium. % RDI: 2% calcium, 16% iron, 0% vit A, 0% vit C, 4% folate.

FIVE FAST MARINADES FOR FISH, POULTRY AND MEAT

A marinade usually contains an acidic ingredient, such as vinegar, that helps tenderize as it flavors. These marinades were designed to work with any poultry, meat or fish dish.

In small bowl, stir together ingredients for desired marinade (below).

For every 4 servings (1 lb/500 g boneless or 1 1/2 lb/750 g bone-in meat or poultry, or 1 lb/500 g fish), marinate with 1/3 cup (75 mL) marinade.

Cover and refrigerate to marinate meat or poultry for at least 4 hours or for up to 12 hours; marinate fish for no more than 30 minutes.

Adobo Marinade

This flavorful, spicy marinade is especially good for pork, chicken or turkey dishes.

1/4 cup	orange juice	50 mL
1 tsp	grated lime rind	5 mL
2 tbsp	lime juice	25 mL
2	cloves garlic, minced	2
1	jalapeño pepper, seeded and minced	1
2 tsp	dried oregano	10 mL
1 tsp	ground cumin	5 mL

Combine all ingredients.
Makes about 1/3 cup (75 mL).

Chimichurri Marinade

Sharp and piquant, this marinade works well with beef, pork, chicken and turkey. It can also be used for fish but be careful to marinate just a short while, up to 20 minutes.

2 cups	packed fresh parsley	500 mL
1/3 cup	olive oil	75 mL
1/4 cup	packed fresh oregano	50 mL
1/4 cup	wine vinegar	50 mL
1	jalapeño pepper, seeded	1
4	cloves garlic	4
1/2 tsp	each salt and pepper	2 mL

In food processor or mini-chopper, finely chop ingredients.
Makes 1 cup (250 mL).

Moroccan Marinade

This piquant marinade is great with fish and chicken but also with lamb.

3 tbsp	olive oil	50 mL
2 tbsp	each ground cumin and paprika	25 mL
2 tbsp	granulated sugar	25 mL
2 tbsp	lemon juice	25 mL
2	cloves garlic, minced	2
1/2 tsp	each salt and pepper	2 mL
1/4 tsp	cinnamon	1 mL

Combine all ingredients.
Makes about 1/3 cup (75 mL).

Red Wine Marinade

Use this mild, slightly acidic marinade with beef, lamb, duck or game.

1/4 cup	dry red wine	50 mL
2 tbsp	wine vinegar	25 mL
1 tbsp	olive oil	15 mL
2	cloves garlic, minced	2
1	bay leaf	1
1/4 tsp	each salt and pepper	1 mL

Combine all ingredients.
Makes about 1/3 cup (75 mL).

Teriyaki Marinade

This savory and slightly sweet marinade is particularly suited for full-flavored fish such as salmon and chicken or beef.

3/4 cup	chicken or vegetable stock	175 mL
1/2 cup	soy sauce	125 mL
1/3 cup	mirin (Japanese sweet rice wine)	75 mL
2 tbsp	granulated sugar	25 mL
3	slices gingerroot	3
2 tbsp	cold water	25 mL
1 tbsp	cornstarch	15 mL

In saucepan, stir stock, soy sauce, mirin, sugar and ginger. Bring to boil. Reduce heat; simmer for 20 minutes or until reduced by about half. Whisk cold water with cornstarch; add to pan and cook, stirring, for about 2 minutes or until thick enough to coat back of spoon. Discard ginger. Let cool.
Makes about 1/3 cup (75 mL).

Endnotes

Step 2

1. La Rue, A et al. "Nutritional status and cognitive functioning in a normally aging sample: a 6-y reassessment." *Am J Clin Nutr* 1997; 65(1):20–29.

2. Kaplan, RJ et al. "Dietary protein, carbohydrate, and fat enhance memory performance in the healthy elderly." *Am J Clin Nutr* 2001; 74(5):687–693.

3. Hannan, MT et al. "Effect of dietary protein on bone loss in elderly men and women: the Framingham Osteoporosis Study." *J Bone Min Res* 2000; 15(12):2504–2512.

4. Munger, RG et al. "Prospective study of dietary protein intake and risk of hip fracture in postmenopausal women." *Am J Clin Nutr* 1999; 69(1):147–152.

5. Schurch, MA et al. "Protein supplements increase serum insulin-like growth factor-I levels and attenuate proximal femur bone loss in patients with recent hip fracture. A randomized, double-blind, placebo-controlled trial." *Ann Intern Med* 1998; 128(10):801–809.

6. Cooper, C et al. "Dietary protein intake and bone mass in women." *Calcif Tissue Int* 1996; 58(5):320–325.

7. Hajjar, IM et al. "Impact of diet on blood pressure and age-related changes in blood pressure in the US population: analysis of NHANES II." *Arch Intern Med* 2001; 161(4):589–593.

8. Feskanich, D et al. "Protein consumption and bone fractures in women." *Am J Epidemiol* 1996; 143(5):472–479.

9. Sellmeyer, DE et al. "A high ratio of dietary animal protein to vegetable protein increases the rate of bone loss and the risk of fracture in postmenopausal women." *Am J Clin Nutr* 2001; 73(1):118–122.

10. Shiell, AW et al. "Diet late in pregnancy and glucose-insulin metabolism of the offspring 40 years later." *BJOG* 2000; 107(7):890–895.

11. Shiell, AW et al. "High-meat, low-carbohydrate diet in pregnancy: relation to adult blood pressure in the offspring." *Hypertension* 2001; 38(6):1282–1288.

12. Zhang, S et al. "Dietary fat and protein in relation to risk of non-Hodgkin's lymphoma among women." *J Natl Cancer Inst* 1999; 91(20):1751–1758.

13. Tavani, A et al. "Red meat intake and cancer risk: a study in Italy." *Int J Cancer* 2000; 86(3):425–428.

14. Fraser, GE. "Associations between diet and cancer, ischemic heart disease, and all-cause mortality in non-Hispanic white California Seventh-day Adventists." *Am J Clin Nutr* 1999; 70 (3 Suppl):532S–538S.

15. Appleby, PN et al. "The Oxford Vegetarian Study: an overview." *Am J Clin Nutr* 1999 70(3 Suppl):525S–531S.

16. National Institute of Nutrition. *Tracking Nutrition Trends IV. An Update on Canadians' Nutrition-Related Attitudes, Knowledge and Actions, 2001* (Ottawa, April 2002).

17. *Canadians and Food Safety.* IPSOS-Reid. Toronto, ON, October 2001.

18. National Institute of Nutrition. *Tracking Nutrition Trends IV. An Update on Canadians' Nutrition-Related Attitudes, Knowledge and Actions, 2001* (Ottawa, April 2002).

19. Khachatourians, GG. "Agricultural use of antibiotics and the evolution and transfer of antibiotic-resistant bacteria." *CMAJ* 1998; 159(9):1129–1136.

20. White, DG et al. "The isolation of antibiotic-resistant salmonella from retail ground meats." *N Eng J Med* 2001; 345(16):1147–1154.

21. Bazzano, LA et al. "Legume consumption and risk of coronary heart disease in US men and women: NHANES I Epidemiologic Follow-up Study." *Arch Intern Med* 2001; 161(21):2573–2578.

22. Hu, FB, MJ Stampfer et al. "Frequent nut consumption and risk of coronary heart disease in women: prospective cohort study." *BMJ* 1998; 317(7169): 1341–1345.

Step 3

1. Meyer, KA et al. "Carbohydrates, dietary fiber, and incident type 2 diabetes in older women." *Am J Clin Nutr* 2000; 71(4):921–930.

2. Liu, S et al. "A prospective study of whole-grain intake and risk of type 2 diabetes mellitus in US women." *Am J Public Health* 2000; 90(9):1409–1415.

3. Jacobs, DR Jr et al. "Whole-grain intake may reduce the risk of ischemic heart disease death in post-menopausal women: the Iowa Women's Health Study." *Am J Clin Nutr* 1998; 68(2):248–257.

4. Liu, S et al. "Whole-grain consumption and risk of coronary heart disease: results from the Nurses' Health Study." *Am J Clin Nutr* 1999; 70(3):412–419.

5. Liu, S et al. "Whole grain consumption and risk of ischemic stroke in women: a prospective study." *JAMA* 2000; 284(12):1534–1540.

6. Levi, F et al. "Food groups and colorectal cancer risk." *Br J Cancer* 1999; 79(7–8):1283–1287.

7. Chatenoud, L et al. "Refined cereal intake and risk of selected cancers in Italy." *Am J Clin Nutr* 1999; 70(6):1107–1110.

8. Levi, F et al. "Refined cereals and whole grain cereals and the risk of oral, oesophageal and laryngeal cancer." *Eur J Clin Nutr* 2000; 54(6):487–489.

9. Jacobs, DR Jr et al. "Is whole grain intake associated with reduced total and cause-specific death rates in older women? The Iowa Women's Health Study." *Am J Public Health* 1999; 89(3):322–329.

10. Lui, S et al. "Dietary glycemic load assessed by food frequency questionnaire in relation to plasma high-density-lipoprotein cholesterol and fasting plasma triaglycerols in postmenopausal women." *Am J Clin Nutr* 2001; 73(3):560–566.

11. Liu, S et al. "Relation between a diet with a high glycemic load and plasma concentrations of high sensitivity C-reactive protein in middle-aged women." *Am J Clin Nutr* 2002; 75(5):492–498.

12. Salmeron, J et al. "Dietary fiber, glycemic load, and the risk of NIDDM in men." *Diabetes Care* 1997; 20(4):545–550.

13. Salmeron, J et al. "Dietary fiber, glycemic load, and the risk of non-insulin-dependent diabetes mellitus in women." *JAMA* 1997; 277(6):472–477.

14. Franceschi, S et al. "Dietary glycemic load and colorectal cancer risk." *Ann Oncol* 2001; 12(2):173–178.

15. Ludwig, DS et al. "High glycemic index foods, overeating and obesity." *Pediatrics* 1999; 103(3):E26.

16. Spieth, LE et al. "A low-glycemic index diet in the treatment of pediatric obesity." *Arch Pediatr Adolesc Med* 2000; 154(9):947–951.

17. Wender, EH and MV Solanto. "Effects of sugar on aggressive and inattentive behavior in children with attention deficit disorder with hyperactivity and normal children." *Pediatrics* 1991; 88(5):960–966.

Step 4

1. Heart and Stroke Foundation of Canada. "Report Cards on Health." Available at **www.heartandstroke.ca**.

2. Block, G et al. "Fruit, vegetables, and cancer prevention: a review of the epidemiological evidence." *Nutr Cancer* 1992; 18(1):1–29.

3. World Cancer research Fund/American Institute for Cancer Research. *Food, Nutrition and the Prevention of Cancer: a Global Perspective* (Washington, DC: American Institute for Cancer Research, 1997).

4. Health Canada. *Health Canada Scientific Summary of the U.S. Health Claim Regarding Fruit, Vegetables and Cancer* (Ottawa: Supply and Services Canada 2000).

5. Ness, AR and JW Powles. "Fruit and vegetables, and cardiovascular disease: a review." *Int J Epidemiol* 1997; 26(1):1–13.

6. Joshipura, KJ et al. "Fruit and vegetable intake in relation to risk of ischemic stroke." *JAMA* 1999; 282(13):1233–1239.

7. Liu, S et al. "Intake of vegetables rich in carotenoids and risk of coronary heart disease in men: the Physicians' Health Study." *Int J Epidemiol* 2001; 30(1):130–135.

8. Appel, LJ et al. "A clinical trial of the effects of dietary patterns on blood pressure." *N Eng J Med* 1997; 65(Suppl):643S–651S.

9. Conlin, PR et al. "The effect of dietary patterns on blood pressure control in hypertensive patients: results from the Dietary Approaches to Stop Hypertension (DASH) trial." *AM J Hypertens* 2000; 13(9):949–955.

10. Jacques, PF and LT Chylack Jr. "Epidemiologic evidence of a role for the antioxidant vitamins and carotenoids in cataract prevention." *Am J Clin Nutr* 1991; 53(1 Suppl):352S–355S.

11. Seddon, JM et al. "Dietary carotenoids, vitamins A, C and E, and advanced age-related macular degeneration." *JAMA* 1994; 272(18):1413–1420.

12. Fuchs, CS et al. "The influence of folate and multivitamin use on the familiar risk of colon cancer in women." *Cancer Epidemiol Biomarkers Prev* 2002; 11(3):227–234.

13. Zhang, S et al. "A prospective study of folate intake and the risk of breast cancer." *JAMA* 1999; 281(17):1632–1637.

14. Speizer, FE et al. "Prospective study of smoking, antioxidant intake, and lung cancer in middle-aged women." *Cancer Causes Control* 1999; 10(5):475–482.

15. Galli, RL et al. "Fruit polyphenolics and brain aging: nutritional interventions targeting age-related neuronal and behavioral deficits." *Ann N Y Acad Sci* 2002; 959:128–132.

16. Kolonel, LN et al. "Vegetables, fruits, legumes and prostate cancer: a multiethnic case-control study." *Cancer Epidemiol Biomarkers Prev* 2000; 9(8):795–804.

17. Knekt, P et al. "Dietary flavonoids and the risk of lung cancer and other malignant neoplasms." *Am J Epidemiol* 1997; 146(3):223–230.

18. Le Marchand, L et al. "Intake of flavonoids and lung cancer." *J Natl Cancer Inst* 2000; 92(2):154–160.

19. Knekt, P et al. "Quercetin and the incidence of cerebrovascular disease." *Eur J Clin Nutr* 2000; 54(5):415–417.

20. Seddon, JM et al. "Dietary carotenoids, vitamins A, C and E, and advanced age-related macular degeneration." *JAMA* 1994; 272(18):1413–1420.

21. Richer, S. "ARMD–pilot (case series) environmental intervention data." *J Am Optom Assoc* 1999; 70(1):24–36.

22. Chasan-Taber, L et al. "A prospective study of carotenoid and vitamin A intakes and risk of cataract extraction among US women." *Am J Clin Nutr* 1999; 70(4):509–516.

23. Brown, L et al. "A prospective study of carotenoid intake and risk of cataract extraction in US men." *Am J Clin Nutr* 1999; 70(4):517–524.

24. Giovannucci, E et al. "Intake of carotenoids and retinol in relation to risk of prostate cancer." *J Natl Cancer Inst* 1995; 87(23):1767–1776.

25. Giovannucci, E et al. "A prospective study of tomato products, lycopene and prostate cancer risk." *J Natl Cancer Inst* 2002; 94(5):391–398.

26. Kantesky, PA et al. "Dietary intake and blood levels of lycopene: association with cervical dysplasia among non-Hispanic, black women." *Nutr Cancer* 1998; 31(1):31–40.

27. Steinmetz, KA, LH Kushi et al. "Vegetables, fruit, and colon cancer in the Iowa Women's Health Study." *Am J Epidemiol* 1994; 139(1):1–15.

28. Canadian Produce Marketing Association. "Stats, Facts and Research." Available at **www.5to10aday.com/eng/media_stats.htm**.

29. *Crop Protection in Context* (Toronto: Crop Protection Institute of Canada, 2002). Available at **www.cropro.org/english/resourcecentre/resourcecentrepest.html**.

30. Duell EJ et al. "A population-based case-control study of farming and breast cancer in North Carolina." *Epidemiology* 2000; 11(5):523–531.

31. Ritter, L. "Report of a panel on the relationship between public exposure to pesticides and cancer. Ad Hoc Panel on Pesticides and Cancer. National Cancer Institute of Canada." *Cancer* 1997; 80(10):2019–2033.

32. Laden, F et al. "Plasma organochlorine levels and the risk of breast cancer: an extended follow-up in the Nurses' Health Study." *Int J Cancer* 2001; 91(4):568–574.

33. Zheng, T et al. "DDE and DDT in breast adipose tissue and risk of female breast cancer." *Am J Epidemiol* 1999; 150(5):453–458.

34. van't Veer, P et al. "DDT (dicophane) and post-menopausal breast cancer in Europe: case-control study." *BMJ* 1997; 315(7100):81–85.

Step 5

1. Oomen, CM et al. "Association between trans fatty acid intake and 10-year risk of coronary heart disease in the Zutphen Elderly Study: a prospective population-based study." *Lancet* 2001; 357(9258):746–751.

2. Willett, WC et al. "Intake of trans fatty acids and risk of coronary heart disease among women." *Lancet* 1993; 341(8845):581–585.

3. Gillman, MW et al. "Margarine intake and subsequent coronary heart disease in men." *Epidemiology* 1997; 8(2):144–149.

4. Tavani, A et al. "Margarine intake and risk of nonfatal acute myocardial infarction in Italian women." *Eur J Clin Nutr* 1997; 51(1):30–32.

5. Salmeron, J et al. "Dietary fat intake and risk of type 2 diabetes in women." *Am J Clin Nutr* 2001; 73(6):1019–1026.

6. Siscovick, DS et al. "Dietary intake of long-chain n-3 polyunsaturated fatty acids and the risk of primary cardiac arrest." *Am J Clin Nutr* 2000; 71(1 Suppl): 208S–212S.

7. Hu, FB et al. "Fish and omega-3 fatty acid intake and risk of coronary heart disease in women." *JAMA* 2002; 287(14):1815–1821.

8. Oomen, CM et al. "Fish consumption and coronary heart disease mortality in Finland, Italy and The Netherlands." *Am J Epidemiol* 2000; 151(10): 999–1006.

9. Albert, CM et al. "Fish consumption and risk of sudden cardiac death." *JAMA* 1998; 279(1):23–28.

10. Djousse L, et al. "Relation between dietary linolenic acid and coronary artery disease in the National Heart, Lung, and Blood Institute Family Heart Study." *Am J Clin Nutr* 2001; 74(5):612–619.

11. Hu, FB et al. "Dietary intake of alpha linolenic acid and the risk of fatal ischemic heart disease among women." *Am J Clin Nutr* 1999; 69(5):890–897.

12. Klein, V et al. "Low alpha-linolenic acid content of adipose breast tissue is associated with an increased risk of breast cancer." *Eur J Cancer* 2000; 36(3): 335–340.

13. de Lorgeril, M et al. "Mediterranean diet, traditional risk factors, and the rate of cardiovascular complications after myocardial infarction: final report of the Lyon Diet Heart Study." *Circulation* 1999; 99(6): 779–785.

Step 6

1. National Institute of Nutrition. Tracking Nutrition Trends IV. An Update on Canadians' Nutrition-Related Attitudes, Knowledge and Actions, 2001 (Ottawa, April 2002).

2. "Quick Facts. Osteoporosis Online." Osteoporosis Society of Canada, 2002. Available at **www.osteo porosis.ca/OSTEO/D05.html#prev**.

3. Deegan, H. "Assessment of iron status in adolescents" (Masters of Science thesis, University of Alberta, 2000).

4. Gibson, RS et al. "Are young women with low iron stores at risk of zinc as well as iron deficiency?" in *Trace Elements in Man and Animals 10*, ed. Roussel AM et al. (Klower Academic/Plenum Publishers, New York, 2000):323–328.

5. Rimm, EB et al. "Folate and vitamin B6 from diet and supplements in relation to risk of coronary heart disease among women." *JAMA* 1998; 279(5):359–364.

6. Voutilainen, S et al. "Low dietary folate intake is associated with an excess of incidence of acute coronary events: The Kuopio Ischemic Heart Disease Risk Factor Study." Circulation 2001; 103(22):2674–2680.

7. Zhang, S et al. "A prospective study of folate intake and the risk of breast cancer." *JAMA* 1999; 281(17):1632–1637.

8. Sellers, TA et al. "Dietary folate intake, alcohol, and risk of breast cancer in a prospective study of post-menopausal women." Epidemiology 2001; 12(4):420–428.

9. Su, LJ and L Arab. "Nutritional status of folate and colon cancer risk: evidence from NHANES I epidemiologic follow-up study." Ann Epidemiol 2001; 11(1):65–72.

10. Giovannucci, E et al. "Multivitamin use, folate, and colon cancer in women in the Nurses' Health Study." Ann Intern Med 1998; 129(7):517–524.

11. Fuchs, CS et al. "The influence of folate and multivitamin use in familiar risk of colon cancer in women." Cancer Epidemiol Biomarkers Prev 2002; 11(3):227–234.

Step 7

1. Pollitt, E et al. "Fasting and cognition in well- and undernourished schoolchildren: a review of three experimental studies." *Am J Clin Nutr* 1998; 67(4 Suppl):779S–784S.

2. Vaisman, N et al. "Effect of breakfast timing on the cognitive functions of elementary school students." *Arch Pediatr Adolesc Med* 1996; 150(10):1089–1092.

3. Michaud, C et al. "Effects of breakfast-size on short-term memory, concentration, mood and blood glucose." *J Adolesc Health* 1991; 12(1):53–57.

4. Lombard, CB. "What is the role of food in preventing depression and improving mood, performance and cognitive function?" *Med J Aust* 2000; 173(Suppl): 104S–105S.

5. Benton D, and PY Parker. "Breakfast, blood glucose, and cognition." *Am J Clin Nutr* 1998; 67(Suppl): 772S–778S.

6. Nicklas, TA et al. "Breakfast consumption with and without vitamin-mineral supplement use favourably impacts daily nutrient intake of ninth-grade students." *J Adolesc Health* 2000; 27(5):314–321.

7. Preziosi, P et al. "Breakfast type, daily nutrient intakes and vitamin and mineral status of French children, adolescents, and adults." *J Am Coll Nutr* 1999; 18(2):171–178.

8. Nicklas, TA et al. "Impact of breakfast consumption on nutritional adequacy of the diets of young adults in Bogalusa, Louisiana: ethnic and gender constraints." *J Am Diet Assoc* 1998; 98(12):1432–1438.

9. Ortega, RM et al. "The importance of breakfast in meeting daily recommended calcium intake in a group of schoolchildren." *J Am Coll Nutr* 1998; 17(1):19–24.

10. Nicklas, TA et al. "Efficiency of breakfast consumption patterns of ninth graders: nutrient-to-cost comparisons." *J Am Diet Assoc* 2002; 102(2):226–233.

11. McNulty, H et al. "Nutrient intakes and impact of fortified breakfast cereals in schoolchildren." *Arch Dis Child* 1996; 75(6):474–481.

12. Lee, CJ et al. "Meal skipping patterns and nutrient intakes of rural southern elderly." *J Nutr Elder* 1996; 15(2):1–14.

13. Jenkins, DJ et al. "Nibbling versus gorging: metabolic advantages of increased meal frequency." *N Eng J Med* 321(14):929–933.

14. Titan, SM et al. "Frequency of eating and concentrations of serum cholesterol in the Norfolk population of the European prospective investigation into cancer (EPIC-Norfolk): cross sectional study." *BMJ* 2001; 323(7324):1286–1288.

15. McGrath, SA and MJ Gibney. "The effects of altered frequency of eating on plasma lipids in free-living healthy males on normal self-selected diets." *Eur J Clin Nutr* 1994; 48(6):402–407.

16. Edelstein, SL et al. "Increased meal frequency associated with decreased cholesterol concentrations; Rancho Bernardo, CA, 1984–1987." *Am J Clin Nutr* 1992; 55(3):664–669.

17. Speechly, DP et al. "Acute appetite reduction associated with an increased frequency of eating in obese males." *Int J Obes Relat Metab Disord* 1999; 23(11):1151–1159.

18. Speechly, DP and P Buffenstein. "Greater appetite control associated with an increased frequency of eating in lean males." *Appetite* 1999; 33(3):285–297.

19. Fabry, P et al. "The frequency of meals: its relation to overweight, hypercholesterolaemia, and decreased glucose tolerance." *Lancet* 1964; ii:614–615.

20. Fabry, P et al. "Effect of meal frequency in schoolchildren: changes in weight-height proportion and skinfold thickness." *Am J Clin Nutr* 1966; 18(5):358–361.

21. Iwoa, S et al. "Effects of meal frequency on body composition during weight control in boxers." *Scand J Med Sci Sports* 1996; 6(5):265–272.

22. Debry, G et al. "Ponderal losses in obese subjects submitted to restricted diets differing by nibbling and by lipid and carbohydrate" in *Energy Balance in Man*, ed. M. Apfelbaum (Paris: Masson, 1973):305–310.

23. Redondo, MR et al. "Food, energy and nutrient intake at breakfast in a group of elderly persons. Most common problems and difference related to body mass index." *Arch Latinoam Nutr* 1996; 46(4):275–281. [Spanish]

24. O'Dea, JA and P Caputi. "Association between socioeconomic status, weight, age and gender, and the body image and weight control practices of 6- to 19-year-old children and adolescents." *Health Educ Res* 2001; 16(5):521–532.

25. Ortega, RM et al. "Difference in the breakfast habits of overweight/obese and normal weight schoolchildren." *Int J Vitam Nutr Res* 1998; 68(2):125–132.

26. Wyatt, HR et al. "Long-term weight loss and breakfast in subjects in the National Weight Control Registry." *Obes Res* 2002; 10(2):78–82.

27. Gluck, ME at al. "Night eating syndrome is associated with depression, low self-esteem, reduced daytime hunger, and less weight loss in obese outpatients." *Obes Res* 2001; 9(4):264–267.

28. Romon, M et al. "Circadian variation of diet-induced thermogenesis." *Am J Clin Nutr* 1993; 57(4):476–480.

Step 8

1. Michaud, DS et al. "Fluid intake and the risk of bladder cancer." *N Eng J Med* 1999; 340(18):1390–1397.

2. Wilkens, LR et al. "Risk factors for lower urinary tract cancer: the role of total fluid consumption, nitrites and nitrosamines, and selected foods." *Cancer Epidemiol Biomarkers Prev* 1996; 5(3):161–166.

3. Slattery, ML et al. "Intake of fluids and methylxanthine-containing beverages: associations with colon cancer." *Int J Cancer* 1999; 81(12):199–204.

4. Tang, R et al. "Physical activity, water intake and risk of colorectal cancer in Taiwan: a hospital-based case-control study." *Int J Cancer* 1999; 82(4):484–489.

5. Lubin, F et al. "Nutritional and lifestyle habits and water-fiber interaction in colorectal adenoma etiology." *Cancer Epidemiol Biomarkers Prev* 1997; 6(2):79–85.

6. Shannon, J et al. "Relationship of food groups and water intake to colon cancer risk." *Cancer Epidemiol Biomarkers Prev* 1996; 5(7):495–502.

7. Stookey, JD et al. "Correspondence re: J. Shannon et al., Relationship of food groups and water intake to colon cancer risk." *Cancer Epidemiol Biomarkers Prev* Vol. 5(7):495–502." *Cancer Epidemiol Biomarkers Prev* 1997; 6(8):657–658.

8. Chan, J et al. "Water, other fluids, and fatal coronary heart disease: the Adventist Health Study." *Am J Epidemiol* 2002; 155(9):827–833.

9. Borghi, L et al. "Urinary volume, water and recurrences in idiopathic calcium nephrolithiasis: a 5-year randomized prospective study." *J Urol* 1996; 155(3):839–843.

10. Embon, OM et al. "Chronic dehydration and stone disease." *Br J Urol* 1990; 66(4):357–362.

11. Curhan, GC et al. "Beverage use and risk for kidney stones in women." *Ann Intern Med* 1998; 128(7):534–540.

12. Hirvonen, T et al. "Nutrient intake and use of beverages and the risk of kidney stones among male smokers." *Am J Epidemiol* 1999; 150(2):187–194.

13. Curhan, CG et al. "Prospective study of beverage use and the risk of kidney stones." *Am J Epidemiol* 1996; 143(3):240–247.

14. Seltzer, MA et al. "Dietary manipulation with lemonade to treat hypocitraturic calcium nephrolithiasis." *J Urol* 1996; 156(3):907–909.

15. Convertino, VA et al. "American College of Sports Medicine position stand. Exercise and fluid replacement." *Med Sci Sports Exerc* 1996; 28(1):i–vii.

16. Kleiner, SM. "Water: An essential but overlooked nutrient." *JADA* 1999; 99(2):200–206.

17. Lloyd, T et al. "Dietary caffeine intake and bone status of postmenopausal women." *Am J Clin Nutr* 1997; 65(6):1826–1830.

18. Harris, SS and B Dawson-Hughes. "Caffeine and bone loss in healthy menopausal women." *Am J Clin Nutr* 1994; 60(4):573–578.

19. Hansen, SA et al. "Association of fractures with caffeine and alcohol in postmenopausal women: the Iowa Women's Health Study." *Public Health Nutr* 2000; 3(3):253–261.

20. "Caffeine, even in small doses, may hurt arteries." Reuter's Health Information, May 17, 2002. Available at **www.reutershealth.com/frame2/eline.html**.

21. Barbieri, RL. "The initial fertility consultation: recommendations concerning cigarette smoking, body mass index, and alcohol and caffeine consumption." *Am J Obstet Gynecol* 2001; 185(5):1168–1173.

22. Cnattingius, S et al. "Caffeine intake and the risk of first-trimester spontaneous abortion." *N Eng J Med* 2000; 343(25):1839–1845.

23. Wen, W et al. "The associations of maternal caffeine consumption and nausea with spontaneous abortion." *Epidemiology* 2001; 12(1):38–42.

24. Infante-Rivard, C et al. "Fetal loss associated with caffeine intake before and during pregnancy." *JAMA* 1993; 270(24):2940–2943.

25. Fenster, L et al. "Caffeine consumption during pregnancy and spontaneous abortion." *Epidemiology* 1991; 2(3):168–174.

26. Cao, G et al. "Antioxidant capacity of tea and common vegetables." *Journal of Agriculture and Food Chemistry* 1996; 44(11):3426–3431.

27. Geleijnse, JM et al. "Inverse association of tea and flavonoid intakes with incident myocardial infarction: the Rotterdam Study." *Am J Clin Nutr* 2002; 75(5):880–886.

28. Sesso, HD et al. "Coffee and tea intake and the risk of myocardial infarction." *Am J Epidemiol* 1999; 149(2):162–167.

29. Hunter, DJ et al. "A prospective study of caffeine, coffee, tea and breast cancer." *Am J Epidemiol* 1992; 136:1000–1001. [Abstract]

Step 9

1. Tremblay, MS et al. "Temporal trends in overweight and obesity in Canada, 1981–1996." *Int J Obes* 2002; 26(4):538–543.

2. Ibid.

3. Tremblay, MS and JD Willms. "Secular trends in the body mass index of Canadian children." *CMAJ* 2000; 163(11):1429–1433.

4. Field, AE et al. "Impact of overweight on the risk of developing common chronic diseases during a 10-year period." *Arch Intern Med* 2001; 161(13):1581–1586.

5. Folsom, AR et al. "Associations of general and abdominal obesity with multiple health outcomes in older women: the Iowa Women's Health Study." *Arch Intern Med* 2000; 160(14):2117–2128.

6. Kramer, FM et al. "Long-term follow-up of behavioural treatment for obesity: patterns of weight regain among men and women." *Int J Obes* 1989; 13(2):123–136.

7. Wadden, TA. "Treatment of obesity by moderate and severe caloric restriction: results from clinical research trials." *Ann Intern Med* 1993; 119(7 part 2):688–693.

8. Young, LR and M Nestle. "Variation in perceptions of a 'medium' food portion: implications for dietary guidance." *J Am Diet Assoc* 1998; 98(4):458–459.

9. Klem, ML et al. "Does weight loss maintenance become easier over time?" *Obes Res* 2000; 8(6):438–444.

10. McGuire, MT et al. "Behavioural strategies of individuals who have maintained long-term weight losses." *Obes Res* 1999; 7(4):334–341.

Step 10

1. Dimeo, F et al. "Benefits of aerobic exercise in patients with major depression: a pilot study." *Br J Sports Med* 2001; 35(2):114–117.

2. Babyak, M et al. "Exercise treatment for major depression: maintenance of therapeutic benefit at 10 months." *Psychosom Med* 2000; 62(5):633–638.

3. Peters, EM. "Exercise, immunology and upper respiratory tract infections." *Int J Sports Med* 1997; 18(1 Suppl):69S–77S.

4. Nieman, DC et al. "Infectious episodes in runners before and after a roadrace." *J Sports Med Phys Fitness* 1989; 29(3):289–296.

5. Nieman, DC et al. "Immune response to exercise training and/or energy restriction in obese women." *Med Sci Sports Exerc* 1998; 30(5):679–686.

6. Pan, XR et al. "Effects of diet and exercise in preventing NIDDM in people with impaired glucose tolerance. The Da Qing IGT and Diabetes Study." *Diabetes Care* 1997; 20(4):537–544.

7. Hu, FB et al. "Walking compared with vigorous physical activity and risk of type 2 diabetes in women: a prospective study." *JAMA* 1999; 282(15):1433–1439.

8. Manson, JE et al. "A prospective study of exercise and incidence of diabetes among US male physicians." *JAMA* 1992; 268(1):63–67.

9. Manson, JE et al. "A prospective study of walking as compared with vigorous exercise in the prevention of coronary heart disease in women." *N Eng J Med* 1999; 341(9):650–658.

10. Hu, FB et al. "Physical activity and the risk of stroke in women." *JAMA* 2000; 283(22):2961–2967.

11. Martinez, ME et al. "Leisure-time physical activity, body size, and colon cancer in women. Nurses' Health Study Research Group." *J Natl Cancer Inst* 1997; 89(13):948–955.

12. Slatterly, ML et al. "Lifestyle and colon cancer: an assessment of factors associated with risk." *Am J Epidemiol* 1999; 150(8):869–877.

13. White, E et al. "Physical activity in relation to colon cancer in middle-aged men and women." *Am J Epidemiol* 1996; 144(1):42–50.

14. Rockhill, B et al. "A prospective study of recreational activity and breast cancer risk." *Arch Intern Med* 1999; 159(19):2290–2296.

15. Wolff, I et al. "The effect of exercise training programs on bone mass: a meta-analysis of published controlled trials in pre- and postmenopausal women." *Osteoporosis Int* 1999; 9(1):1–12.

16. Dalsky, GP et al. "Weight-bearing exercise training and lumbar bone mineral content in postmenopausal women." *Ann Intern Med* 1988; 108(6):824–828.

17. Pruitt, LA et al. "Weight-training effects on bone mineral density in early postmenopausal women." *J Bone Min Res* 1992; 7(2):179–185.

18. Winett, RA and RN Carpinelli. "Potential health-related benefits of resistance training." *Prev Med* 2001; 33(5):503–513.

General Index

A
acesulfame K, 58
action stage, 4
activated aluminum oxide
  filters, 138
adequate intakes (AI)
  see also recommended
    dietary allowance (RDA)
  vitamin D, 107
alcohol, 144–145
alpha-linolenic acid, 85, 93
American Institute for Cancer
  Research, 62
amino acids, 20, 21, 28
anemia, 109
animal protein, 25–26, 29–32
anthocyanins, 68
antibiotic residues, 30–31
antibiotic resistance, 78
appetite reduction, 123–124
artesian water, 139
artificial sweeteners, 57–58
aspartame, 57
athletes, 109

B
bacteria strains, 31, 72
barriers to success, 7–8
beans. *See* legumes
beef, 30–31
beta-carotene, 66
beverages, 13
  see also fluids
Biotech Century (Rifkin), 78

biotech foods
  antibiotic resistance, 78
  concerns, 78–79
  described, 76–77
  food allergies, 78
  future of, 79
  lack of labelling, 79
  in marketplace, 77
  super bugs, super weeds
    and super viruses, 78
bladder cancer, 132
blood cholesterol
  control, 123
  and fats, 88
  HDL cholesterol, 88
  hydrogenation and, 91
  LDL cholesterol, 88, 95
  levels, 70
  triglycerides, 88
blood pressure, 63, 142
body fat measurements,
  150–151
body mass index (BMI),
  148–149
body measurements, 153
bone density, 25, 65, 141
bone meal, 106
bottled water, 139–140
brain power, 121–122
breakfast, 125–127, 126
breast cancer, 64, 74, 113,
  133
breastfeeding, and fluid
  intake, 135

buckwheat, 47
bulgur, 47

C
caffeine
  and blood pressure, 142
  and bone health, 141
  daily upper limit, 142–143
  and pregnancy, 142
  and sleep, 142
calcium, 103–106, 117
calcium carbonate, 106
calcium citrate, 106
Camplyobacter, 31, 34
Canadian Food Inspection
  Agency, 30, 32–33
*Canadian Medical Association
  Journal*, 31
Canadian Organic Producers
  Association, 76
cancer prevention
  anthocyanins, 68
  beta-carotene, 66
  cruciferous compounds, 68
  exercise, 166–167
  flavonoids, 68
  folate, 64, 113
  fruits and vegetables, health
    benefits of, 62
  lycopene, 69
  omega-3 fats, 92–93
  sulfur compounds, 70
  tea, 144
  vitamin C, 65

water, 132–133
and whole-grain foods, 45–46
cancers
and alcohol, 144–145
and artificial sweeteners, 57
bladder cancer, 132
breast cancer, 64, 74, 113, 133
colon cancer, 49, 64, 113, 133, 166
lung cancer, 66
and meat consumption, 25–26
and pesticide residues, 74
canned tuna, 32
canola oil, 77
carbadox, 31
carbohydrates
added sugar, 54–56
artificial sweeteners, 57–58
dietary fibers, 42
fiber, 52–54
high-carbohydrate diets, 43–44
and insulin, 48–52
nutrition IQ quiz, 41, 59
refined, 44
simple sugars, 42
starches, 42
tips for incorporating into diet, 58–59
types, 42
whole-grain foods, 45–48
carbonated bottled water, 139
cardiovascular exercises, 172–173
cataracts, 63–64, 69
certification bodies, 76
certified personal trainer, 176
cervical dysplasia, 69

change, stages of
action stage, 4
contemplation stage, 3
maintenance stage, 10
pre-contemplation stage, 2–3
preparation stage, 4
changing your diet quiz, 1, 16
children
fat intake, recommended, 88
ready-to-eat breakfast cereals, 122
sugar and, 56
water, 134
Children's Hospital (Boston), 49
cholesterol. *See* blood cholesterol; dietary cholesterol
cholesterol content of foods, 95
clothing size, 153
colon cancer, 49, 64, 113, 133, 166
Colorado Potato Beetle, 77
complementary vegetarian proteins, 29
condiments, 13
contemplation stage, 3
convenience, 72–73
cracked wheat, 47
Crop Protection Institute of Canada, 73
cruciferous compounds, 68
cyclamate, 57

D
daily weight monitoring, 161
dairy products, 13
DDT, 74
dehydration, 135, 136–137

Demeter, 76
dental caries, 56
DHA, 92, 93
diabetes, 45, 52, 56, 57, 91, 165–166
Dietary Approaches to Stop Hypertension (DASH) diet study, 63
dietary cholesterol, 94–95
dietary fiber. *See* fiber
disaccharides, 42
distillation systems, 138
dolomite, 106
dressings, 13

E
E. coli, 31, 34
eating more often
appetite reduction, 123–124
avoid large meals after 8 p.m., 128–129
brain power, 121–122
breakfast, 125–127
cholesterol control, 123
energy, 121
every three to four hours, 127
frequency, 125–129
grazing, 123, 129
improved nutrition, 122
reasons for, 121–125
snack guidelines, 127–128
tips, 129–130
weight management, 160, 124–125
effervescent calcium, 106
eggs, 12
eicosanoids, 93
energy, 21, 121
Environmental Defence Canada, 33

enzymes, 20
EPA, 92, 93
European Union, 30
exercise
  and bone loss, 167
  boredom and, 168–169
  cancer prevention, 166–167
  cardiovascular, 172–173
  doctor's recommendations, 171
  excuses for not exercising, 167–169
  flexibility, 174
  fluid intake, 135–136
  and heart disease, 166
  lifestyle approach, 169
  making time for, 167–168
  motivation, 169–170
  nutrition IQ quiz, 163, 178
  program, 171–176
  reasons for, 164–167
  self-consciousness, 168
  strength, 174–176
  target heart rate zone, 173
  timing of, 176
  tips for becoming more active, 177
  weight management and, 161, 164
eyesight, 63–64, 65, 69

F
fad diets, 151–152
fat-free foods, 43–44
fat free label, 43
fats
  alpha-linolenic acid, 93
  and blood cholesterol, 88
  chemistry of, 84
  children's recommended intake, 88
  cutting back, 85–86
  dietary cholesterol, 94–95
  excessive amounts, 85
  label reading, 86–88
  monounsaturated fats, 93–94
  need for, 84–85
  nutrition IQ quiz, 83, 99
  omega-3 fats, 92–93
  omega-6 fats, 93
  polyunsaturated fats, 91–92
  recommended intake, 95–96
  saturated fats, 89–90
  serving size, 86
  tips for choosing healthier fats and oils, 96–99
  trans fat, 90–91
  types of, 89–94
fatty acids, 84, 89
fertility, 142
fiber, 42, 52–54, 66–67
fish
  antibiotic residues, 30–31
  omega-3 fats, 92–93
  as protein source, 35
  as staple, 12
  toxins in, 32
fitness level, 153
flavonoids, 68
flexibility exercise, 174
fluids
  alcohol, 144–145
  bottled water, 139–140
  during breastfeeding, 135
  caffeinated beverages, 141–144
  coffee, 141–143
  dehydration, 135, 136–137
  exercise and, 135–136
  during illness, 136
  juices, 140–141
  milk, soy and rice beverages, 140
  nutrition IQ quiz, 131, 146
  during pregnancy, 135
  recommended daily intake, 135–136
  recommended types of, 137–141
  tap water, 137–138
  tea, 143–144
  tips for improving intake, 145
  water, 132–134
folate, 64–65, 112–115, 118
folic acid. See folate
food allergies, 78
food content
  caffeine, 143
  calcium, 104–105
  cholesterol, 95
  fiber, 53–54
  folate, 114
  iron, 111
  protein, 22–23
  vitamin D, 108
food diary, 9, 160
food labels
  biotech foods, 79
  information on, 86–88
  ingredients list, 87
  nutrition labels, 86–88
food safety issues
  animal protein, 29–32
  antibiotic residues, 30–31
  bacteria strains, 31
  biotech foods, 78–79
  fruits and vegetables, 72–75
  genetically modified foods, 78–79
  growth hormone residues in beef, 30

home-based solutions, 33–35
mercury contamination, 32
monitoring, 32–33
organic option, 34, 76–77
pesticide residues, 73–75
plant-based diet option, 33–34
safe food handling, 34–35
toxins in fish, 32
14-day meal plan, 182–183
Framingham Osteoporosis Study, 24
free radical damage, 65
freezer, 12, 73
frequent eating. *See* eating more often
frozen foods, 72–73
fructose, 42
fruits
    beta-carotene, 66
    biotech, 76–79
    blood pressure management, 63
    cancer prevention, 62
    convenience, 72–73
    eyesight, 63–64
    fiber content, 66–67
    folate, 64–65
    frozen, 72–73
    genetically modified, 76–79
    health benefits, 62–64
    and heart disease, 62–63
    juices, 140–141
    nutrition IQ quiz, 61, 81
    organic option, 76–77
    pesticide residues, 73–75
    phytochemicals, 67–70
    planning ahead, 71–72
    safety issues, 72–75

    serving size, 70–71
    as staple, 12
    strategies to eat more, 70–73
    tips for eating more, 79–81
    vitamin C, 65

G

galactose, 42
genetically modified foods, 76–79
glucose, 42, 121
glycemic index
    definition, 48
    food selection and, 50–52
    and health, 49
    values of foods, 50–52
    whole-grain foods, 126
goal setting, 4–7, 153–154
grain foods, 12
grazing, 123, 129
    see also eating more often
grocery shopping, weekly, 11–13
growth hormone residues, 30

H

handling food safely, 34–35
Harvard Medical School study, 69
HDL cholesterol, 88
Health Canada, 30, 32, 33, 57, 73, 95, 115, 142
health measurements, 153
healthy tools, 14–15, 181
heart disease
    exercise and, 166
    folate, 64–65
    folate and, 112–113
    fruits and vegetables, 62–63
    Mediterranean diet, 94

omega-3 fats, 92
tea and, 143
trans fats, 91
and water, 133
whole grains and, 45
hectic lifestyle, 120–121
heme sources of iron, 110
heterocyclic amines, 26
high blood pressure, 25, 142
high-carbohydrate, low-fat diets, 160
high-carbohydrate diets, 43–44
high cholesterol levels, 95
high-protein diets, 25–26
homocysteine levels, 64–65
hormones, 20
hunger signals, 155
hydrogenated fat, 90–91

I

illness, and fluid requirements, 136
immunity, 165
ingredients list, 87
insoluble fiber, 52
insulin, 48–52, 121, 123
intensity levels of various activities, 172
Iowa Women's Health Study, 45, 46, 150
iron, 109–112, 117–118
iron deficiency, 109

K

kale, 63–64
kamut, 47
kasha, 47
kidney stones, 134
kitchen tools, healthy, 14–15

L

lacto-ovo vegetarians, 27
lacto vegetarians, 27
lactose, 42
large meals after 8 p.m.,
  128–129
LDL cholesterol, 88, 95
leftover planning, 14, 181
legumes
  cooking facts, 38
  as protein source, 37–38
  soaking methods, 37–38
  as staple, 13
linoleic acid, 85
Loma Linda University
  (Calif.), 26
low-protein diets, 24–25
lung cancer, 66
lutein, 69
lycopene, 69–70
Lyon Diet Heart Study, 94

M

maintenance stage, 10
maltose, 42
Mayo Clinic, 24–25
meal skipping, 122
meat, 12, 30–31
Mediterranean diet, 93–94
memory, 24
menu planning, 11, 182–183
mercury contamination, 32
milk, 140
mineral water, 139
minerals. *See* vitamins and
  minerals
monosaccharides, 42
monounsaturated fats, 93–94
mood improvement, 164–165
motivation, 8, 169–170
multivitamin supplements,
  115–116

N

National Cancer Institute of
  Canada, 74
national food safety program,
  32–33
National Institute of
  Nutrition, 102
National Research Council,
  135
National Weight Control
  Registry, 160
*New England Journal of
  Medicine*, 31, 123
night eating syndrome, 128
Nurses' Health Study, 25, 38,
  45, 64, 74, 91, 92, 93, 113,
  166
nutrition IQ quiz
  carbohydrates, 41, 59
  changing your diet, 1, 17
  eating for energy and
    health, 119, 130
  exercise, 163, 178
  fats and oils, 83, 99
  fluids, 131, 146
  fruits and vegetables,
    61, 81
  protein, 19, 40
  vitamins and minerals, 101,
    118
  weight management, 147,
    162
nutrition knowledge, 161
nutrition labels, 86–88
nutrition supplements,
  102–103
  calcium, 106
  choosing, 116
  folic acid, 114–115
  iron, 111–112
  necessity of, 115
  purchasing, 116

vitamin D, 108
nuts, 38–39

O

oils
  see also fats
  nutrition IQ quiz, 83, 99
  serving size, 86
  as staple, 13
omega-3 fats, 92–93
omega-6 fats, 93
once-a-week grocery shopping,
  11–13, 180
Organic Crop Improvement
  Association (OCIA), 76
Organic Crop Producers and
  Processors, 76
organic option, 34, 76–77
organizational strategies
  fruits and vegetables, 71–72
  healthy tools, 14–15
  leftover planning, 14
  once-a-week grocery shop-
    ping, 11–13
  plan weekly menus ahead,
    11
  pre-prepared foods, 13–14
  staple foods, 12–13
osteoporosis, 24, 65, 103, 107,
  142, 167
Osteoporosis Society of
  Canada, 108
overeating causes, 155–156
Oxford Vegetarian Study, 26
oyster shell calcium, 106

P

peak mass, 103
percentage body fat standards,
  151
pesco-vegetarians, 27

Pest Management Regulatory Agency, 73
pesticide residues, 73–75
phytochemicals, 67–70
pitcher-type products, 138
plant-based diet, 27, 33–34
point-of-entry devices, 138
point-of-use treatment, 138
polyunsaturated fats, 91–92
pork, 31
poultry, 12, 30–31
pre-contemplation stage, 2–3
pre-prepared foods, 13–14, 180
pregnancy
    and caffeine, 142
    fish consumption, 32
    fluids during, 135
    folate needs, 112
    iron needs, 109
    protein needs, 23, 25
preparation stage, 4
progress tracking, 9
protein
    amount in diet, 21–22
    animal protein, 25–26
    bone fracture, 24
    calculation of intake, 22
    content in foods, 22–23
    daily requirements, 21
    deficiency in diet, 24–25
    excessive amounts, 25–26
    fish, 35
    legumes, 37–38
    need for, 20–21
    nutrition IQ quiz, 19, 40
    nuts, 38–39
    and osteoporosis, 24
    soy foods, 35–37
    during special stages in life cycle, 23

tips for incorporating into diet, 39–40
    top protein foods, 35–39
    in vegetarian diet, 28–29
purified water, 139

Q

Quality Assurance International, 76
quinois, 48

R

realistic goals, 4–7, 153–154, 170
recommended dietary allowance (RDA)
    see also adequate intakes (AI)
    calcium, 104
    folate, 113
    iron, 109–110
relapses, 10
repetitions, 175–176
reverse osmosis, 138
rewards, 8
rice beverages, 140
Rifkin, Jeremy, 78
Roundup, 77

S

saccharin, 57
safe food handling, 34–35
safety. See food safety issues
salmonella, 31, 34, 35, 72
satiety signals, 155
saturated fats, 89–90
self-denial, 160
self-rewards, 170
semi-vegetarians, 27
serving size
    fats and oils, 86

fruits and vegetables, 70–71
    portion distortion, 154–155
    weight management, 157–158
    whole grain, 46
sets, 175–176
simple sugars, 42
sleep, and caffeine, 142
SMART goal setting, 5–6
smoking, 66
snack guidelines, 127–128
soluble fiber, 52
soy beverages, 36, 140
soy flour, 36
soy foods, 13, 35–37
soy meats, 36
soy nuts, 36
soy protein powders, 36–37
soybeans, 36
spelt, 48
spices, 13
spinach, 63–64
spring water, 139
stages of change. See change, stages of
staple foods, 12–13
starches, 42
strategies for success
    barriers to success, identification of, 7–8
    goal setting, 4–7
    progress tracking, 9
    rewards, 8
    support, 8–9
strength exercise, 174–176
sucralose, 57–58
sucrose, 42
sugar
    added, 54–55
    calories in foods, 55–56
    children's diets, 56

dental caries, 56
and diabetes, 56
and weight control, 55
sulfur compounds, 70
super bugs, super weeds and
super viruses, 78
supplements. *See* nutrition
supplements
support, 8–9, 170
sweets, 13
synthetic dyes, 32

T

talk test, 173
tap water, 137–138
target heart rate zone, 173
tea, 143–144
tempeh, 36
texturized vegetable protein
(TVP), 36
tofu, 36
trans fat, 90–91
triglycerides, 84
tryglycerides, 88
Tufts University (Boston),
63, 68

U

University of Pennsylvania
School of Medicine, 69
urinary tract infections, 68
U.S. Federal Drug
Administration, 32

V

vegans, 27
vegetables
beta-carotene, 66
biotech, 76–79
blood pressure manage-
ment, 63

cancer prevention, 62
convenience, 72–73
eyesight, 63–64
fiber content, 66–67
folate, 64–65
frozen, 72–73
genetically modified, 76–79
health benefits, 62–64
and heart disease, 62–63
juices, 140–141
nutrition IQ quiz, 61, 81
organic option, 76–77
pesticide residues, 73–75
phytochemicals, 67–70
planning ahead, 71–72
safety issues, 72–75
serving size, 70–71
as staple, 12
strategies to eat more,
70–73
tips for eating more, 79–81
vitamin C, 65
vegetarian diet
complementary vegetarian
proteins, 29
plant protein vs. animal
protein, 26–27
protein quality, 28–29
types of, 27–28
vitamin C, 65
vitamin D, 107–108, 117
vitamins and minerals
calcium, 103–106, 117
folate, 64–65, 112–115, 118
iron, 109–112, 117–118
nutrition IQ quiz, 101, 118
supplements, 102–103
tips for boosting nutrient
intake, 117–118
vitamin C, 65
vitamin D, 107–108, 117

W

waist-hip ratio, 150
water
bottled, 139–140
and cancer, 132–133
children, 134
health benefits, 132–134
and heart disease, 133
kidney stones, 134
tap, 137–138
treatment devices for home
use, 138
and weight management,
134
weekly menus, 11, 182–183
weight-loss plans, 156–157
weight-loss program, 158–159
weight management
eating more often, 124–125
exercise. *See* exercise
and fad diets, 151–152
hunger signals, 155
maintenance strategies,
159–161
necessity of, 148–151
nutrition IQ quiz, 147, 162
overeating causes, 155–156
realistic goals, 153—154
satiety signals, 155
serving size, 157–158
serving sizes, 154–155
tips for, 161–162
and water, 134
weight-loss plans, 156–157
weight-loss program,
158–159
Weight Watchers, 8, 158
whole-grain foods, 45–48, 126
World Cancer Research Fund,
62
written goals, 5

Recipe Index

A

adobo marinade, 221
apples
   and cinnamon oatmeal
     porridge, 199
   oat muffins, 201
   with kale and onion, 194
apricot orange loaf, 202
artichoke pizza, 207
Asian fish steaks, 215
asparagus leek braise, 191

B

balsamic honey pork tenderloin, 220
banana sandwich, French-
   toasted, 204
banana strawberry smoothie,
   213
barley, 204
bean spread, 187
beets, honey lemon, 193
berry melon fruit salad, 198
beverages. *See* drinks
bran muffins, date, 202
breads. *See* quick breads
broccoli and red pepper,
   roasted, 196
broccoli salad, lemon, 194
buttermilk berry pancake
   mix, 203

C

carrots
   cumin carrot tofu patties,
     210
   curried, 192
   soup, creamy, 185
cereals
   apple cinnamon oatmeal
     porridge, 199
   granola, 201
   maple walnut multigrain
     porridge, 200
   orange date oat bran por-
     ridge, 199
   snack mix, 200
   toppings, 200
cheese pita pockets, 187
cherry tomato and mushroom
   sauté, 191
chicken. *See* poultry
chickpea, turkey sausage and
   tomato soup, 186
chili, vegetarian with squash,
   212
chimichurri marinade, 221
citrus mustard chicken, 219
couscous, 205
cucumber, mango and red
   pepper salad, 195
cumin carrot tofu patties, 210
curried carrots, 192

D

date and orange oat bran porridge, 199
date bran muffins, 202
drinks
   strawberry banana
     smoothie, 213
   tropical fruit shake, 213

E

eggs
   frittata, 214
   western omelet pockets,
     214

F

fajitas, chicken, 218
fish
   Asian fish steaks, 215
   garlic gratin, 215
   marinades, 221
   Mediterranean tuna pasta,
     216
   roasted Cajun halibut, 217
   roasted salmon fillets with
     orange caramelized
     onions, 217
   salmon melt, 189
   tuna and pepper panini
     melt, 189
French-toasted banana sandwich, 204
frittata, 214
fruit
   melon berry fruit salad, 198
   stewed, 198
   tropical fruit shake, 213

G

garlic dressing, 197
garlic gratin fish, 215
garlic horseradish sirloin
   roast, 220
ginger pepper peas, 197

grain foods
    apple cinnamon oatmeal
      porridge, 199
    apple oat muffins, 201
    barley, 204
    buttermilk berry pancake
      mix, 203
    couscous, 205
    date bran muffins, 202
    French-toasted banana
      sandwich, 204
    granola, 201
    great ideas for, 206
    kasha, 205
    maple walnut multigrain
      porridge, 200
    orange apricot loaf, 202
    orange date oat bran por-
      ridge, 199
    snack mix, 200
    wheat berries, 206
granola, 201
green beans gremolata, 193
green peas
    ginger pepper, 197
    honey almond, 197
    lemon dill, 197
    mint red pepper, 197

H
halibut
    Asian steaks, 215
    roasted Cajun, 217
honey almond peas, 197
honey lemon beets, 193

K
kale with apples and onion,
    194
kasha, 205

L
lasagna, vegetarian, 209
leek asparagus braise, 191
legumes
    bean spread, 187
    chili, vegetarian with
      squash, 212
    potato lentil soup, 185
    Sicilian beans with pasta,
      210
    southwestern three-bean
      salad, 211
    turkey sausage, tomato and
      chickpea soup, 186
lemon broccoli salad, 194
lemon dill peas, 197
lentil potato soup, 185

M
mango chicken wrap, 188
mango, cucumber and red
    pepper salad, 195
maple walnut multigrain por-
    ridge, 200
marinades
    adobo marinade, 221
    chimichurri marinade, 221
    Moroccan marinade, 221
    red wine marinade, 221
    teriyaki marinade, 221
meat
    marinades, 221
    pork tenderloin, balsamic
      honey, 220
    sirloin roast, garlic horse-
      radish, 220
Mediterranean tuna pasta, 216
melon berry fruit salad, 198
Moroccan marinade, 221

O
oat bran porridge, with orange
    and dates, 199
oat muffins, apple, 201
orange and date oat bran por-
    ridge, 199
orange apricot loaf, 202
orzo salad, 195

P
pancakes, buttermilk berry,
    203
pasta
    couscous, 205
    Mediterranean tuna pasta,
      216
    orzo salad, 195
    vegetarian lasagna, 209
    with Sicilian beans, 210
peanut sauce, 211
pita pockets, cheese, 187
pizza
    artichoke, 207
    dough, 207
    hot and spicy, 208
    vegetarian spinach, 208
pork tenderloin, balsamic
    honey, 220
porridge
    apple cinnamon oatmeal
      porridge, 199
    maple walnut multigrain
      porridge, 200
    orange date oat bran
      porridge, 199
potato lentil soup, 185
poultry
    chicken club pita, 188
    chicken fajitas, 218

chicken in spicy spinach
sauce, 219
citrus mustard chicken, 219
mango chicken wrap, 188
marinades, 221
marinated chicken breasts,
218

Q

quick breads
apple oat muffins, 201
date bran muffins, 202
orange apricot loaf, 202

R

rapini with lemon anchovy
vinaigrette, 196
red pepper
and mango and cucumber
salad, 195
and roasted broccoli, 196
and snow peas, 197
mint peas, 197
red wine marinade, 221
roasted Cajun halibut, 217
roasted garlic dressing, 197

S

salads
broccoli salad, lemon, 194
mango, cucumber and red
pepper salad, 195
melon berry fruit salad, 198
orzo salad, 195
rapini with lemon anchovy
vinaigrette, 196
roasted garlic dressing, 197
roasted root vegetables, 197
Swiss chard leaves, cold
sesame, 192

three-bean, southwestern,
211
vegetable tofu salad, 212
salmon
Asian fish steaks, 215
fillets, roasted, with orange
caramelized onions, 217
melt, 189
sandwiches and wraps
bean spread and veggie
sandwich, 187
cheese pita pockets, 187
chicken club pita, 188
fast sandwich ideas, 190
French-toasted banana
sandwich, 204
mango chicken wrap, 188
salmon melt, 189
tuna and pepper panini
melt, 189
tuna wrap, 190
western omelet pockets,
214
sesame Swiss chard
leaves, 192
Sicilian beans with pasta, 210
side dishes
barley, 204
couscous, 205
kasha, 205
wheat berries, 206
sirloin roast, garlic
horseradish, 220
snack mix, 200
snow peas and peppers, 197
soups
carrot, 185
potato lentil soup, 185
turkey sausage, tomato and
chickpea soup, 186

southwestern three-bean
salad, 211
soy foods
cumin carrot tofu patties,
210
tofu and vegetable skewers
with peanut sauce, 211
tropical fruit shake, 213
vegetable tofu salad, 212
spinach sauce, spicy, 219
spinach veggie pizza, 208
squash, with vegetarian
chili, 212
stewed fruit, 198
strawberry banana smoothie,
213
Swiss chard leaves, cold
sesame, 192

T

teriyaki marinade, 221
tofu
and vegetable skewers with
peanut sauce, 211
patties, with cumin and
carrots, 210
tropical fruit shake, 213
vegetable tofu salad, 212
tomato (cherry) and mush-
room sauté, 191
tomato, turkey sausage and
chickpea soup, 186
tropical fruit shake, 213
tuna
and pepper panini melt,
189
Mediterranean tuna pasta,
216
wrap, 190

turkey sausage, tomato and
chickpea soup, 186

V

vegetables
asparagus leek braise, 191
bean spread and veggie
sandwich, 187
beets, honey lemon, 193
broccoli and red pepper,
roasted, 196
cherry tomato and mush-
room sauté, 191
chili, vegetarian with
squash, 212
curried carrots, 192
ginger pepper peas, 197
green beans gremolata, 193
honey almond peas, 197
kale with apples and
onion, 194
lasagna, vegetarian, 209
lemon dill peas, 197
mint red pepper peas, 197
pizzas (*See* pizza)
rapini with lemon anchovy
vinaigrette, 196
root vegetables, roasted,
197
salads (See salads)
snow peas and peppers, 197
tofu and vegetable skewers
with peanut sauce, 211

W

walnut maple multigrain
porridge, 200
western omelet pockets, 214
wheat berries, 206